THE NEW FLORIDA CUISINE

MIAMI SPICE

STEVEN RAICHLEN

ILLUSTRATED BY ROBIN ZINGONE

WORKMAN PUBLISHING • NEW YORK

Dedication

To Barbara, Betsy, and Jake,
the reasons I moved
to Miami

@@@

Library of Congress Cataloging-in-Publication Data
Raichlen,Steven.
Miami spice: the new Florida cuisine/by Steven Raichlen;
illustrations by Robin Zingone.
p. cm.
Includes index. ISBN 1-56305-519-8 (cloth) ISBN 1-56305-346-2 (paper)
1. Cookery, American. 2. Cookery–Florida–

Cover and book design: Lisa Hollander with Lori S. Malkin
Cover and book illustration: Robin Zingone

Workman books are available at special discounts when purchased in bulk for
premiums and sales promotions as well as for fund-raising or educational use.
Special editions or book excerpts can also be created to specification. For
details, contact the Special Sales Director at the address below.

Workman Publishing Company, Inc.
708 Broadway
New York, NY 10003

Manufactured in the United States of America

First printing September 1993
10 9 8 7 6 5 4 3 2 1

ACKNOWLEDGMENTS

This book began with a romance between a cooking teacher and his student. The year was 1979. Into my class walked that most rare of creatures, a Miamian who was actually born and raised there. Our encounter led to a romance with nightly long distance phone calls (I was living in Cambridge, Massachusettes at the time). The calls led to more than thirty trips to Florida.

Over the next ten years of our long distance courtship and the three years I've lived in south Florida, I've watched Miami blossom from a gastronomic backwater to a culinary hot spot. I've also met hundreds of extraordinary and talented people who have nurtured this book at every step along the way.

The first thanks goes to my wife, Barbara, for waiting all those years for a Yankee to decide to move to the tropics—and for putting up with a steady assault of recipe testing on our kitchen. Daughter Betsy and son Jake cheerfully endured a steady diet of strange tropical fruits and vegetables.

Elida Proenza, who seems more like a family member than a friend, graced this book with dozens of recipes and food lore from her native Cuba. Michelle Bernstein proved to be a recipe tester extraordinaire. Marc and Kiki Ellenby of the LNB Groves kept me supplied with exotic fruits, while Maricel Presilla generously shared her encyclopedic knowledge of Hispanic history.

Many gifted chefs and restaurateurs contributed their recipes and vision of Floridian cuisine. Mark Militello of Mark's Place in North Miami was an endless source of inspiration and dining pleasure and a good friend to boot. There simply would not be a new Floridian cuisine without the creativity of individuals like Robbin Haas of the Colony Bistro, Doug Rodriguez of Yuca, Mark Rodriguez of Jordan's Grove, Allen Susser of Chef Allen's, Sonia Zaldivar of Victor's Café, and roving chef Norman Van Aken.

Many farmers and fruit growers shared their horticultural expertise with me, including Pal Brooks, Stephanie Johnson, Keith Mitchell, Reed Olszack, and Bill Schaefer of J.R. Brooks & Son, Inc.; Jim Shine of the Florida Sugar Cane League; Richard Campbell of the Fairchild Tropical Garden; Quentin J. Roe of Wm. G. Roe & Sons, Inc.; Jonathan H. Crane, Ph.D. of the University of Florida; Chris Rollins of the Tropical Fruit and Spice Park; and Bill Lessard of the W.O. Lessard Nursery.

Equally generous with their knowledge were Florida's seafood experts and fisherfolk, including Daniel McLister of Manatee Bay Shellfish, Inc.; Ed Froehlich of Froehlich's Gator Farm; Joey Durante of Mariner Seafoods; Rick Madrigal of Clayton's Crab; Clare Vanderbeek of the National Fisheries Institute, and frog and 'gator hunter, Norman Padget.

I'd also like to thank baking guru Maida Heatter, *Miami Herald* food editor Felicia Gressette, restaurant critic Lucy Cooper, *Jacksonville Union* writer Jonathan Rogers, Tim and Brigid Schmand, and the Coconut Grove Writer's Group for their expertise and support.

Suzanne Rafer graced my manuscript with her skillful and painstaking editing. Further polishing came from copy editor Mardee Regan. Lisa Hollander gave my words a design that says "Florida's hot" and wisely chose Robin Zingone to create the cover and book illustrations. I'd also like to thank Peter Workman, Andrea Glickson, and the whole Workman staff for their enthusiasm and support.

Contents

a great catch from Florida's waters. A gazeteer of tropical fish, from amberjack to wahoo.

Hot! Hot! Hot!

It was bound to happen. The regional food movement sweeping the nation had to arrive in Florida. After decades of dishing up "Continental" and "California" foods, Floridians have finally discovered the gastronomic treasures in their own backyard. In the process, we've captivated the taste of a nation that is hungry for fun, vibrant, tropical food that is loaded with flavor and healthy to boot.

If ever there was an area ripe for a culinary revolution, it is Florida. The Sunshine State has everything a cook could want: The Atlantic Ocean and Gulf of Mexico supply impeccably fresh stone crabs, spiny lobsters, Gulf shrimp, Apalachicola Bay oysters, and more than 500 varieties of finfish. The nation's largest freshwater swamp, the Everglades, yields such rustic delicacies as alligator, frogs' legs, and hearts of palm.

Florida's semitropical climate supports a year-round growing season. (Where else can you find ripe farmstand tomatoes in December?) Citrus groves in central Florida furnish the rest of the country with the bulk of our oranges, grapefruits, tangerines, and kumquats. More recently, Homestead, Florida (a farming community near Miami) has become the nation's exotic fruit capital, specializing in mangos, star fruit, lychees, passion fruit, sapotes, and mameys. The Spanish explorer Ponce de Leon had the right idea when he named the region Florida, which stems from the Latin word "flowering."

South Florida is the crossroads of the Caribbean and Latin America. Miami has a Cuban population of

250,000, a Nicaraguan population of 150,000. Our Haitian and Colombian communities are the largest in the nation. Nearly 50 percent of Dade County is Hispanic. Latin American food pervades the Floridian diet. Most street corners in Miami have their *loncherias*, Cuban snack bars. Mainstream supermarkets in Florida sell calabazas (West Indian pumpkins), boniatos (Cuban sweet potatoes), plantains, cassava, and other Hispanic produce.

Florida restaurant-goers have a staggering choice of Cuban, Colombian, Nicaraguan, Honduran, Peruvian, Argentinan, Haitian, Bajan, Jamaican, and Trinidadian restaurants. Miamians munch on *arepas* (Columbian grilled cheese sandwiches) and *tres leches* (Nicaraguan "three milks" cake) the way Texans eat burritos and San Franciscans down dim sum. Nor is Hispanic dining here limited to ethnic holes-in-the-wall. A new breed of restaurant, epitomized by Miami's Yuca and Victor's Café, has raised ethnic food to the level of fine dining.

Given the superlative raw materials, the cultural richness and ethnic diversity, the local preference for high-flavor low-fat cooking methods dictated by the warm weather (and craved by health-conscious Americans), it's no surprise that the Sunshine State would give rise to a new regional cuisine. What is astonishing is that it didn't happen sooner. Of the top twenty restaurants in South Florida, fifteen didn't exist just a few years ago. Virtually overnight, Miami has gone from being a cultural backwater to an acclaimed culinary trendsetter.

But there's more to Floridian cooking than just America's latest food trend. The Sunshine State is pioneering foods that

the rest of country will eat in the twenty-first century. Hispanic root vegetables, exotic tropical fruits, under-utilized seafoods, seasonings from the Caribbean Basin: These are everyday fare in Florida. More and more of these foods are turning up in mainstream super-markets across the U.S. As the Hispanification of American culture increases, so will the popularity of Florida's Hispano-American cuisine.

What's more, Floridian food is generally health-ful food. Our collective fondness for salads and seafood and for marinating and grilling are very much in keeping with modern American health-conscious-ness. It's only natural. We all but invented beach cul-ture and our cuisine is designed to keep you looking good in the sun!

Thirst Quenchers

Rum Runner

Banana Mojito

Mamey Daiquiri

South Beach Sangria

Victor's Café occupies a sprawling neo-Colonial building on a busy street in Miami. But take a seat at the bar and you can imagine yourself in Havana in the glory days of the fifties. Musicians in *guaracheras* (puff-shouldered jackets tied at the waist) croon mambo songs of love. Bartenders in white jackets with pink bow ties expertly mix daiquiris, *presidentés*, and *mulatas*. And just about everyone, at some time or other, orders a mint-flavored thirst quencher known as a *mojito*. Welcome to one of the world's best watering holes!

As Hemingway knew, Florida is a drinking man's paradise. Even during Prohibition, smugglers, like the character Harry Morgan in *To Have and Have Not*, kept Sunshine Staters stocked with their favorite libation: rum. Their memory lives on in a pastel-colored drink popular throughout the Florida Keys, the Rum Runner. Today, Miami is the corporate headquarters of the world's largest rum company, Bacardi.

Castro's rise to power in 1959 marked a red-letter date in Florida mixology. For three decades, exiles have streamed to Miami from Cuba, bringing with them a thirst for such traditional island beverages as *guarapo* (sugarcane juice) and *batidos* (fruit shakes). The bartenders of Miami's Calle Ocho (Little Havana) or Tampa's Ybor City still make the drinks they enjoyed in the old country. Cubans are also passionate coffee drinkers. Thimble-size cups of sugary black *café cubano* can be sipped on virtually any street corner. Cuban coffee is Miami's answer to espresso—enjoyed by Anglos and Hispanics alike.

But if Florida is a barfly's paradise, it is also a haven for bartenders. The lime groves in the Redlands and orange groves in Indian River supply fresh fruit juices for mixing. We even make our own sugar, thanks to the cane fields around Lake Okeechobee. Twelve months a year, we have warm weather and plenty of sunshine to make you thirsty. Our 2,120 miles of stunning coast-line offer a great waterfront setting for drinks to toast the sunset.

So, pull up a chair and reach for your glass. The party's about to begin.

Mango Nectar

It's hard to believe that a fruit as luxurious as a mango would be so cheap people practically give it away. But at the height of mango season in Florida, roadside stands sell the abundant fruit for as little as three for one dollar. Mango nectar is very easy to make at home, and it's a great way to use up bruised or overly fibrous mangos.

MAKES 6 CUPS

1 large ripe mango (1¼ to 1½ pounds)
1 to 2 tablespoons sugar, or to taste
1 to 2 tablespoons fresh lime juice, or
    to taste
4 cups water

1. Peel the mango and cut the flesh off the seed (for easy preparation, see page 80). Place the flesh in a blender with the sugar, lime juice, and water. Purée until smooth. (This can be done in batches. Correct the seasoning, adding sugar or lime juice to taste.)
2. Strain the mango nectar into a pitcher and refrigerate until serving time. Stir well just before serving.

Tamarind Nectar

The fruity tartness of tamarind makes it an excellent refresher. Fresh tamarind is in season from May to November. If unavailable, look for packaged tamarind pulp in a Hispanic or Asian market.

MAKES 6 CUPS

6 to 8 fresh tamarind pods, or 4 ounces peeled tamarind pulp
2 cups hot water (heated, not tap)
4 cups cold water
⅓ cup sugar, or to taste

1. Skin the tamarind pods, scraping off the peel with a paring knife.

2. Place the pulp in the bowl of a blender with the hot water. Let stand for 10 minutes. Blend the mixture in short bursts at low speed until the seeds are free of pulp, 30 to 60 seconds.

3. Pour the tamarind mixture through a fine-mesh strainer into a bowl or pitcher, pressing hard with a wooden spoon to extract the juices, and scraping the bottom of the strainer with a rubber spatula. Set the tamarind water aside.

4. Return the seeds and pulp that remain in the strainer to the blender and blend with the cold water and sugar. Strain this mixture into the tamarind water and chill.

5. Just before serving, season the nectar to taste, adding sugar if it's too sour or water if it's too strong. Shake or stir well before serving.

PIQUANT PODS

When I first moved to Florida, I was puzzled by the crescent-shaped, fuzzy brown seed pods in the produce section of our local market. Our Cuban friend, Elida Proenza, explained their identity to me: *tamarindo*, fresh tamarind pods.

The tamarind tree grows throughout the Caribbean, where the orangish brown flesh of its seed pods is prized as a flavoring for drinks and sauces. Tamarind tastes like a cross between lime juice and prunes.

Tamarind is too sticky and fibrous to use in its natural state. The first step is to turn the stringy flesh into "tamarind water" (also known as "tamarind purée"). If you use fresh pods, trim off the skin with a paring knife. Hispanic and Asian markets sell plastic-wrapped packages of peeled tamarind pulp. To make 2 cups of tamarind water, you'll need 6 to 8 fresh pods or 4 ounces of peeled pulp.

Break the pulp into small pieces and place them in a blender with 1½ cups boiling water. Let this mixture stand for 8 to 10 minutes, to soften the pulp. Run the blender in short bursts at low speed for 30 to 60 seconds to obtain a thick brown liquid. (Blend briefly: You don't want to chop the seeds—they're bitter.) Pour this liquid through a fine-mesh strainer into a bowl, pressing hard with a wooden spoon to extract the juices, and scraping the bottom of the strainer with a spatula.

Return the pulp from the strainer to the blender and add ¼ cup hot water. Blend briefly, again, and pour the mixture though the strainer, pressing well to extract the juices. You should wind up with about 2 cups of tamarind "water," or purée. It will keep for 1 week in the refrigerator. I freeze it in ice cube trays to have 2-tablespoon portions of tamarind water whenever I need it.

If you live in an area with a large Hispanic population, you may be able to find frozen strained tamarind purée, thereby eliminating the above preparation steps. The Cuban grocery store in my neighborhood sells it by the name of *pulpa de tamarindo*. An 8-ounce bag costs less than $2.

Orange and Carrot Juice

I first tasted this drink in a now-defunct Nicaraguan restaurant called Momotombo. I've since enjoyed it at many Cuban and Colombian restaurants, not to mention at juice bars from St. Augustine to Key West. The combination may sound bizarre, but it's really quite refreshing. The nutmeg is my touch and can be omitted for the sake of authenticity.

SERVES 1

Crushed ice
½ cup fresh orange juice
½ cup fresh carrot juice
Freshly grated nutmeg

Fill a large (12 ounce) glass with crushed ice. Add the juices and stir well with a long-handled spoon. Grate a little nutmeg on top, and serve at once.

Banana-Strawberry Batido

This is one of the most popular *batidos*. For the best results, use very ripe bananas and fragrant, ripe strawberries.

SERVES 2

1 cup hulled strawberries, plus 2 large berries for garnish
1 banana
1 tablespoon sweetened condensed milk
1 to 2 tablespoons sugar, or to taste
1 tablespoon fresh lime juice, or to taste
1½ cups crushed ice

1. Combine all of the ingredients except the strawberry garnish in a blender, and purée until smooth. Taste for sweetness, adding sugar or lime juice as necessary.

2. Pour the *batidos* into tall glasses. Garnish each with a whole strawberry and serve at once.

Melon-Papaya Batido

A slightly more exotic shake, this recipe unites watermelon and papaya. To check the latter for ripeness, squeeze it. It should be gently yielding to the touch.

SERVES 2

1 cup diced, seeded watermelon, plus 2 small wedges
    for garnish
1 cup diced ripe papaya
1 tablespoon sweetened condensed milk
1 to 2 tablespoons sugar, or to taste
1 tablespoon fresh lime juice, or to taste
1½ cups crushed ice

BATIDOS: MILK SHAKES THE HISPANIC WAY

When most North Americans think of milk shakes, they envision a thick ice cream-based beverage rich enough to double as dessert. Floridians are more likely to drink *batidos*. Served at juice bars and *loncherias* (Cuban snack bars) throughout the state, *batidos* are a cross between a smoothie and a milk shake. The name comes from the Spanish word *bater*, to beat or purée.

Batidos differ from milk shakes in two essential ways. The main ingredient of a *batido* is fresh fruit, not dairy products. The primary chilling agent is ice, not ice cream. This makes *batidos* lighter and lower in fat than their North American counterparts—no small advantage in the Florida summer, when it's 90 degrees in the shade.

Some juice bar jockeys enrich their *batidos* with a spoonful of sweetened condensed milk. This, too, is dictated by the climate. Before the widespread availability of refrigeration (still the case in parts of the Caribbean and Central America), this was the only dairy product that

1. Combine all of the ingredients except the watermelon garnish in a blender, and purée until smooth. Taste for sweetness, adding sugar or lime juice as necessary.

2. Pour the *batidos* into tall glasses. Garnish each with a watermelon wedge and serve at once.

wouldn't spoil in the heat.

Batidos are made with a cornucopia of exotic Floridian fruits. Where else in the U.S. would you find shakes made with atemoya or mamey? The former looks like a puffed-up artichoke and tastes like a cross between melon, grapes, and vanilla pudding. The latter has the shape of an elongated coconut and the flavor of a baked sweet potato. These and other tropical fruits are whirred into creamy shakes that evoke the flavor of the Caribbean.

Of course, *batidos* are also made with more plebeian ingredients, like pineapples, strawberries, and bananas. Then, there are more offbeat versions, like *batido de trigo*, a curious "wheat" *batido,* made by blending ice, sugar, milk, and puffed wheat breakfast cereal.

Wherever the sun creates thirst and there's an electrical outlet handy for plugging in a blender, you will find someone serving these refreshing Floridian drinks.

Puffed Wheat Batido

Of all the *batidos* enjoyed by Florida's Hispanic-Americans, this is the most unusual. I like to think of it as a liquid breakfast. The recipe comes from one of the best places to sample *batidos*, the Mappy restaurant, located on Ocean Drive in the heart of the Art Deco District of Miami Beach.

SERVES 1

1 cup puffed wheat cereal
½ cup milk
½ cup crushed ice
2 tablespoons sugar, or to taste
Pinch of salt

Combine all of the ingredients in a blender and purée until smooth. Serve at once.

Pineapple-Mint Batido

This recipe is a cross between a piña colada and a *Mojito* (see page 12). *Batidos* don't normally contain rum, but you could always add an ounce or so to this one, if you like.

SERVES 2

1½ cups diced fresh pineapple
1½ cups crushed ice
⅓ cup canned sweetened coconut cream, such as Coco Lopez
¼ cup fresh mint leaves, or 1½ teaspoons dried, plus 2 large
     sprigs for garnish

1. Combine all of the ingredients except the garnish in a blender, and purée until smooth.

2. Pour the *batidos* into tall glasses and garnish each with a sprig of mint.

CUBAN COCKTAILS

Like so much of Caribbean culture, the Cuban cocktail began with the fateful encounter of the Old World and New World in 1492. Columbus and his successors brought many Old World and African foods to the New World, foremost among them sugar cane. By the eighteenth century, sugar cane was cultivated throughout the Caribbean, and by the nineteenth century, it was Cuba's primary industry. And wherever sugar cane grows, you find rum.

Columbus was also responsible for bringing the second crucial cocktail ingredient to the Caribbean: the lime. It arrived here in 1493 and its antiscorbutic properties were much prized by European seafarers. Within a century, it had spread across the Caribbean to Central and South America.

The harshness of the early rums made mixing desirable, if not mandatory. With lime juice and sugar in place, the stage was set for the invention of Cuba's most famous drink: the Daiquiri. History books credit an American, one Jennings S. Cox, with the drink's discovery. Cox belonged to a contingent of American engineers who ran the Daiquiri iron mines in southeast Cuba after the Spanish-American War. Legend has it that Cox created the drink at the Venus Hotel in Santiago de Cuba. In all likelihood, he simply coined a name for a drink that had been enjoyed throughout Cuba for decades if not for centuries.

The Daiquiri wasn't the only Cuban cocktail invented by Americans around the time of the Spanish-American War. Roosevelt's Rough Riders introduced Cuba to a new soft drink invented by Atlanta pharmacist Dr. John Smyth Pemberton: Coca-Cola. Originally, coke and rum were combined with sugar and lime juice to toast the liberation of Havana. The result was the Cuba Libre (free Cuba).

If Cuban bartending was born during the Spanish-American War, it reached its heyday during Prohibition. Pan Am seaplane flights would roar off from Dinner Key, a tiny peninsula in Coconut Grove, ferrying American revelers to Havana. Bartenders became celebrities, creating new drinks, which they named for American movie stars. The Mary Pickford (rum, pineapple juice, grenadine, and maraschino liqueur) dates from this period, as does the Douglas Fairbanks (apricot brandy, lemon juice, egg white, and gin). Hemingway was both a fan and symbol of Prohibition-era Havana, where, legend has it, he would stop at the Floridita Bar for his daily Daiquiri, then La Bodeguita del Medio for his *mojito.*

The *mojito* is the most famous Cuban cocktail, although it's ignored by most Anglos and virtually unknown in the States outside of Miami. A rum and lime spritzer, it owes its unique flavor to an herb called *yerbabuena*, a cousin of North America's spearmint. One theory holds that the *mojito* is named for the popular Cuban table sauce *mojo*. Alternatively, the name may come from the Spanish verb *mojar*, to wet or moisten.

The traditional accompaniment for a *mojito* is *chicharrónes,* bite-size nuggets of deep-fried pork rind. While *chicharrónes* may not fit into the health-conscious North American diet, the fat helps slow the body's alcohol absorption—and the speed with which you get drunk!

Rum Runner

Rum running was a widespread and honorable profession in the Florida Keys during Prohibition, immortalized in Hemingway's novel, *To Have and Have Not*. Rum is legal, of course, these days, and an enormous amount of it is consumed in the Florida Keys in the form of the Rum Runner, a frozen drink made with three types of rum and an assortment of fruit liqueurs. Warning: Rum Runners go down with astonishing ease. When partaking, make sure you have a designated driver!

SERVES 2

1 ounce light rum

1 ounce dark rum

½ ounce 151° rum

1½ ounces banana liqueur

1 ounce blackberry brandy or sloe gin

½ ounce grenadine

1½ ounces fresh lime juice, plus 2 lime wedges
for garnish

1½ cups crushed ice

1. Combine all of the ingredients except the lime wedges in a blender, and purée until smooth.

2. Pour into tumblers and garnish with the lime wedges.

South Beach Sangria

angría turns up at innumerable Spanish, Nicaraguan, and Cuban restaurants in South Florida. This one features the tropical fruits for which Dade County is becoming so famous.

SERVES 8

1 bottle (750 ml/25.4 ounces) dry red wine
¼ cup (packed) light brown sugar, or to taste
4 cinnamon sticks, 2 inches each
1 cup fresh orange juice
1 orange, thinly sliced and seeded
1 lemon, thinly sliced and seeded
2 star fruits, thinly sliced
1 mango, peeled, seeded, and diced (see page 80)
1 atemoya, peeled, seeded, and diced, or other exotic fruit
16 ounces club soda or 7-Up

1. Combine the wine, brown sugar, and cinnamon sticks in a large pitcher. Stir with a wooden spoon until the sugar dissolves. Stir in the orange juice and fruits. (The sangría can be prepared up to 30 minutes ahead to this stage. Indeed, it will taste richer if you let the fruit macerate for 30 minutes.)

2. Just before serving, stir in the club soda. Correct the flavorings, adding sugar or orange juice to taste.

Mojito (Rum Spritzer)

Mojito is one of the most refreshing drinks ever to grace a bar glass. To be strictly authentic, you'll need *yerbabuena* (*Mentha nemorosa* in Latin), an herb in the mint family, whose name literally means "good herb" in Spanish. If you live in a city with a Cuban neighborhood, *yerbabuena* can be found at a botanica (herb shop) or Hispanic food market. It's a little less sweet than American mint and has a slightly bitter aftertaste. Fresh spearmint, peppermint, or even sweet basil make acceptable substitutes.

....
SERVES 1
....

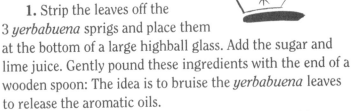

*3 sprigs yerbabuena or mint
    (10 to 12 leaves), plus 1 large
    sprig for garnish*
1 tablespoon sugar, or to taste
1½ tablespoons fresh lime juice
1½ ounces light rum
1 cup ice cubes
About 1 cup club soda

1. Strip the leaves off the 3 *yerbabuena* sprigs and place them at the bottom of a large highball glass. Add the sugar and lime juice. Gently pound these ingredients with the end of a wooden spoon: The idea is to bruise the *yerbabuena* leaves to release the aromatic oils.

2. Stir in the rum, followed by the ice cubes. Add enough club soda to fill the glass. Stir the *mojito* with a long-handled spoon until the sugar dissolves. Garnish the glass with the remaining *yerbabuena* sprig and serve at once.

GUARAPO: FRESH SUGAR CANE JUICE

Sidle up to a Cuban snack bar and you'll observe a curious ritual. When a customer orders *guarapo* (wa-RA-po), the vendor takes a 3-foot length of fresh sugar cane and feeds it into a stainless steel box-like pressing device. A minute later a greenish liquid emerges from the chute at the bottom: *guarapo*—fresh sugar cane juice.

Cane juice isn't nearly as sugary as you'd expect, for the sweetness is offset by an earthy mineral flavor and a delicate green taste, like alfalfa sprouts. Served over ice in a paper cup, it's one of the best thirst quenchers under the Florida sun.

Guarapo can be purchased at many Hispanic markets and

Banana Mojito

Here's a drink of my own invention, which is really a cross between a *mojito* and banana *batido*.

....

SERVES 4

....

1 very ripe banana
3 ounces light rum
3 tablespoons fresh lime juice
3 tablespoons sugar, or to taste
3 tablespoons chopped fresh mint leaves,
    plus 4 mint sprigs for garnish
1 cup crushed ice
2 cups club soda

1. Peel and dice the banana and place it in a blender with the rum, lime juice, sugar, chopped mint, and ice. Blend until smooth and creamy.

2. Add the club soda and blend for a few seconds to mix. Pour the *mojito* into 4 tall glasses. Garnish each with a sprig of mint.

Mamey Daiquiri

Frozen daiquiris have, of course, become standard fare at any North American bar. There's no mistaking the Cuban origins of this daiquiri, a specialty of Miami's famous Victor's Café, made with a

juice bars. Canned cane juice can be found in Asian markets. Boiled down to a thick, honey-like syrup, it is delectable on tea breads, pancakes, and waffles. You can also use it for curing fish. *Guarapo* is also the starting point of a famous Cuban cocktail. Just add light rum and fresh lime juice in equal portions.

tropical fruit that looks and tastes like a cross between a melon and baked sweet potato. A similar daiquiri could be made with mango, papaya, or strawberries. The nutmeg—my own addition—is optional.

SERVES 1

*5 tablespoons chopped mamey, or other fruit
    mentioned above*
1½ ounces light rum
2 tablespoons half-and-half
2 tablespoons fresh lime juice
1 to 2 tablespoons sugar, or to taste
1 cup crushed ice
Freshly grated nutmeg

1. Combine all of the ingredients except the nutmeg in a blender, and blend until smooth.

2. Pour the daiquiri into a shallow champagne glass and lightly dust with freshly grated nutmeg.

Saoco

Saoco (sa-OH-ko) is traditionally made with the water (the clear liquid) of a green coconut. Green coconuts can be found at Hispanic markets. To open them, whack off the top with a cleaver or large chef's knife. You can also make *saoco* with the liquid in a ripe (hard brown) coconut. To open the latter, punch in the "eyes" (round dots on the top of the shell) with a screwdriver, then drain the coconut over a glass.

2 to 3 ounces coconut water
1½ ounces light rum
2 teaspoons fresh lime juice, or to taste
2 teaspoons sugar, or to taste
Ice cubes

Combine all of the ingredients except the ice in a shaker glass, and stir with a spoon until the sugar dissolves. Pour the mixture into a stemmed glass filled with ice.

Mulata

Chocolate and lime aren't ingredients one would readily think of combining, but they go together well in this classic Cuban cocktail. Traditionally, a Mulata is served straight up, but you can also make a frozen Mulata by puréeing the ingredients in a blender.

1½ ounces light rum
¾ ounce dark crème de cacao
1 tablespoon fresh lime juice, or to taste
1 cup ice cubes

Combine all of the ingredients in a bar shaker, cover, and shake well. Strain the Mulata into a martini glass.

Cuban Coffee

*L*et the Italians have their espresso, the French their café au lait: I raise my cup for *café cubano*. I'm certainly not alone. This dark, dulcet brew is one of the official drinks of Miami, sipped by the thousands from thimble-size plastic cups. In most American cities, only "Yupscale" restaurants or cafés have commercial espresso machines. In Miami, such equipment is found at the lowliest lunch counter. Elsewhere in the country people pay 1 to 2 dollars for a cup of espresso; Miamians pay an average of 30 cents a shot for *café cubano*!

Cuban coffee is something of a misnomer, as the most popular brands, Café Pilon and Café Bustelo, use beans from Ecuador, Colombia, Brazil, and other countries, but not Cuba. What makes the coffee Cuban is its intensity and sweetness. Cuban coffee is always served presweetened. To make true Cuban coffee, with the characteristic froth on top, you really need a commercial espresso machine. But good results can be obtained with a home model.

SERVES 4

3 tablespoons finely ground dark roast coffee
1 cup water
2 to 3 teaspoons sugar, or to taste

Make the coffee in an espresso machine, following the manufacturer's instructions. Have the sugar in the receiving cup. Stir well and serve at once.

HOW TO DRINK COFFEE LIKE A CUBAN

*B*lack as night, sweet as sin, frothy as a sea squall, and dear to Floridians of all ethnic persuasions, that's *café cubano*—Cuban coffee.

Cuban coffee comes in a variety of forms and sizes. Here's the lingo you need to drink it like a native.

CAFE CUBANO: Sweetened black coffee for one person. (In other cities, it would be called espresso.) It's usually served in a demitasse and is always served sweetened. (To order it without sugar, say *sin azúcar*.)

COLADA: An order of Cuban coffee to be shared with office companions or friends. Coladas are usually ordered to go. You will be given a small styrofoam cup of coffee and a half-dozen thimble-size plastic serving cups.

CAFE CON LECHE: Roughly equal parts Cuban coffee and hot milk. This is the Cuban equivalent of French *café au lait*.

CAFE CORTADITO: Cuban coffee with a little milk.

CAFE CARAJILLO: Cuban coffee with brandy.

Starters, Snacks, and Fritters

Conch Fritters

Black Bean Salsa

Nicaraguan Meat Pies

Tamales

Caribbean Tuber Chips

Gator Guacamole

In Spain they're known as *tapas*, in Nicaragua *antejitos*. But whatever you call them, they mean bar food unlike any you'll find elsewhere in the U.S. Floridians are great fans of Hispanic hors d'oeuvres, partaking of them with gusto at Nicaraguan steak houses, Spanish and Cuban restaurants in Miami's Little Havana, and seaside pubs from Panama City to Key West.

The term *tapas* comes from *tapar*, the Spanish verb meaning "to cover." The first *tapas* were served on small plates that acted as covers for drink glasses. In time, the food on these plates became delicacies in their own right. Spanish *tapas* have profoundly influenced Floridian bar fare. Popular hors d'oeuvre flavorings, for example, include *chorizo* (Spanish sausage), *jamón serrano* (mountain-style ham), and *queso manchego* (Spanish sheep's milk cheese).

Other Floridian starters have more direct Caribbean roots. Consider the Caribbean vegetable chips served at popular Hispanic restaurants, such as Miami's Yuca and Cafe Tu Tu Tango. Chips and dips have been around, of course, as long as potatoes and tortillas have. But only in Florida are they made with such exotic vegetables as yuca, malanga, boniato, and plantain.

Fritters, too, loom large on Florida's culinary landscape. Hush puppies are a mainstay among rural Floridians from the central and northern part of the state. Key Westers are partial to conch fritters, made with giant sea snails that once teemed in south Florida's waters. (Today, most of our conch comes from the Bahamas.) Salt cod fritters turn up in our Bajan (Barbadian) and Jamaican restaurants. Fried plantains and plantain fritters are immensely popular among Miami's Hispano-Americans. But Floridians will turn just about any food into fritters, from alligator to olives.

Also popular with Florida snackers are *tamales*, *empanadas*, and *arepas*. The first are savory snacks cooked inside corn husks. *Empanadas* are crisp-fried turnovers that come with a variety of fillings, from spiced beef to guava paste and cheese. *Arepas* are a gift of our Colombian community, a cross between polenta and a grilled cheese sandwich. All turn up at street fairs, where they're enjoyed by Anglos and Hispanics alike.

Here's a look at some of the most popular Floridian snack foods. It's a long way from nachos!

Floridian Tuber Chips

To most Americans, a chip means one of two essential American snack foods: a potato chip or a corn chip. Here in Florida we make chips from a host of tropical vegetables, from boniatos to plantains. You don't even have to go to an ethnic restaurant to enjoy our unusual chips. Stop at a traffic light in a Hispanic neighborhood in Miami and you may be approached by a *mariquita* man, selling paper bags of crisp plantain chips.

SERVES 4

3 to 4 cups canola or peanut oil, for frying
1 pound boniato, malanga, yam, dasheen (taro),
*   or other Hispanic root vegetables*
Salt

1. Pour the oil to a depth of 2 to 3 inches in a deep-fat fryer, dutch oven, or deep heavy skillet and heat to 350°F.

2. Peel the tubers. Slice them as thinly as possible across the grain on a mandoline. If you have a lightweight mandoline, slice the chips directly into the hot fat in small batches so as not to crowd the pan. Alternatively, slice the chips onto a plate or dish towel, then add them to the fat.

3. Fry the chips until golden brown, a total of 1 to 2 minutes, turning with a wire skimmer. Drain the chips on paper towels. Sprinkle with salt and serve at once.

Note: A mandoline is a flat wooden, metal, or plastic slicer with an adjustable metal blade in the center. Slice the chips as thinly as possible. The fine slicing blade of a food processor will work in a pinch, but the slices won't be as even. Most Hispanic grocery stores sell inexpensive wooden mandolines.

Mariquitas

ariquita is the Cuban name for a crisp-fried green plantain chip, reminiscent in taste to the potato chip. Nicaraguans call them *tajadas*. The plantains are sliced lengthwise to create a long, slender, wavy chip. Stand the chips upright in your favorite dip to create a whimsical hors d'oeuvre.

SERVES 4

3 to 4 cups canola or peanut oil, for frying
2 green plantains
Salt or garlic salt

1. Pour the oil to a depth of 2 to 3 inches in a deep-fat

HISPANIC TUBERS

You may have seen them at the supermarket. Strange looking tubers. Bizarre roots. Inscrutable produce arranged alongside the more commonplace potatoes and carrots. They are Latin American vegetables and they are being added to America's melting pot with increasing fervor and frequency.

These foods were once available only at ethnic markets and specialty shops. Due to the influx of Hispanic immigrants in the last fifteen years, they've become available closer to home. For the cook, it's a whole new ballgame. Here's a scorecard to help you identify the players.

BONIATO: Sweet-potato-like, but harder, drier, and considerably less sweet than the North American varieties. Also known as *batata*, *camote*, and Cuban sweet potato, this turnip-shaped or elongated root has patchy reddish or purplish brown skin. The flavor has the mealy sweetness of chestnuts.

DASHEEN: This barrel-shaped tuber with its shaggy, bark-like skin and concentric, ring-like markings is known by a myriad of names, including *tannia*, *tannier*, *taro*, and *eddo*. (Dasheen is a corruption of the French words *de la Chine*, "from China.") The flesh may be white, cream colored, or even lavender and turns purplish or gray when cooked. The flavor is similar to potato, with hints of artichoke and chestnut.

MALANGA: Also known as *yautia*, this gnarled, elongated, brown-skinned root looks like a carrot that's been through the wringer. The pink, yellow, or cream-colored flesh has an aroma reminiscent of a musty cellar. For me, this one is an acquired taste, but it's much beloved in Miami.

YAM: Most of what passes for yam in the United States is actually sweet potato. There's no mistaking the Afro-Hispanic yam (also called *ñame* or *gname*). Its color ranges from white to ivory to pale yellow, and when freshly sliced, it exudes a sticky juice. The flavor recalls potato with a faint hint of chestnut. But yams are never sweet. Yams can grow up to 6 feet in length, so it's customary to buy them in pieces.

fryer, dutch oven, or deep heavy skillet and heat to 350°F.

2. Peel the plantains (see the sidebar, page 28). Slice lengthwise as thinly as possible on a mandoline. If you have a lightweight mandoline, slice the strips directly into the hot fat in small batches so as not to crowd the pan. Alternatively, slice the chips onto a plate or dish towel, then add them to the fat.

3. Fry the strips until golden brown, a total of 1 to 2 minutes, turning with a wire skimmer. Drain the *mariquitas* on paper towels. Sprinkle with salt and serve at once.

Black Bean Salsa

The Southwest meets the Sunshine State in this colorful "Floribbean" salsa. Serve it with the *Mariquitas* or Floridian Tuber Chips in the preceding recipes or even with tortilla chips.

SERVES 4 TO 6

2 cups Firm-Cooked Black Beans (see page 269)

2 to 3 tablespoons extra-virgin olive oil

3 to 4 tablespoons fresh lime juice, or to taste

½ cup cooked corn kernels

1 ripe avocado, peeled, pitted, and finely diced

1 poblano chili or ½ green bell pepper, cored, seeded, and finely diced

½ red bell pepper, cored, seeded, and finely diced

½ cup finely diced red onion

½ scotch bonnet chili or 1 to 2 jalapeño chilies, seeded and minced

½ teaspoon ground cumin

½ cup finely chopped fresh cilantro or mint leaves

Salt and freshly ground black pepper, to taste

Combine all of the ingredients in a mixing bowl and toss well. Correct the seasonings, adding salt or lime juice to taste. The salsa should be highly seasoned.

Gator Guacamole

Florida avocados, or alligator pears, as they're sometimes called, are larger, rounder, and sweeter than the California varieties, but either will work fine. I like to serve *Mariquitas* (page 20) with this guacamole, which is medium-hot to hot, depending on the amount of chili you decide to use.

SERVES 4 TO 6

2 ripe avocados (preferably Florida avocados)
3 to 4 tablespoons sour orange juice (see page 72)
      or fresh lime juice
1 clove garlic, minced
½ to 1 scotch bonnet chili, seeded and
      minced
4 scallions, trimmed and finely chopped
2 tablespoons extra-virgin olive oil
¼ cup chopped fresh cilantro or mint leaves
Salt and freshly ground black pepper, to taste
1 cup Firm-Cooked Black Beans (see page 269)

1. Peel, pit, and finely dice the avocados, then toss them with 1 tablespoon of the sour orange juice to prevent discoloring.

2. Place half the avocados in a bowl with the garlic, chili, and scallions. Mash with a fork to a smooth paste. Beat in the olive oil, the remaining sour orange juice, cilantro, and salt and pepper.

3. Gently fold in the black beans and remaining diced avocado. Correct the seasonings, adding salt, olive oil, or sour orange juice. Spoon the guacamole into a bowl and stand some of the plantain chips upright in it. Arrange the remaining chips in a basket at the side of the guacamole.

Smoked Mullet Dip

S moked mullet is a specialty of the northwest coast of Florida, especially Cedar Key, where it's mixed with cream cheese and sour cream to make an outrageously savory dip. Smoked mullet can be found at select fishmongers and some Greek markets. If unavailable, smoked bluefish or mackerel make acceptable substitutes. Serve with crackers, bagel chips, or thin slices of crusty bread.

SERVES 4

8 ounces smoked mullet

4 ounces cream cheese, at room temperature

½ cup sour cream

> *Dash of Tabasco sauce*
>
> *Salt and freshly ground black pepper, to taste*

1. Remove the skin and any bones from the mullet and purée the fish in a food processor. Work in all of the remaining ingredients.

2. Correct the seasonings, adding Tabasco sauce and salt or pepper to taste. Transfer to a serving bowl and refrigerate, covered, until serving time.

Floridian Tortilla

In most parts of the country, *tortilla* means a Mexican-style flatbread made of cornmeal or flour. In Florida, the term often refers to a traditional Spanish snack, a sort of frittata made with onions and potatoes. My version differs from traditional *tortilla espagnola* in two ways. First, I use boniato (Cuban sweet potato) in place of potato. (If boniato is unavailable, use Yukon golds or Idaho potatoes.) Second, to make the dish lighter, I cook the boniatos by boiling instead of deep-frying.

SERVES 8 TO 10

3 pounds boniato or potatoes, peeled and cut into
    ¼-inch-thick slices
Salt
3 tablespoons extra-virgin olive oil
2 onions, thinly sliced
6 eggs, beaten
Freshly ground black pepper

1. Preheat the oven to 375°F.

2. Place the boniato slices in a large pot with cold water to cover and 1 teaspoon salt. Bring to a boil. Reduce the heat and simmer the boniato until tender, 10 minutes. Drain in a colander and rinse with cold water. Drain well.

3. Heat 2 tablespoons of the olive oil in a 10-inch non-stick ovenproof frying pan. Add the onions and cook over medium heat until golden brown, about 5 minutes.

4. Transfer the onions with a slotted spoon to a mixing bowl. Stir in the boniato, eggs, and salt and pepper to taste. The tortilla mixture should be highly seasoned.

5. Heat the remaining 1 tablespoon oil

OUT OF THE FRYING PAN

Deep-frying is hardly a fashionable cooking method in these health-conscious 1990s. But without it, there would be no conch fritters, no hush puppies, and none of that Cuban snack favorite, *croquetas*. In short, Florida's cuisine would be considerably impoverished without fritters. Eat them in moderate quantities and the pleasure you derive may well offset any deleterious effects from the fat.

There's no great mystery to the popularity of fritters here in the tropics. Quick to prepare and cooked at the last minute, fritters are the ideal street food. The speed of preparation makes them ideal party fare as well. Most fritters are highly seasoned, making them the perfect companion to Florida's bounty of festive mixed drinks.

Deep-frying is easy, but there are a few watchpoints.

Boniato

First, use a neutral-tasting oil with a high smoking point: peanut or canola oil is ideal. Second, heat the oil to the proper temperature (350° to 375°F). If the oil is too cool, the fritters will be soggy. If too hot, the exterior of the fritter will burn before the inside has a chance to cook.

There's a simple way to test the temperature of the oil, even if you don't have a deep-frying thermometer. Add a slice of garlic: If bubbles dance around it vigorously for 20 seconds without browning the garlic, the oil is the proper temperature for frying. If the garlic sinks to the bottom, the oil is too cool. If it browns immediately, the oil is too hot.

Cook fritters in small batches: Crowding the pan lowers the overall temperature of the oil and prevents the fritters from cooking properly. Let the oil reheat before adding another batch. Finally, place the fritters on paper towels to drain before serving.

in the frying pan over medium heat. Add all of the tortilla mixture and pat with a spatula into a pancake shape. Lightly brown the bottom of the tortilla, about 2 minutes. Transfer the frying pan to the oven and bake the tortilla until the egg is set, about 30 minutes. When cooked, an inserted skewer will come out clean.

6. Remove the pan from the oven and let cool for 5 minutes. Invert the tortilla onto a round platter. The tortilla can be served warm or at room temperature. Cut into wedges for serving.

Conch Fritters

Conch fritters are a mainstay in the Florida Keys, and there are probably as many versions as there are seaside bars to serve them. Conch has a mild, sweet taste—like an ethereal scallop. If it tastes fishy or ammoniated, it's no good. Virtually all the conch sold in the U.S. comes trimmed, but if any black or orange membranes slipped by the processor, they should be removed. (For a full discussion of conch, see page 174.) Should conch be unavailable in your area, you could use equal parts shrimp and scallops. The Caribbean Cocktail Sauce on page 113 makes a good accompaniment.

MAKES 24 TO 28

8 ounces conch (see page 172), cut into ½ inch pieces
1 cup all-purpose flour
1 teaspoon sugar
1 teaspoon baking powder
1 egg, beaten
6 to 8 tablespoons buttermilk or milk
1 pickled jalapeño chili, minced
¼ cup finely chopped onion
¼ cup finely chopped red bell pepper
¼ cup minced celery
1 clove garlic, minced
Salt and freshly ground black pepper, to taste
About 2 cups vegetable oil, for frying

1. Finely grind the conch in a food processor or meat grinder.

2. Combine the flour, sugar, baking powder, and egg in a large bowl and beat well, adding buttermilk as necessary to obtain a thick paste. The mixture should be the consistency of muffin batter. Stir in the conch, vegetables, and salt and pepper.

3. Just before serving, pour the oil to a depth of at least 1 inch in a small frying pan or electric skillet, and heat to 350°F. Using 2 spoons or a small ice cream scoop, drop 1-inch balls of batter into the oil. Fry, turning with a slotted spoon or wire skimmer, until golden brown, about 2 minutes total. Work in several batches, so as not to crowd the pan.

4. Using a slotted spoon, transfer the fritters to paper towels to drain. Arrange the fritters on a platter lined with a doily and serve at once.

Plantain Fried Olives

This recipe uses ripe plantains, which are sweet and fruity, like bananas. Cuban tradition calls for them to be filled with *picadillo* (spiced stewed ground beef or other meat). If you have the time, such fritters are delicious. This recipe achieves the same contrast of sweet and salty in considerably less time by stuffing plantains with olives, capers, and raisins. For the best results, use *pintones*, sweet, semi-ripe plantains. The Banana-Molasses Ketchup on page 128 would make a good accompaniment.

....

MAKES 24

....

2 semi-ripe plantains (skin is yellow with
*   black spots)*
24 bottled pitted jumbo green olives
24 raisins
24 capers
About 1 cup all-purpose flour
1 egg, beaten
About 1 cup fine dry bread crumbs
About 2 cups vegetable oil, for frying

1. Peel the plantains (see sidebar, page 28) and cut them into 1-inch pieces. Cook in 1 quart of boiling water in a medium-size saucepan until soft, 10 to 15 minutes. Drain the plantains well in a strainer and return to the pan. Mash the plantains with a potato masher or fork and let cool.

2. Stuff each olive with a raisin and a caper. Pinch off 1 inch pieces of mashed plantain and pat each into a 2-inch disk. Wrap each olive in a plantain disk, rolling it between the palms of your hands to form a smooth ball. (The fritters can be prepared up to 6 hours ahead to this stage and stored, covered, in the refrigerator.)

3. Place the flour in a shallow bowl, the egg in a second bowl, and the bread crumbs in a third.

4. Just before serving, pour the oil to a depth of at least 1 inch, in a small frying pan or electric skillet and heat to 350°F. Using 2 forks, dip each plantain ball in flour to cover. Shake off the excess and dip the balls in the beaten egg to cover, then roll in the bread crumbs, shaking off the excess.

5. Fry the fritters, turning with a skimmer, until golden brown on all sides, about 2 minutes total. Work in several batches, so as not to crowd the pan.

6. Using a slotted spoon, transfer the fritters to paper towels to drain. Arrange the fritters on a platter lined with a doily and serve at once.

Plantain Spiders

These crisp, garlicky fritters make a great introduction to green plantain. The long strands of grated plantain look a little like the legs of a spider, whence the fritter's curious name. This recipe was inspired by Puerto Rican-born Miami chef Carmen Gonzales. The Tamarind Cream Sauce on page 126 would make a good accompaniment.

MAKES 24 TO 30

2 large green plantains
1 piece (1 inch) fresh ginger, peeled
6 cloves garlic, minced
About 2 cups vegetable oil, for frying
Salt and freshly ground black pepper, to taste

THE BANANA'S JUMBO COUSIN

To the untrained eye, the plantain (accent on the first syllable) could easily be mistaken for a banana. But woe betide the unsuspecting eater who slices one onto his corn flakes! Shaped like a banana and with a banana smell, the plantain is rarely eaten in its raw state. But fry, boil, or bake it and it becomes an epicure's morsel.

I didn't realize how popular plantains were until I moved to Miami. This jumbo cousin of the banana turns up at our ethnic grocery stores and mainstream supermarkets, at humble sandwich shops and exclusive restaurants, at ethnic eateries of a dozen nationalities. *Tostones, mariquitas, maduros,* and other plantain preparations are as popular here in the Caribbean basin as french fries are in the North.

When green, the plantain is bland and starchy, like a yuca or potato. As it ripens, it becomes sweeter, tasting more and more like a banana. But even when fully ripe, it remains firm, which makes it very useful for cooking.

As the name suggests, a green plantain will have a hard

bright green skin. A semi-ripe plantain (known as *pinton* in Spanish) will be yellow with black spots, while a ripe one will be completely black. Like many tropical fruits, the plantain is at its sweetest when it is so ripe it looks like you should throw it out! It takes 6 to 8 days for a green plantain to ripen fully.

Plantains are more difficult to peel than bananas, especially when green. With a paring knife, slice off the ends and cut the fruit into 3-inch sections. Make a lengthwise slit in the skin of each section. Slide your thumbnails under the slit to pry off the skin. Some chefs soak the plantain sections in a bowl of ice water before skinning. Others skin the plantains under running water to wash away the milky liquid that sometimes seeps from the skin. If you do, pat the plantain sections dry with paper towels.

Plantains are widely available—even in northern cities. Look for them in the produce section of your supermarket or in any store that caters to a Caribbean or Latin American clientele.

1. Peel the plantains as described in the accompanying sidebar and grate on the coarse side of a hand grater or in a food processor fitted with the julienne disk. Cut the ginger into the thinnest possible slivers.

2. Combine the plantain, ginger, and garlic in a mixing bowl and toss with 2 spoons to mix.

3. Just before serving, pour oil to a depth of at least 1 inch in a small frying pan or electric skillet, and heat to 350°F.

4. Using 2 spoons or your fingertips, form 1-inch balls of the plantain mixture and lower them into the oil. Don't pack the plantain shreds too tightly; the fritters should look spiky and lacy. Fry the spiders, turning with a skimmer or slotted spoon, until golden brown, about 2 minutes total. Work in several batches, so as not to crowd the pan.

5. Transfer the fritters to paper towels to drain. Sprinkle with salt and pepper and serve at once.

Black-Eyed Pea Fritters

I first tasted these fritters at a streetside fry shop in Key West, where they go by the Cuban name *bollos*. Made from ground black-eyed peas, they resemble a famous Brazilian fritter called *acarajé*. The traditional recipe calls for the peas to be skinned, a process that's as boring as it is time-consuming, but I prefer the speckled effect that results from leaving the skins intact. I've jazzed up the traditional recipe by adding cilantro and scotch bonnet chili.

MAKES ABOUT 40

1 cup dried black-eyed peas
8 to 10 cloves garlic
1 very small onion, quartered
½ scotch bonnet chili or 1 to 2 jalapeño chilies,
    seeded and minced (optional; for even
    spicier fritters, leave the seeds in)
3 tablespoons minced fresh cilantro or
    Italian (flat-leaf) parsley
2 eggs
Salt and freshly ground black pepper, to taste
½ teaspoon baking powder
About 2 cups vegetable oil, for frying

1. Spread out the black-eyed peas on a tray and pick through them, removing any stones or stems. Place the peas in a colander and rinse thoroughly under cold water. Transfer the peas to a large bowl with cold water to cover by 2 inches. Soak overnight in the refrigerator.

2. The next day, thoroughly drain the peas in a colander. Place the peas, garlic, onion, and chili in a food processor and grind to a smooth paste. You'll need to run the machine for several minutes, stopping to scrape the sides of the bowl several times with a rubber spatula. Add the cilantro, eggs, and plenty of salt and pepper. Purée again to a smooth paste, 2 to 3 minutes. Transfer the batter to a bowl, cover, and let rest for 30 minutes.

3. Beat the baking powder into the batter with a wooden spoon. Continue beating the batter for 1 to 2 minutes to incorporate air and make the fritters light.

4. Just before serving, pour the oil to a depth of at least 1 inch in a small frying pan or electric skillet, and heat to 350°F. Using 2 spoons, drop 1-inch balls of batter into the oil. Fry, turning with a slotted spoon or wire skimmer, until golden brown, about 2 minutes total. Work in several batches, so as not to crowd the pan.

5. Using a slotted spoon, transfer the fritters to paper towels to drain. Arrange the fritters on a platter lined with a doily and serve at once.

Note: Unused batter can be kept for several days in the refrigerator. Stir in an additional ½ teaspoon baking powder for every cup of batter you have left. Beat well before frying.

Yuca Fritters

Crisp on the outside, soft and chewy inside, these fritters exemplify the delectably doughy texture of cooked yuca. You can spice up these fritters virtually any way you desire: with chopped cilantro or other herbs, minced chilies, saffron, or grated cheese. The Sunshine Aioli on page 122 makes a good dipping sauce.

MAKES ABOUT 20

1 pound yuca
3 cloves garlic, chopped
3 tablespoons chopped onion
1 jalapeño chili, seeded and minced (optional)
1 egg
1 tablespoon cornstarch
½ teaspoon baking powder
½ to 1 teaspoon hot sauce, or to taste
Salt and freshly ground black pepper, to taste
About 2 cups vegetable oil, for frying

1. Peel the yuca as described in the accompanying sidebar. Cut it into 1-inch pieces and grind to a coarse paste in a food processor. Add the garlic, onion, chili, egg, cornstarch, baking powder, hot sauce, and salt and pepper and process until mixed.

2. Just before serving, pour the oil to a depth of at least 1 inch in a small frying pan or electric skillet, and heat to 350°F. Using 2 spoons, drop ¾-inch balls of batter into the oil. Fry, turning with a slotted spoon or wire skimmer, until golden brown, about 2 minutes total. Work in several batches, so as not to crowd the pan.

3. Drain the fritters on paper towels. Transfer to a doily-lined platter and serve at once.

Yuca Fingers

While the preceding recipe emphasized yuca's doughy properties, this one reflects its ability to fry up firm and crisp. The peeled frozen yuca from the Dominican Republic you find in Hispanic and West Indian markets works fine for this recipe. The Fresh Carrot Sauce on page 120 makes a good accompaniment.

MAKES ABOUT 20, ENOUGH TO SERVE 4

1 pound yuca
Salt
About 2 cups vegetable oil, for frying

1. Peel the yuca as described in the accompanying sidebar and cut it crosswise into 3-inch sections. Cut a shallow *X* in the end of each section to help the yuca expand while cooking.

YUCA: THE VERSATILE VEGETABLE

Not too many North Americans have yet heard of yuca (also known as cassava and manioc). And few West Indians or Latin Americans would willingly live without it. This starchy root vegetable is enjoyed from Port-au-Prince to São Paolo. It's so popular here in Miami, the vegetable has given its name to a celebrated Cuban restaurant called Yuca.

Yuca (pronounced DJOO-ka or YOO-ka) is one of the most versatile roots in the vegetable kingdom. It's the root from which tapioca is made. It also yields cassava flour, which is used to make a Caribbean flat bread. When boiled, yuca becomes soft and fluffy, almost like a baked potato. (Eat it slathered with *mojo* or butter.) It fries up crisp on the outside, while remaining soft in the center, making it ideal for dipping in spicy sauces.

A long (4 to 16 inches), tapered, cylindrical root, yuca has bone-white flesh covered with a brown, bark-like skin. Its texture is pleasingly starchy, while the taste is mild and buttery. This delicately flavored tuber makes a perfect foil for the vibrant flavors of garlic, cilantro, and lime juice. When buying yuca, look

for firm heavy roots covered with unbroken skin. Avoid tubers with cracks, soft spots, mold, or an unpleasant or ammoniated odor. The flesh should be white—do not use yuca with brown spots or grayish or bluish veins. It's not unreasonable to ask the produce person to cut one open for you. Frozen yuca is acceptable for most recipes and has the advantage of being already peeled.

When preparing yuca, cut it crosswise into 2- to 3-inch rounds. Pare off the bark-like skin and pink layer underneath. Remove the fibers in the center either before or after cooking. Like other Hispanic tubers, yuca should be served at once: It becomes dry and mealy when it sits.

2. Place the yuca in a medium-size saucepan with 1 teaspoon salt and cold water to cover. Boil the yuca until tender but not soft (the pieces will begin to split in half), about 15 minutes. Drain the yuca in a colander, refresh under cold water, and drain again.

3. Cut the yuca pieces lengthwise in half, then lengthwise into finger-size strips. Using the tip of a paring knife or your fingers, remove any fibers running the length of the yuca pieces. Gently squeeze the yuca strips in the palm of your hand to form compact cylinders. (The recipe can be prepared up to 48 hours ahead to this stage. Store the yuca fingers, covered, in the refrigerator.)

4. Just before serving, pour the oil to a depth of at least 1 inch in a small frying pan or electric skillet, and heat to 350°F. Fry the yuca fingers, turning with a slotted spoon or wire skimmer, until golden brown, about 2 minutes total. Work in several batches, so as not to crowd the pan.

5. Drain the yuca fingers on paper towels. Transfer to a doily-lined platter and serve at once.

Grilled Corn Hush Puppies

To most people, Floridian cuisine means the cosmopolitan cooking of our southern cities, like Miami. But a meal at a roadhouse or breakfast joint in more backwater parts of the state will quickly remind you that Florida is part of the Deep South. I'm not sure what a north Floridian would make of these hush puppies, which features such newfangled additives as grilled corn and pickled chilies, but in our house, they're always devoured with gusto. Instructions for grilling corn are found on page 245. For the best results use a stone-ground cornmeal, preferably organic.

MAKES ABOUT 20

¾ cup stone-ground cornmeal

⅓ cup all-purpose flour

1 teaspoon baking powder

1 teaspoon baking soda

¾ teaspoon salt

¼ cup cooked corn kernels (preferably grilled)

¼ green bell pepper, very finely chopped

3 scallions, trimmed and minced

1 clove garlic, minced

1 pickled jalapeño chili, minced
(optional)

1 egg, beaten

About ½ cup buttermilk or milk

About 2 cups vegetable oil, for frying

1. Combine the cornmeal, flour, baking powder, baking soda, and salt in a mixing bowl and whisk to mix. Whisk in the corn, bell pepper, scallions, garlic, and chili.

2. Make a well in the center and add the egg and buttermilk. Whisk just to mix, adding buttermilk as necessary to obtain a thickish batter. Mix as little as possible.

3. Just before serving, pour the oil to a depth of at least 1 inch in a small frying pan or electric skillet, and heat to 350°F. Using 2 spoons, drop 1-inch balls of batter into the oil. Fry, turning with a slotted spoon or wire skimmer, until golden brown, about 2 minutes total. Work in several batches, so as not to crowd the pan.

4. Using a slotted spoon, transfer the hush puppies to paper towels to drain. Arrange the fritters on a platter lined with a doily and serve at once.

ALLIGATOR GOURMET

Froehlich's Gator Farm in Christmas, Florida, is situated midway between Orlando and Cape Canaveral. But few of the cars that streak by on their way to Disney World would suspect the presence of more than 5,000 live alligators raised in dank hothouses and open-air pens on this otherwise bucolic central Florida farm. Gators are becoming big business: The Sunshine State currently boasts over 40 alligator farms.

The focus of all this activity is a toothy carnivore whose appearance on earth predates that of dinosaurs. Stories and statistics bear grim testimony to the reptile's will to survive. The jaws of an alligator snap shut at something on the order of 3,000 pounds of pressure per square inch. Gators have been known to bite boats in half. In 1956, a 17½-foot-long gator was captured in Lake Apopka in central Florida. It's still not uncommon to find gators that measure 12 to 14 feet.

Alligator tastes like a cross between pork and a freshwater fish, like perch. Gator meat can be cooked pretty much any way you'd prepare either. The preferred method here in the South is deep-frying. But alligator can also be roasted, stewed, and sautéed. Gator ribs are great, braised with barbecue sauce. Gator's chief drawback is its tendency to be tough. Most chefs tenderize it by pounding it with a meat mallet, and then marinating it in an acid, like lemon juice. Before cooking alligator, you should trim off all visible traces of fat.

Gator is generally sold frozen—even in Florida.

Fortunately, the dense meat freezes well and will keep in the freezer for several months. Alligator can be found at select gourmet shops around the country, especially ones that carry frozen game. It can also be ordered by mail from Froehlich's Gator Farm (26256 E. Highway 50, Christmas, FL 32709). The minimum order is 20 pounds, so you may wish to get together and buy it with friends.

There's another reason for eating gator, besides its distinctive flavor. It's good for you. Alligator meat is 29 percent protein (as much as chicken and more than fish), but only 3 percent fat (beef contains 10 percent, chicken 7). One hundred grams (3.5 ounces) of gator meat contains 143 calories (as compared with 220 in beef and 190 in chicken) but only 65 milligrams of cholesterol (as compared to 90 milligrams in beef and 89 in chicken). Obviously, you lose these benefits if you deep-fry the gator.

Alligator is also high in monounsaturated fatty acids (the "good" fat), niacin, vitamin B_{12}, phosphorus, and potassium.

Gator Bites

The most popular way of cooking alligator here in Florida is deep-frying. These small, crisp, appetizer-size nuggets of gator are ideal for people who aren't quite ready to set fork to a whole alligator steak. A mail-order source for alligator is on page 35. The Tropical Tartar Sauce on page 125 would make a good accompaniment.

SERVES 4

1 pound frozen alligator, thawed, or pork loin

¼ cup fresh lime juice

3 cloves garlic, minced

Salt and freshly ground black pepper, to taste

1 cup all-purpose flour

1 teaspoon cayenne pepper

1 teaspoon chili powder

About 2 cups vegetable oil, for frying

1. Cut the alligator into ½-inch-thick steaks and tenderize by pounding with a meat mallet for a minute or two. Cut each steak into strips the size of your baby finger.

2. Combine the lime juice, garlic, and salt and pepper in a mixing bowl. Add the alligator, making sure it is coated with the marinade. Marinate the alligator in this mixture for 30 minutes in the refrigerator, turning once during this time.

3. Combine the flour, 1 teaspoon salt, 1 teaspoon pepper, the cayenne pepper, and the chili powder in a bowl and whisk to mix.

4. Just before serving, pour the oil to a depth of at least 1 inch in a small frying pan or electric skillet, and heat to

SALT COD: ITS SMELL IS DECEIVING

Salt cod may not be the most fashionable ingredient these days, but before refrigeration, it was the world's most available and affordable form of fish. Salt cod played a particularly important role in Caribbean cooking and it turns up at Spanish, Cuban, and West Indian restaurants throughout the Sunshine State.

Despite its popularity, salt cod is anything but appealing. Its aroma might charitably be likened to a hamper full of dirty gym socks. Some varieties are as stiff and hard as a board. Nonetheless, salt cod makes some of the world's best stews and fritters.

When buying salt cod,

look for thick pieces cut from the center of the fish. (The tail pieces remain tough and stringy, even with prolonged soaking.) Choose slightly flexible pieces over stiff pieces, slightly yellowish pieces over white: They contain less salt. Salt cod can be found in the seafood department of most supermarkets, but you'll get better quality if you seek it out at a Hispanic, Italian, or Iberian market. The Spanish name is *bacalao.*

Salt cod must be soaked overnight to soften the fish and remove the salt before cooking. Place it in cold water to cover for 24 hours (if possible, but no less than 12), changing the water three or four times. Then simmer the salt cod in water until soft.

If you're in a hurry, rinse the salt cod under cold running water for 15 minutes. Place in a pot with cold water to cover and gradually bring to a boil. Drain the fish and rinse in cold water. Repeat the boiling and rinsing two or three times, or to taste.

Last of all, run your fingers over the fish to feel for bones. Remove any you encounter with needle-nose pliers or tweezers.

350°F. Drain the alligator and blot dry. Dredge the alligator pieces in flour to cover, shaking off the excess.

5. Fry the alligator pieces, turning with a slotted spoon or wire skimmer, until golden brown, 1 to 2 minutes total. Work in several batches, so as not to crowd the pan. Drain on paper towels and serve at once.

Cod Puffs

Salt cod fritters turn up wherever Caribbean immigrants gather in south Florida. Every islander has his preferred version, from Jamaica's Stamp 'n Go to Guadaloupe's *accras.* My favorite are *bacalaitos* from Cuba and the Dominican Republic. The fritters owe their rich flavor to the use of the cooking liquid from the salt cod.

MAKES ABOUT 30

6 ounces dried salt cod
1 egg, beaten
2 to 3 tablespoons minced onion
1 clove garlic, minced
½ scotch bonnet chili or other hot chili, seeded and
  minced (optional)
2 scallions, trimmed and minced
3 tablespoons finely chopped Italian (flat-leaf) parsley
½ to ⅔ cup all-purpose flour
½ teaspoon baking powder
Salt and freshly ground black pepper, to taste
About 2 cups vegetable oil, for frying

1. Soak the salt cod in cold water to cover for at least 12 hours, or overnight, changing the water three times.

2. Drain the cod and place it in a small saucepan with enough fresh water to cover. Bring the water to a boil, then lower the heat and simmer until soft, about 10 minutes. Remove the pan from the heat. Transfer the fish to a plate to cool, reserving ½ cup of the cooking liquid.

3. Finely chop the fish by hand or in a food processor. Alternatively, the fish can be coarsely pounded in a mortar with a pestle.

4. Add the egg to the cod with the onion, garlic, chili, scallions, parsley, and the reserved ½ cup salt cod cooking liquid. Beat in enough flour to obtain a thick paste—it should be a little thinner than soft ice cream. Stir in the baking powder and salt and pepper to taste. You won't need much salt, as the cod is quite salty to begin with.

5. Just before serving, pour the oil to a depth of 1 inch in a small frying pan or electric skillet, and heat to 350°F. Using 2 spoons, drop spoonfuls of batter into the oil to form 1-inch balls. Fry the fritters, turning with a skimmer, until golden brown on all sides, about 2 minutes total. Work in several batches, so as not to crowd the pan.

6. Using a slotted spoon, transfer the fritters to paper towels to drain. Arrange the fritters on a platter lined with a doily and serve at once.

Pastelitos
(Nicaraguan Meat Pies)

hese tiny meat pies turn up at all sorts of Nicaraguan social events: birthdays, communions, and anniversaries. *Pastelitos* reflect the Nicaraguan fondness for dishes that are both salty and sweet: The tiny, meat-filled pastries are traditionally dusted with sugar after frying. Odd as it may sound, the contrast is very pleasing. This recipe was inspired by Miami caterer, Carmen Zampieri.

MAKES ABOUT 40

DOUGH:

½ cup solid vegetable shortening

¾ teaspoon salt

2 cups all-purpose flour

About ½ cup warm water

FILLING:

6 ounces boneless, skinless chicken breast
*   or pork, diced*

½ tomato, peeled, seeded, and finely chopped

¼ cup minced onion

½ green bell pepper, cored, seeded, and minced

½ rib celery, minced

1 tablespoon tomato paste

Salt and freshly ground black pepper, to taste

1½ tablespoons dried currants

4 pitted green olives, coarsely chopped

About 1 cup water

1 to 2 tablespoons fine, dried bread crumbs
*   (optional)*

About 2 cups vegetable oil, for frying

½ cup sugar, for dusting

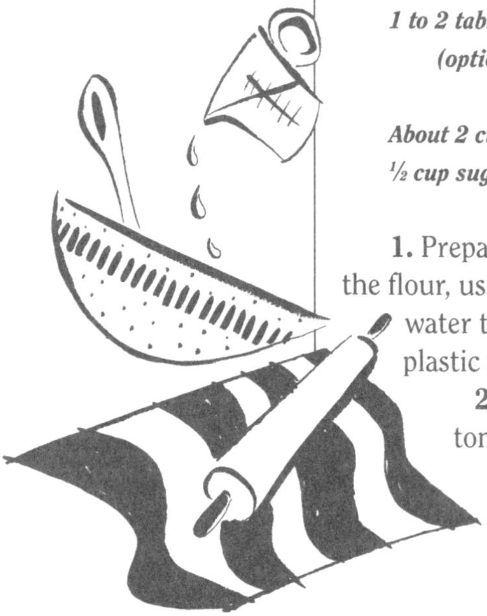

1. Prepare the dough: Cut the shortening and salt into the flour, using two knives or a food processor. Add enough water to make a soft pliable dough. Wrap the dough in plastic and let rest at room temperature for 2 hours.

2. Prepare the filling: Combine the chicken, tomato, onion, bell pepper, celery, tomato paste, and salt and pepper in a nonreactive large saucepan. Add enough water just to cover.

Gently simmer the mixture until the chicken is tender, about 20 minutes. Drain the filling in a colander, reserving the cooking liquid.

3. Coarsely chop the filling in a food processor to the consistency of ground beef. Stir in the currants, olives, and salt and pepper to taste. If the mixture is too dry, add a little of the reserved cooking liquid. If it's too runny, stir in the bread crumbs.

4. On a lightly floured surface, roll out half of the dough as thin as possible. Cut out 2-inch circles, using a cookie cutter. Roll out the remaining dough and cut out 1¾-inch circles. Gather up the scraps into a ball, roll out and cut, until all of the dough is used.

5. Assemble the *pastelitos:* Brush the smaller dough circles with water and place a small spoonful of filling in the center of each. Place the larger circle on top. Seal the dough circles by crimping the edges with a fork. (The *pastelitos* can be prepared ahead to this stage and frozen.)

6. Just before serving, pour the oil to a depth of 1 inch in a heavy skillet or frying pan and heat to 350°F. Fry the *pastelitos* until golden brown on both sides, 2 to 3 minutes total. Work in several batches so as not to crowd the pan. Drain the *pastelitos* on paper towels. Lightly sprinkle the *pastelitos* with the sugar and serve at once.

Note: For a healthier, although less succulent version, the *pastelitos* can be baked instead of fried. Brush with a beaten egg, sprinkle lightly with sugar, and bake in a preheated 400°F oven until golden brown, about 20 minutes.

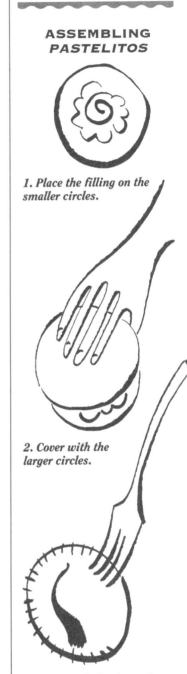

ASSEMBLING PASTELITOS

1. Place the filling on the smaller circles.

2. Cover with the larger circles.

3. Press with the tines of a fork to seal.

Empanadas

mpanadas, fried turnovers, are enjoyed throughout the Spanish Caribbean and Latin America. The traditional filling is *picadillo* (minced beef with olives, capers, and raisins) or one of its numerous variations—mine is made with ground turkey. The contrast of sweet and salty flavors in *picadillo* is echoed in another popular filling: guava paste and cheese. Other fillings are limited only by your imagination.

MAKES ABOUT 40

DOUGH:

2 cups all-purpose flour

1 teaspoon salt

1 teaspoon sugar

5 tablespoons solid vegetable shortening

1 egg, beaten

About ⅓ cup dry white wine

Filling of your choice (recipes follow)

About 2 cups vegetable oil, for frying

1. Prepare the dough: Place the flour, salt, and sugar in a food processor and cut in the shortening, running the machine in spurts. The mixture should be sandy, like cornmeal. Add the egg and ⅓ cup wine and pulse just until the dough comes together into a ball. The dough should be softly pliable; if necessary, add a little more wine.

2. On a lightly floured surface, roll out the dough ⅛ inch thick. Using a round cookie cutter, cut out 3-inch circles. Gather up the scraps into a ball, roll out and cut, until all of the dough is used.

3. Lightly brush the top of each circle with water. Place a spoonful of your chosen filling in the center and fold the circle in half to form a turnover. Seal the edges by pleating with your fingertips or pinching with a fork.

4. Just before serving, pour the oil to a depth of 1 inch in a heavy skillet or electric frying pan and heat to 350°F. Fry the *empanadas,* turning with a slotted spoon, until golden brown on both sides, about 2 minutes total. Work in several batches, so as not to crowd the pan. Drain the *empanadas* on paper towels and serve at once.

SMOKED CHEESE FILLING

Douglas Rodriguez, chef of Miami's celebrated Yuca restaurant, serves smoked cheese *empanadas* with his *ajiaco* (Cuban root vegetable stew).

MAKES ENOUGH TO FILL 40 *EMPANADAS*

10 ounces smoked mozzarella cheese, finely diced

Place a spoonful of the diced cheese in each *empanada.* Fold and seal. Fry as described above.

PICADILLO FILLING

The secret to a moist *empanada* is to chill the *picadillo* so the juices solidify. That way the *empanada* won't leak when you're filling them, but will be very juicy when you bite into them. I

GUAVA PASTE

Guava paste is a thick red jelly, made from a perfumed fruit called guava. Although most North Americans have never heard of it, it is a mainstay in the Latin American diet. It's available in this country at Hispanic markets and at an increasing number of supermarkets.

The guava is an egg-shaped fruit with a flavor that hints of honey, melon, and strawberries. Unfortunately, the fruit contains a multitude of tiny, hard, round seeds, which makes eating out of hand a messy and frustrating experience. That's why the bulk of the guava crop is consumed in the form of guava paste and guava nectar.

Guava paste is thick enough to slice and eat with a knife and fork. It's often served with salty cheese (*queso blanco*) for dessert. The saltiness of the cheese balances the sweetness of the guava paste. I also like to use it as a base for barbecue sauce.

The best grade of guava paste is a translucent jelly sold in flat 21 ounce tins. It keeps forever—even after the can is opened. Simply transfer any leftovers to a zip-lock-type bag and store it in the refrigerator.

Here in Miami you can also buy a cheaper grade of guava paste with a creamy pink-white appearance that's sold in cardboard boxes. Its flavor isn't as good and it tends to fall apart when it is cooked. The canned paste only costs a little more and is definitely worth it.

learned this trick from my assistant's mother, Martha Bernstein.

MAKES ENOUGH TO FILL 40 *EMPANADAS*

½ recipe Picadillo (See page 217)

1. Prepare the *picadillo,* using ground chicken, turkey, pork, veal, or beef. Chill well.

2. Place a spoonful of *picadillo* in each *empanada.* Fold and seal. Fry as described above.

GUAVA PASTE AND QUESO BLANCO FILLING

These *empanadas* are a popular snack for breakfast and Cuban coffee breaks. For the best results, use the jelly-like guava paste that comes in flat tins. Look for it at Hispanic markets or in the canned fruit section of many supermarkets. The creamy guava paste sold in cardboard packages is too sweet. *Queso blanco* is a salty white cheese sold at Hispanic markets.

MAKES ENOUGH TO FILL 40 *EMPANADAS*

5 ounces guava paste
2 to 3 ounces queso blanco *or cream cheese*

1. Cut the guava paste into 40 small pieces. Do the same with the cheese.

2. Place 1 piece of guava paste and 1 piece of cheese in each *empanada.* Fold and seal. Fry as described above.

Basic Tamales

When our friend, Elida Proenza, makes *tamales*, she scours Cuban markets for fresh ears of starchy yellow corn. White corn, she claims, is too sweet and watery. She grates the yellow corn to a milky paste on a hand grater. The process is laborious and time-consuming, but it produces a *tamal* of exceptional delicacy. One day, unable to find starchy yellow corn, she puréed canned corn kernels in the food processor and came up with *tamales* that were almost as delicious. Here's a simplified version of her recipe that the purist can prepare with fresh corn and the convenience-minded cook can make with canned or frozen. Dried corn husks can be found at Hispanic markets and in some supermarkets.

....

MAKES 12

....

24 dried or fresh corn husks

2 cups drained yellow corn kernels

2 tablespoons packing liquid from frozen
      or canned corn, or milky liquid from fresh grated

2 to 3 tablespoons unsalted butter, at room temperature

²/₃ to 1 cup stone-ground yellow cornmeal

Salt and freshly ground black pepper, to taste

1 teaspoon sugar (optional)

Filling of your choice (recipes follow)

FOR COOKING THE TAMALES:

½ teaspoon ground cumin

½ teaspoon freshly ground white pepper

3 sprigs of fresh cilantro

2 bay leaves

1 teaspoon salt

TAMALES AND PASTELES, FLORIDA-STYLE

Say *tamal* to most Americans and they'll think of Mexican or Southwestern cooking. But these savories, which are cooked inside a corn husk, are also an important part of Florida's cuisine. Visit a *loncheria* (Cuban snack bar) in Miami's Little Havana and you'll find a double boiler or Crockpot filled with steaming *tamales*. The Nicaraguan restaurant down the block may call them *nacatamales*, the nearby Dominican eatery *pasteles*, but the principle is the same.

That principle lies at the core of one of the most popular snacks of the Caribbean Basin. Its invention is probably as old as the cultivation of corn itself. A *tamal* features a corn- or cornmeal-filling cooked in a corn husk. The fillings can be as simple or as elaborate as you desire.

Cuban *tamales*, for example, are scented with cumin, garlic, and *cachucha* chilies— the ingredients of the ubiquitous *sofrito*. Nicaraguan *nacatamales* boast the characteristic aromas of annatto seed and *yerbabuena* (a plant similar to spearmint). Historically, corn didn't grow in Puerto Rico, so cooks there made the dough with grated green plantain and cooked it in banana leaves instead of corn husks. The result was called a *pastel,* and it's still a popular snack in the Spanish West Indies.

Florida's Cuban-American *tamales* differ from their Mexican counterparts in two essential and—for me—very appealing ways: First, they're made with fresh corn in addition to or even in place of *masa harina* (dried, ground, processed corn kernels). Second, they contain little or no fat, compared to the 1 to 2 ratio of fat to flour found in a traditional Mexican *tamal.* Finally, in Florida the "dough" is mixed with the filling, whereas in Mexican *tamales* they are separate.

The *tamal* fillings in this chapter include a classic Cuban formula, followed by two Hispano-Caribbean improvisations.

1. Place the corn husks in a large bowl with cold water to cover. Let soak until soft, about 2 hours.

2. Purée the corn kernels, their liquid, and the butter in a food processor. Work in enough of the cornmeal to obtain a firm but moist dough. Add salt and pepper and sugar, if desired, to taste.

3. Stir the chosen filling into the corn mixture.

4. Lay one of the corn husks flat on a work surface, tapered end toward you. Mound 3 heaping tablespoonfuls of the corn mixture in the center of the top half of the corn husk. Fold the tapered half over the top to encase the filling.

5. Lay another corn husk flat on the work surface, tapered end away from you. Place the filled husk in the center of the bottom half of the second husk. Fold the tapered end over the bottom to encase the *tamal.* Tie the bundle into a neat rectangle, using an 12-inch piece of string. Make sure you fold up the sides when you tie up the *tamal.*

Place the filling on the corn husk.   **Fold up tapered end.**   **Place the filled corn husk on a second husk.**

Fold down the tapered end.   **Tie the tamal with string, folding up the sides to enclose the filling.**

Continue forming the *tamales* in this fashion until all of the filling and corn husks are used.

6. Bring 2 quarts water to a boil in a large saucepan with the cumin, white pepper, cilantro, bay leaf, and salt. Add the *tamales*. Cover and gently simmer for 1 hour.

7. To serve, remove the *tamales* from the pan and drain in a colander. Cut the strings. Let each guest open the *tamal* and eat the filling with a fork. Do not attempt to eat the husk!

CHICKEN SOFRITO FILLING

This is the classic Cuban filling for a *tamal*. The *cachucha* is an aromatic, but not particularly piquant chili shaped like a miniature pattypan squash. Look for it in Hispanic markets or substitute green bell pepper.

MAKES ENOUGH TO FILL 12 *TAMALES*

12 cachucha chilies (see sidebar) or ½ green bell pepper, cored, seeded, and minced

8 cloves garlic

½ teaspoon ground cumin

½ teaspoon freshly ground white pepper

2 tablespoons olive oil

¼ cup minced onion

1 tablespoon finely chopped fresh cilantro leaves

½ cup peeled, seeded, and diced tomato

10 ounces boneless, skinless chicken breast, cut into ½-inch dice

Salt, to taste

1. Place the chilies and garlic in a mortar and pound to

IF YOU CAN'T TAKE THE HEAT: CACHUCHA CHILIES

Visit a Hispanic greengrocer, not to mention the produce section of many a Miami supermarket, and you'll find a tiny chili pepper with a scalloped crown that looks like a pattypan squash. In Cuban Spanish it's called *cachucha*. Elsewhere in the Caribbean it's known as *rocotillo* pepper or *aji dulce*.

Whatever you call it, the *cachucha* chili is great news for people who like the aromatic flavor of a scotch bonnet chili but can't take the latter's fiery bite. For the distinctively flavored *cachucha* has none of the hotness associated with other Caribbean chilies. It looks hot and smells hot, but actually it's as mild as a common bell pepper.

Cachucha chiles are usually light green in color, but occasionally you'll find a yellow or red one mixed in. When buying *cachuchas,* look for fresh, springy looking chilies free of shriveling or black spots.

To ready *cachuchas* for cooking, remove the stems. Many Cuban cooks tear the chilies open and remove the seeds as well. If *cachucha* chilies are unavailable, green bell peppers or cubanelle peppers make an acceptable substitute.

a coarse paste. (You can also do this in a food processor.) Pound in the cumin and white pepper.

2. Heat the oil in a nonreactive small skillet over medium heat. Add the onion and chili mixture and cook until soft but not brown, about 2 minutes. Stir in the cilantro, tomato, chicken, and salt. Cook until the chicken is done, about 5 minutes. Correct the seasonings, adding salt and white pepper to taste.

CURRIED SHRIMP FILLING

his filling was inspired by the curried shrimp mixtures found in Bajan and Trinidadian *rotis*. A *roti* is a cross between a sandwich and a burrito. It's a popular snack in the south Caribbean.

MAKES ENOUGH TO FILL 12 *TAMALES*

2 tablespoons unsalted butter or olive oil
1 small onion, minced
3 cloves garlic, minced
2 teaspoons minced fresh ginger
2 to 3 teaspoons curry powder
10 ounces shrimp, peeled, deveined, and cut into ½-inch dice
½ cup peeled, seeded, and diced tomato
3 tablespoons finely chopped fresh cilantro
Salt and freshly ground black pepper, to taste

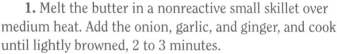

1. Melt the butter in a nonreactive small skillet over medium heat. Add the onion, garlic, and ginger, and cook until lightly browned, 2 to 3 minutes.

2. Stir in the curry powder, shrimp, tomato, cilantro, and salt and pepper. Cook until the shrimp is done, about 1 minute. Correct the seasonings, adding salt or curry powder to taste.

SWEET CORN FILLING

*T*his filling takes its inspiration from the dessert *tamales* served in the American Southwest. When making these sweet corn *tamales*, omit the spices from the cooking liquid on page 44.

....
MAKES ENOUGH TO FILL 12 *TAMALES*
....

½ cup dried currants or raisins

¼ cup light rum

3 tablespoons unsalted butter

1 cup drained corn kernels

⅓ cup toasted pine nuts (see page 311)

¼ cup minced citron or other candied fruit (optional)

½ teaspoon grated fresh lemon zest

3 to 4 tablespoons sugar, or to taste

½ teaspoon ground cinnamon

½ teaspoon vanilla extract

1. Combine the currants and rum in a small bowl and let stand until soft, about 30 minutes.

2. Melt the butter in a small skillet over medium heat. Add the corn and sauté until soft, about 2 minutes. Stir in the currants and soaking liquid, pine nuts, citron, lemon zest, sugar, cinnamon, and vanilla extract. Bring to a boil, then remove the pan from the heat. Correct the flavorings, adding sugar or spices to taste.

Sunshine Soups

Black Bean Soup

Bahamian Conch Chowder

Bellyache Soup

Alligator Pear Soup

Peanut Soup with Fried Leek

Cedar Key Crab Bisque

Soup—the very word evokes feelings of comfort and contentment. Soup can be a prelude to the entrée or a rib-sticking meal in itself. It can be as sophisticated as consommé or as earthy as a bowl of borscht. The restorative powers of chicken soup have earned it the sobriquet "Jewish penicillin." Lewis Carroll's Mock Turtle had the right idea when he spoke of "Soup, beautiful soup."

The importance of soup here in Florida is reflected in its diverseness. Every ethnic subculture has its specialty: Cuban black bean soup, West Indian pumpkin soup, coastal crab bisque, and Bahamian conch chowder. In most parts of the country, cold soups are served only during the summer months. In Florida, they're a year-round favorite. Gazpacho, vichyssoise, plus a wide range of fruit soups are never out of season in this mecca of tropical dining.

Florida soups are influenced by our unique supply of ingredients. The Gulf of Mexico gives us blue crab, stone crab, spiny lobster, and Key West pinks (a type of shrimp). Cedar Key, Apalachicola Bay, and the Indian River are renowned for their clams and oysters. And while conch can no longer legally be fished in Florida due to a short supply, our cuisine recalls the days when it was abundant here.

Florida's exotic fruits and vegetables also enter the soup pot. Nothing tastes better on a hot summer evening than an icy bowl of avocado soup or "Mango-spacho." Cubans make soups with red, white, and black beans. Why, we even have a soup made with that cousin of the plantain, the banana.

Soups are well suited to Florida's laissez-faire style of cooking. Soup recipes are forgiving: you needn't have every ingredient on hand or slavishly follow the cooking times. Putting on the soup pot is a great excuse for cleaning out the refrigerator. Some of the best soups I've ever made have been impromptu creations—the result of using up leftovers.

Here's a selection of Florida soups. Use them to cool you down on a warm summer day—or give you courage during a hurricane!

Smoked Gazpacho

More gazpacho is probably consumed in Florida than anywhere else in the country. The reasons are logical enough: gorgeous locally grown tomatoes, a large Hispanic population, warm weather year-round, and a statewide obsession with low-calorie dining. This recipe grew out of my experiments with a Chanukah present, a Cameron Stovetop Smoker. Available at cookware shops or via mail (C.M. International, P.O. Box 60220, Colorado Springs, CO 80960), this box-like metal device enables you to smoke foods quickly and easily indoors. But it's easy to rig up a smoker with a roasting pan or even a wok, as explained in the sidebar on page 52.

SERVES 6

4 large ripe tomatoes, cut crosswise in half

2 yellow or red bell peppers, halved, cored, and seeded

2 cucumbers, peeled, halved lengthwise, and seeded

1 onion, cut in half

4 cloves garlic

4 scallions, trimmed

4 to 5 tablespoons extra-virgin olive oil

4 to 5 tablespoons red wine vinegar, or to taste

*¼ cup chopped fresh herbs, including basil, parsley,
   oregano, and/or thyme*

Salt and freshly ground black pepper, to taste

Cayenne pepper, to taste

GARNISHES:

1 ripe avocado

Juice of ½ lime

3 tablespoons chopped fresh chives or scallion greens

EQUIPMENT:

Stovetop smoker

2 tablespoons apple, oak, or other hardwood chips

1. Place the tomatoes, bell peppers, cucumbers, onion, garlic, and scallions in a smoker, cut side up. Place the smoker over high heat until wisps of smoke begin to appear. Tightly cover the smoker and reduce the heat to medium. Smoke the vegetables until hot and soft, about 30 minutes. Let cool. Be sure to save any juices that collect in the drip pan.

2. Place the smoked vegetables, oil, vinegar, herbs, and seasonings in a blender, and blend at high speed until smooth. Correct the seasonings, adding vinegar, salt, pepper, or cayenne to taste. The gazpacho should be highly seasoned. Refrigerate the soup in a covered container until serving time.

STOVETOP SMOKING

Smoking is easy to do at home—even in an apartment—and you don't have to buy any special equipment. All you need is a wok with a tight-fitting lid and a round cake rack.

Line the wok with aluminum foil. Place a few spoonfuls of hardwood sawdust on the bottom. Place the cake rack in the wok a few inches above the sawdust. Place the vegetables on the rack.

Place the wok on a burner over high heat. As soon as you see a few wisps of smoke, tightly cover the wok and reduce the heat to medium. Smoke the vegetables until hot and soft, 20 to 30 minutes. You may need to work in several batches or use more than one wok.

Note: This method of smoking can generate a lot of smoke. So, be sure to run your exhaust fan on high when using this method. Also, you may need to disconnect your smoke alarm temporarily, but be sure to reconnect it when you're done.

3. Just before serving, peel and pit the avocado and cut it into ½-inch cubes. In a mixing bowl, toss the avocado with the lime juice to prevent discoloring.

4. Ladle the gazpacho into bowls and place a mound of diced avocado in the center of each. Sprinkle with the chopped chives and serve at once.

Mangospacho

I first tasted this dish at the Palm Grill, a cozy courtyard restaurant on a back street in Key West. Chef and co-owner Wayne King reworks classic Spanish gazpacho in a tropical idiom, using juicy Key West mangos. You want to use a light olive oil for this dish: Extra-virgin would be overpowering. If all you have is extra-virgin, dilute it with an equal amount of safflower oil.

SERVES 4

3 large or 6 small ripe mangos, peeled and very finely diced (6 cups)

¼ cup rice vinegar, or to taste

¼ cup light olive oil

About 1 cup water

Salt and freshly ground black pepper, to taste

1 to 2 tablespoons sugar (optional)

¼ cup very finely diced red onion

1 cucumber, peeled, seeded, and very finely chopped

¼ cup finely chopped fresh cilantro

2 tablespoons finely chopped fresh chives

1. Combine half of the mangos (3 cups), the vinegar, olive oil, water, and salt and pepper in a blender and purée. If the mangos are tart, you may wish to add a little sugar. If the purée is too thick, add a little water.

2. Transfer the mixture to a bowl and stir in the onion, cucumber, cilantro, chives, and the remaining diced mango. Correct the seasonings, adding salt, vinegar, or sugar to taste. The soup can be served right away, but it will be better if you refrigerate it for 1 hour to allow the flavors to blend. Adjust the seasonings just before serving.

Alligator Pear Soup

The Florida avocado, or alligator pear as it's affectionately referred to in these parts, is larger and sweeter than the Haas avocado from California. It has the added advantage of being slightly lower in fat. But this soup—a sort of liquid guacamole—can be prepared with either variety.

SERVES 4

1 large or 2 small ripe avocados, peeled, pitted, and diced (2 cups)

2 ripe tomatoes, peeled, seeded, and chopped

¼ cup finely chopped onion

1 large clove garlic, minced

½ scotch bonnet chili or 1 to 2 jalapeño chilies, seeded and minced

⅓ cup finely chopped fresh cilantro leaves

⅓ cup fresh lime juice

⅓ cup light olive oil

1 teaspoon ground cumin, or to taste

Salt and freshly ground black pepper, to taste

About 2 cups milk

2 tablespoons sour cream, for garnish

1 tablespoon chopped fresh chives, for garnish

1. Combine the avocados, tomatoes, onion, garlic, chili,

FLORIDA AVOCADOS

I thought when my childhood ended, I was done with things that go bump in the night. Then I moved to south Florida. All was well during the spring, but at the end of the summer, night after night, my bedroom would echo with resounding thumps. It wasn't until I spied a squirrel nibbling a shiny green fruit in the backyard, that I realized that the enormous tree towering over our house—and pelting our roof—was an avocado.

Avocados are big business here in Florida. And the avocados grown are very different from their California counterparts. So different that the early settlers gave them the colorful name of "alligator pears."

There's no mistaking a Florida avocado for a Californian. Ours are large oval fruits with a smooth, bright green skin. (California avocados, as typified by the Haas, are pear-shaped, with wrinkled dark green skin.) Florida avocados are sweeter, lighter, and moister than most from California. And best of all, according to *Eating Well* magazine, they contain only half the fat and two-thirds the cilantro, lime juice, olive oil, cumin, and salt and pepper in a food processor and purée until smooth.

2. Blend in enough milk to obtain a thick but pourable soup. Correct the seasonings, adding salt, lime juice, or cumin to taste. The soup should be highly seasoned.

3. To serve, ladle the soup into bowls. Garnish each with a dollop of the sour cream and a sprinkling of the chopped chives.

calories (112 in a 3½-ounce serving). Florida avocados are in season from August through January. If unavailable in your area, use California avocados.

When buying avocados, look for unblemished specimens free of bruises, mold, or soft spots. A ripe avocado will yield softly when you squeeze it between your thumb and forefinger. Let unripe avocados ripen at room temperature for 2 to 6 days. To extend the shelf life of a ripe avocado, store it in the refrigerator.

Bellyache Soup

This hearty soup is just the ticket when you're feeling under the weather. Plantain soup is a popular cure for bellyaches throughout the Caribbean. But even if you feel fine, it makes a great pick-me-up on a cool rainy day.

SERVES 4

2 tablespoons extra-virgin olive oil
1 small onion, finely chopped
1 carrot, finely chopped
2 ribs celery, finely chopped
2 cloves garlic, minced
About 5 cups Chicken Stock (see page 329)
*   or veal stock*
2 green plantains, peeled (see sidebar page 28)
*   and diced*
1 bay leaf
1 teaspoon ground cumin
½ cup finely chopped fresh cilantro leaves
Salt and freshly ground black pepper, to taste

1. Heat the olive oil in a large heavy saucepan. Cook the onion, carrot, celery, and garlic over medium heat until soft but not brown, 3 to 4 minutes.

2. Add the stock and bring to a boil. Add the plantains, bay leaf, cumin, half the cilantro, and salt and pepper. Return the soup to a boil. Reduce the heat, and gently simmer, uncovered, until the plantains are very tender, 40 to 50 minutes.

3. Remove and discard the bay leaf. Purée half of the soup in a blender, and return it to the pot. If the soup is too thick, thin it with a little more stock.

4. Just before serving, reheat the soup and correct the seasonings, adding salt or cumin as necessary. Garnish with the remaining chopped cilantro and serve at once.

West Indian Pumpkin Soup
with Spice-Scented Whipped Cream

Having lived in New England for fifteen years, I feel that Thanksgiving simply isn't complete without some sort of squash soup. When I moved to Florida, I added a new squash to my repertory, a large, firm-fleshed, carrot-colored variety called calabaza (also known as West Indian pumpkin). Less watery than most squash, calabaza produces a soup with a glorious velvety consistency and concentrated flavor. Look for calabaza at Hispanic or West Indian markets. If unavailable, a firm northern squash, like Hubbard or butternut, makes an acceptable substitute.

A NEW CURE FOR ULCERS?

Plantains are used as a folk remedy for stomach woes throughout the Caribbean Basin, and whenever someone has an upset stomach at our house, our Cuban friend, Elida, prepares a pot of plantain soup to help ease the discomfort.

In 1984, three researchers at the University of Aston in Birmingham, England, decided it was time to get to the bottom of the plantain's medical powers: They investigated its ability to relieve ulcers.

The researchers discovered that, administered preventively, plantains could reduce the severity of ulcers and, used curatively, could heal them. Plantains, it seems, help thicken the layer of protective gastric mucosa in the stomach.

Besides being served in soup, green plantains can be boiled or baked like potatoes. (When baking them, be sure to make a few slits in the peel to allow the steam to escape.) But for tummy troubles, you must use green plantains, as ripe ones—tasty as they may be—lack these anti-ulcerogenic properties.

1½ to 1¾-pound piece calabaza (West Indian pumpkin)
2 tablespoons unsalted butter
1 onion, diced
1 carrot, diced
2 ribs celery, diced
3 cloves garlic, diced
2 jalapeño chilies, seeded and diced (optional)
4 to 5 cups Chicken Stock (see page 329)
2 bay leaves
2 sprigs fresh thyme or 1 teaspoon dried
¼ cup finely chopped fresh Italian (flat-leaf) parsley
Salt and freshly ground black pepper, to taste
½ cup half-and-half, light cream, or heavy (or whipping) cream

SPICE-SCENTED WHIPPED CREAM AND GARNISH:
½ cup heavy (or whipping) cream
¼ teaspoon ground cumin
¼ teaspoon ground coriander
¼ teaspoon cayenne pepper
Salt and freshly ground black pepper, to taste
1 tablespoon finely chopped fresh chives or scallions

1. Using a sharp knife, cut the rind off the calabaza. Scrape out any seeds with a spoon and cut the flesh into 1-inch pieces.

2. Melt the butter in a large saucepan over medium heat. Sauté the onion, carrot, and celery until soft but not brown, 3 to 4 minutes. Add the garlic and chilies and cook for 1 minute.

3. Stir in the calabaza, 4 cups of the stock, the herbs, and seasonings and bring to a boil. Reduce the heat and simmer the soup, uncovered, until the vegetables are very soft, about 30 minutes. Remove the bay leaves and thyme branches, and purée the soup in a blender.

4. Return the soup to the saucepan and stir in the

cream. If the soup is too thick, add more stock. Correct the seasonings, adding salt or pepper.

5. Prepare the spice-scented whipped cream: Beat the cream to soft peaks in a chilled bowl. Whip in the spices and salt and pepper.

6. To serve, ladle the soup into bowls and place a dollop of the spice-scented whipped cream in the center of each. Sprinkle the cream with the chives and serve at once.

Black Bean Soup

Black bean soup could be thought of as Florida's official soup. It turns up in highbrow restaurants and homey ethnic eateries, sometimes enjoyed as an appetizer, sometimes as a meal in itself. Usually it's served in a bowl and eaten the way most Americans eat soup. But sometimes, it's spooned over white rice to be enjoyed as a vegetable side dish. The Cuban version of the soup differs in one interesting way from other recipes: The beans and vegetables are cooked separately and combined at the end. This creates a more intense flavor.

SERVES 8

BLACK BEAN CHIC

Foods, like clothes, go in and out of fashion. Consider black beans. When I was growing up, they were regarded with indifference, if not disdain. Today, black beans turn up at the nation's trendiest restaurants, playing star roles in everything from appetizers to entrées.

Down home cooks in the Caribbean and Latin America would be astonished to learn of the black bean's ascent to stardom. *Frijoles negros*, also known as turtle beans, have been a cornerstone of the Hispano-American diet for centuries. Virtually every Hispanic nation has its own version of rib-sticking black bean soup. And what would a Cuban meal be without *moros* (short for *moros y cristianos*), a dish of black beans and white rice whose whimsical name literally means "Moors and Christians?"

The black bean is a small, blue-black, kidney-shaped legume with a tiny white eye and white interior. Prized for its striking black color, it has an earthy flavor that reminds some people of mushrooms. Black beans are equally at home in soups, stews, and side dishes. A new generation of Floridian chefs has seen fit to include them in salads, sauces, and even salsas.

There's more to the black bean's appeal than good looks. Like all legumes, black beans are rich in protein (23 percent) and soluble fiber. (The latter is believed to help lower harmful blood cholesterol levels.) A ½-cup serving of black beans contains 142 calories, 13 grams of fiber, 41 milligrams of calcium, 4 milligrams of iron, and 10 grams of protein.

BEANS:

1 pound dried black beans

½ green bell pepper, cored and seeded

2 cloves garlic

1 bay leaf

1 small onion, cut in half

1 whole clove

SOUP:

5 ounces bacon, cut into ¼-inch slivers

3 tablespoons extra-virgin olive oil

1 large onion, finely chopped

1 green bell pepper, cored, seeded, and finely chopped

1 carrot, finely chopped

2 ribs celery, finely chopped

4 cloves garlic, minced

½ cup dry white wine

1 tablespoon wine vinegar

1 teaspoon ground cumin, or to taste

1 teaspoon dried oregano, or to taste

2 bay leaves

Salt and freshly ground black pepper, to taste

¼ cup sour cream, for garnish

¼ cup finely chopped scallion greens, for garnish

1. Prepare the beans: The day before cooking, spread the beans on a baking sheet and pick through them, removing any pebbles. Rinse the beans thoroughly in a strainer under cold running water. Place the beans in a large heavy pot and add 8 cups of water. Let soak overnight in the refrigerator.

2. Add the bell pepper and garlic to the pot. Pin the bay leaf to the onion with the clove, and add it to the pot. Bring the water to a boil. Reduce the heat, loosely cover the pan, and simmer the beans, stirring occasionally, until tender, about 1 hour. (The beans can also be cooked in a 6-quart pressure cooker. Black beans shouldn't cause a frothing problem, but watch the pressure. The cooking time will be about 30 to 40 minutes.)

3. Prepare the soup: Brown the bacon in large heavy frying pan, 3 to 4 minutes. Using a slotted spoon, transfer the bacon to paper towels to drain. Pour off the fat from the pan.

4. Add the olive oil to the pan, followed by the onion, bell pepper, carrot, celery, and garlic. Cook over medium heat until the vegetables are soft but not brown, 4 to 5 minutes.

5. Stir the sautéed vegetables and bacon into the beans, along with the wine, vinegar, cumin, oregano, bay leaves, and salt and pepper. Cover and gently simmer the soup, until the beans are very soft, 10 to 15 minutes.

6. Remove and discard the bay leaves. Using a slotted spoon, transfer 2 cups of the beans to a bowl and mash with the back of a wooden spoon or a pestle. Stir this mixture back into the soup to give it a creamy consistency. Correct the seasonings, adding salt, pepper, or vinegar to taste.

7. Ladle the soup into bowls and garnish each with a dollop of the sour cream and a sprinkling of the scallion greens.

Peanut Soup with Fried Leeks

eanuts are another reminder that Florida is still the Deep South. Turn off the interstate highways onto secondary roads and it won't be long before you see a roadside vendor selling fried, roasted, and, my favorite, boiled peanuts. The latter, which are velvety soft and surprisingly sweet, gave me the idea for this soup.

SERVES 6 TO 8

2 tablespoons extra-virgin olive oil
1 onion, finely chopped
4 scallions, trimmed and finely chopped
3 cloves garlic, minced
2 to 3 teaspoons minced fresh ginger
½ scotch bonnet chili or 1 jalapeño chili, seeded and minced
1 tablespoon all-purpose flour
About 3 cups Chicken Stock (see page 329)
3 cups milk
2 cups chunky-style peanut butter
Salt and freshly ground black pepper, to taste
½ cup chopped fresh parsley
1 to 2 tablespoons fresh lime juice

FRIED LEEKS:
2 leeks, trimmed, cut in half, washed well, and dried thoroughly
About 1 cup oil, for frying
Salt

1. Heat the olive oil in a large saucepan over medium heat. Add the onion, scallions, garlic, ginger, and chili, and cook until soft but not brown, 3 to 4 minutes. Stir in the flour and cook for 1 minute. Remove the pan from the heat.

2. Whisk in the chicken stock and bring the soup to a boil. Whisk in the milk, peanut butter, salt and pepper, parsley, and 1 tablespoon of the lime juice. Gently simmer the soup, uncovered, stirring from time to time, until creamy and well flavored, about 10 minutes. Correct the seasonings, adding salt or lime juice to taste. If the soup is too thick, add a little more stock or water.

3. Meanwhile, prepare the fried leeks: Cut the leeks into 2-inch sections. Slice these sections lengthwise as thinly as possible to make toothpick-thin slivers of leeks. Blot well between 2 paper towels.

4. Just before serving, pour the oil to a depth of at least

1 inch in a small frying pan or electric skillet, and heat to 350°F. Fry the leeks, turning with a slotted spoon, until crisp and golden brown, about 1 minute total. Work in several batches, if necessary, so as not to crowd the pan. Transfer the leeks to paper towels to drain. Lightly sprinkle the leeks with salt.

5. Ladle the soup into bowls or a tureen, and garnish with the fried leeks.

Cedar Key Crab Bisque

Crab soup appears in many incarnations around Florida: the gumbo-style stews of the Panhandle, for example, or the sherry-spiked she-crab soup of the grand hotels in Palm Beach, or even the bell pepper and garlic-laced chowders of Miami's Nicaraguans. My favorite of all is the white crab bisque served in Cedar Key on Florida's West Coast. A triumph of simplicity, it consists of crab, cream, and precious little else. The secret, of course, is to obtain fresh snow white lump crabmeat. For an even richer soup, use 1½ pounds crabmeat.

SERVES 4

1 pound fresh lump crabmeat

4 tablespoons (½ stick) unsalted butter

¼ cup minced shallots (about 4)

1 rib celery, minced

2 tablespoons all-purpose flour

4 cups light cream or half-and-half

Salt and freshly ground black pepper, to taste

Pinch of cayenne pepper

2 tablespoons minced fresh chives

1. Gently pick through the crabmeat, removing any bits of shell or cartilage.

2. Melt the butter in a large heavy saucepan. Add the shallots and celery and cook over medium heat until soft but not brown, about 2 minutes.

3. Whisk in the flour and remove the pan from the heat. Whisk in the cream. Return the pan to the heat, and continuing to whisk, gradually bring the mixture to a boil.

4. Reduce the heat. Stir in the crabmeat and gently simmer the soup, uncovered, until well flavored, 8 to 10 minutes. Add salt and pepper, and a whisper of cayenne to taste. (The soup is now ready to eat, but the flavor will improve if you refrigerate it for a few hours and reheat it before serving.)

5. Reheat the soup without boiling. Ladle it into bowls for serving. Sprinkle with the chives and serve at once.

Nicaraguan Crab and Shrimp Soup

This soup is a Thursday special at many home-style Nicaraguan restaurants in Sweetwater, a Miami neighborhood known as "Little Managua." The traditional recipe calls for live blue crabs, which are boiled to make a sort of crab broth. For the sake of convenience, I use lump crabmeat and bottled clam broth or fish stock.

1 pound lump crabmeat, or 4 large live blue crabs

8 ounces small shrimp

4 tablespoons (½ stick) butter

1 onion, finely chopped

1 green bell pepper, cored, seeded, and diced

1 red bell pepper, cored, seeded, and diced

4 cloves garlic, minced

2 cups Fish Stock (see page 330) or bottled clam broth

2 cups light cream or half-and-half

1 cup heavy (whipping) cream

Salt and freshly ground black pepper

¼ cup coarsely chopped fresh Italian (flat-leaf) parsley

1. Pick through the crabmeat, removing any bits of shell or cartilage. Peel and devein the shrimp (see page 164).

2. Melt the butter in a large heavy saucepan. Add the onion, bell peppers, and garlic and cook over medium heat until soft but not brown, 3 to 4 minutes. Add the crabmeat and cook for 1 minute.

3. Stir in the fish stock, light and heavy creams, and the seasonings. Gently simmer the ingredients, uncovered, until well flavored, about 5 minutes. Add the shrimp and cook until firm and pink, about 1 minute. Correct the seasonings, adding salt and pepper to taste.

4. Just before serving, stir in the parsley. Serve at once.

Bahamian Conch Chowder

Conch chowder is as much a part of Florida's heritage as clam chowder is New England's. Actually, our chowder is closer to a Manhattan tomato-based chowder than to creamy New England chowder. Legend has it that the soup originated with Bahamian fishermen who settled in Key West in the last century. For a discussion of conch, see page 174.

SERVES 6 TO 8

1 pound conch, trimmed

3 to 4 tablespoons fresh lime juice

5 tablespoons tomato paste

4 strips bacon, cut into $\frac{1}{4}$-inch slivers

3 tablespoons extra-virgin olive oil

1 onion, finely chopped

1 carrot, finely chopped

2 ribs celery, finely chopped

3 cloves garlic, finely chopped

1 green bell pepper, cored, seeded, and finely chopped

$\frac{1}{2}$ scotch bonnet chili or 1 jalapeño chili, seeded and minced

3 ripe tomatoes, peeled, seeded, and finely chopped

$\frac{1}{4}$ cup dark or golden rum

$\frac{1}{4}$ cup dry sherry

$1\frac{1}{2}$ pounds potatoes, peeled and diced

2 bay leaves

1 teaspoon dried thyme

$\frac{1}{2}$ cup finely chopped fresh Italian (flat-leaf) parsley

8 cups water

1 tablespoon Worcestershire sauce

1 teaspoon Tabasco sauce

Salt and freshly ground black pepper, to taste

1. Pound the conch with a meat mallet for 1 minute to tenderize it (see page 172). Cut the conch into 1-inch pieces and coarsely grind in a meat grinder or food processor. Combine the conch, 2 tablespoons of the lime juice, and the tomato paste in a mixing bowl and mix well. Set aside to marinate while you prepare the remaining ingredients.

2. Brown the bacon in 1 teaspoon of the olive oil in a large heavy pot. Leaving the bacon in the pan, pour off the fat.

3. Add the remaining olive oil, the onion, carrot, celery, garlic, bell pepper, and chili. Cook over medium heat until the vegetables are very lightly browned, 5 to 6 minutes.

4. Stir in the tomatoes. Increase the heat to high, and cook for 1 minute. Stir in the rum and sherry and bring to a boil. Stir in the potatoes, conch mixture, bay leaves, thyme, ¼ cup of the parsley, the water, Worcestershire sauce, Tabasco sauce, and salt and pepper.

5. Bring the soup to a boil. Reduce the heat and gently simmer the chowder, uncovered, until the potatoes and conch are very tender and well flavored, about 1 hour. (The chowder can also be cooked in a 6-quart pressure cooker. Maintaining high pressure, it will take about 20 minutes.)

6. Just before serving, remove and discard the bay leaves. Correct the seasonings, adding salt, pepper, 1 to 2 tablespoons lime juice, Worcestershire or Tabasco sauce, or sherry to taste: The chowder should be highly seasoned. Sprinkle with the remaining parsley and serve at once.

Salad Days

Black Bean Salad with mango & shrimp

Watermelon Salad

Hearts of Palm Salad

Stone Crab, Melon & Cucumber Salad

Where I grew up, salads once meant iceberg lettuce and hothouse tomatoes. My, how times have changed! Today's salad lover has the choice of a dazzling array of greens, from purslane to puntarella, from mizuna to mesclun. Gone are the days when salads served solely as a prelude to the entrée. Here in Florida, we eat salads as an appetizer, main course, side dish, condiment, and even as dessert.

Floridians are unequivocal in their enthusiasm for salads. Our warm climate dictates dishes that are refreshing, light, and easy to digest. When you live in the tropics, bathing suit weather is never far off. We pace our caloric intake accordingly. There's another advantage to being a salad lover in Florida: the availability of locally grown fruits and vegetables 12 months a year. Where else in the U.S. can you find a gorgeous vine-ripened tomato in December?

Floridian salads are also shaped by a number of ingredients found solely or principally in the Sunshine State. One is the heart of the palmetto, more prosaically known as swamp cabbage. Harvested throughout the state, but especially around Lake Okeechobee, Florida hearts of palm dwarf their Brazilian counterparts, measuring 4 to 6 inches in diameter and as much as 3 feet in length. The softly crunchy texture and sweet, mild taste are absolutely unique.

Citrus fruit, of course, plays an important role in Florida salad-making. The Sunshine State leads the nation in orange, grapefruit, tangerine, and tangelo production. Sectioned citrus fruit, a splash of juice, or grated zest does wonders for enlivening a salad.

Seafood is another important component of Florida salads. Blue crab, stone crab, conch, and Gulf shrimp are but a few of our distinctive seafoods that turn up in well-dressed salads.

The following salads are great for summertime. If you live in Florida, you can eat them at any time of the year!

MESCLUN, DEMYSTIFIED

Mesclun is the name given by the French to an assortment of baby salad greens. Many gourmet shops and farmer's markets sell mesclun-type salad mixes, but if unavailable, make your own by combining such greens as arugula, watercress, spinach, leaf lettuces, radicchio, and endive. Remember, the younger and smaller the leaves, the less bitter and more tender they'll be.

Tim's Mesclun Salad with Tangerine Cream

You've probably never heard of Miami herb grower Tim Mumford. But if you've ever dined at Mark's Place or any of the other top Miami restaurants, you've surely tasted his amazing greens. Tim grows all his herbs and lettuces organically—no small feat in steamy, buggy South Florida—and he harvests his mizuna, lollo rosa, and other exotic greens so young, sweet, and tender, he could almost be accused of infanticide. Tim is one of the unsung heros who have helped bring world-class dining to Florida. It gives me great pleasure to dedicate this recipe to him.

SERVES 4

DRESSING:
1½ tablespoons tangerine syrup (see Note)
1½ tablespoons balsamic vinegar
2 tablespoons heavy (or whipping) cream
1 teaspoon soy sauce
Freshly ground black pepper, to taste

5 to 6 cups mesclun (mixed baby salad greens)
2 tablespoons chopped fresh herbs, including chervil,
*   tarragon, and/or Italian (flat-leaf) parsley*
1 tablespoon chopped fresh chives

1. In a large salad bowl, combine the ingredients for the salad dressing and whisk until smooth. Correct the seasonings, adding balsamic vinegar or soy sauce to taste.

2. Tear any of the large greens into bite-size pieces. Leave the small ones whole.

3. Just before serving, add the greens, herbs, and chives to the salad bowl. Toss the salad as gently as possible, just until the greens are coated with dressing.

Note: Tangerine syrup is made by boiling down fresh tangerine juice. I love the flavor of citrus in salads, but straight juice makes the dressing too watery. Follow the instructions for making Orange Syrup, found on page 332.

Spinach, Blood Orange, and Macadamia Nut Salad

*H*ere's a Florida remake of a classic spinach salad. Blood oranges look like juice oranges, but are a little on the small side. Many have darkish red patches on the outside, others don't, but cut into them, and you'll find sweet, crimson-colored flesh. Although most domestic blood oranges are grown in California, Florida growers have developed a large, luscious fruit called the Cara Cara Navel, which is pinkish red inside, like a grapefruit. If blood oranges are unavailable, this salad can be prepared with regular oranges. For the best results, use small bunch spinach, rather than the tough, gnarled leaves sold in cellophane packs.

COOKING WITH CITRUS FRUIT

*C*itrus fruits offer two types of flavors: the aromatic oils in the rind and the sweet-tart juice in the pulp. The oils are concentrated in the zest, the shiny outer peel. The easiest way to remove the zest is in broad thin strips with a vegetable peeler. These strips can then be twisted over drinks like Martinis (colored side down, so that the oil droplets fall into the drink); simmered with milk, cream, or poached fruit; or finely chopped in a spice mill for other uses.

For grating citrus zest, you may wish to buy a zester, a small tool with a rectangular blade that has a row of holes at the end. To work a zester, pull the perforated end of the blade over the fruit to scrape off the oil-rich outer peel. If using a conventional grater, place a sheet of parchment paper over the grater surface before grating the fruit. When you're finished, the zest will be on the paper, not stuck in the teeth of the grater.

My favorite technique for peeling citrus fruit is "to skin it alive" (*peler à vif* in French). First, using a sharp paring knife, cut all the rind off the fruit to expose the flesh. The easiest way to do this is to cut off the rind in a continuous strip, as you would peel an apple.

To remove the individual segments, make V-shaped cuts between the membranes. Work over a bowl to catch the juices. You should wind up with gorgeous skinless segments. Remove any seeds with a fork.

Orange, tangerine, and grapefruit juice are delicious in salad dressings, but used straight, they can make a salad too watery. I like to boil the juice down in a nonreactive heavy saucepan until reduced to one-quarter of its original volume to make an intensely flavored concentrate or syrup.

Although available year-round, oranges and grapefruits are in their prime in the winter. When buying citrus fruits, choose specimens that feel plump and heavy. The best way to store citrus fruit is loosely wrapped in a plastic bag in the refrigerator.

SERVES 4

¾ cup coarsely chopped macadamia nuts
4 blood oranges
5 cups baby spinach leaves, washed, stemmed, dried,
*   and torn into bite-size pieces*
1 cup cooked corn kernels (preferably grilled, see page 245)

DRESSING:
½ clove garlic, minced
1 teaspoon Dijon mustard
Salt and freshly ground black pepper, to taste
1½ tablespoons sherry vinegar
3 tablespoons hazelnut oil
1 to 2 tablespoons fresh blood orange juice
*   (reserved from sectioning*
*   the fruit)*

1. Lightly toast the macadamia nuts until light golden brown and fragrant in a dry skillet over medium heat or in a toaster oven, 2 to 3 minutes. Watch them to make sure they don't burn.

2. Peel and section the blood oranges, as described in the accompanying sidebar. Cut the segments into ½-inch dice. Reserve the juice for the dressing.

3. Just before serving, combine the macadamia nuts, blood oranges, spinach, and corn in a large salad bowl.

4. Prepare the dressing: In a small bowl, place the garlic, mustard, salt, and pepper; mash with a fork to a smooth paste. Add the vinegar and whisk until smooth. Whisk in the oil in a thin stream, until thickened. Whisk in the reserved blood orange juice. Correct the seasonings, adding salt or orange juice to taste. The dressing should be highly seasoned.

5. Pour the dressing over the salad ingredients and toss as gently as possible, just until the spinach is coated with the dressing.

A GUIDE TO FLORIDA CITRUS FRUITS

Florida is the nation's largest producer of oranges, grapefruits, and tangerines. But we also have a host of lesser-known citrus fruits, ranging from kumquats to calamondins. Here are some of the varieties you should know about.

BLOOD ORANGE: Distinguished by its red-, purple-, or burgundy-colored pulp, the aptly named blood orange is the trendiest citrus fruit on the market. Smaller than regular oranges, it has a delicate, sweet flavor with a hint of raspberry or strawberry.

CALAMONDIN: This Floridian fruit (a native of the Philippines) looks like a miniature tangerine, but woe betide the person who tries to eat one raw. Excruciatingly bitter and sour in its natural state, it's delectable in jellies and jams.

KUMQUAT: Many people maintain that this quail egg-size fruit can be eaten raw, rind and all. Such a notion makes my hair stand on end, as I find them unbearably bitter. Kumquats can be made more palatable by poaching them in sugar syrup.

POMELO: Long before there were grapefruits, people enjoyed the grapefruit's ancestor, the pomelo (also written pummelo), also known as shaddock. Large, thick-skinned, round or slightly oval, the pomelo is sweeter and drier than a grapefruit, so you can peel, section, and eat it like a navel orange. You can even tease apart the individual juice sacs in each section. Sprinkled on salads, these sacs crunch when you bite into them, like the seeds of a pomegranate.

SOUR ORANGE: This bumpy green-orange fruit won't win any beauty contests, but Cuban and other Hispanic cuisines would be much impoverished without it. Often sold by its Spanish name, *naranja agria,* it looks like an orange, but tastes like a lime. Sour orange is a primary ingredient in Cuba's national table sauce, *mojo.* Fresh lime juice makes an acceptable substitute.

TANGELO: A grapefruit-tangerine hybrid, a tangelo looks like a dark-skinned orange. The most popular variety, the Minneola, takes its name from a town in central Florida. Also known as Honeybell, Minneolas are large, pineapple-scented, lasciviously juicy fruits with a nipple-like protrusion at one end. Another popular variety is the large, round Orlando tangelo.

TANGERINE: To judge from the name, you might imagine that this fruit originated in North Africa. Its European name—Mandarin—indicates its true birthplace: China. The tangerine is a small, slightly flat citrus fruit with a loosely fitting skin that makes it the easiest to peel of all citrus fruits. A famous Florida grower named Colonel Dancy had the right idea when he called tangerines "kid-gloved oranges." The best-known Florida varieties are the mild, sweet Robinson, the juicy Honey Tangerine, and the acidic, musky Sunburst.

UGLI FRUIT: Another cross between a tangerine and grapefruit, ugli is a large, sort of fat pear-shaped, thick-skinned, green-yellow fruit from Jamaica. Don't be put off by its homely appearance, as the flesh unites the honeyed fragrance of tangerine with the juicy tartness of grapefruit.

Minneola, Arugula, and Olive Salad

inneolas are a type of tangelo, a cross between a tangerine and a grapefruit. If unavailable, you can use oranges or tangerines—you'll need 4 of the former and 6 to 8 of the latter. My favorite olive for this recipe are the raisin-like, dry-cured black olives you find at Italian and Middle Eastern markets.

SERVES 4

4 tangelos
1 bunch of arugula, washed, stemmed, and dried
4 scallions, trimmed and very finely chopped
3 tablespoons chopped fresh Italian (flat-leaf) parsley
½ cup black olives (preferably oil-cured)

DRESSING:
¼ teaspoon salt, or to taste
1½ tablespoons balsamic vinegar
1½ tablespoons extra-virgin olive oil
Freshly ground black pepper, to taste

Hot pepper flakes, for sprinkling

1. Cut the rind off the tangelos, working over a bowl to catch any juices. Cut the tangelos crosswise into ¼-inch slices. Remove any seeds with the tip of a fork.

2. Line a platter with the arugula. Arrange the tangelo slices on top, leaving a border of green arugula showing. Scatter the scallions, parsley, and olives on top.

3. Make the dressing: Combine the salt and vinegar in a small bowl and whisk until the salt completely dissolves. Whisk in any reserved tangelo juice, and add the olive oil in a thin stream, followed by the pepper. Correct the seasonings, adding salt to taste.

4. Drizzle the dressing over the salad. Dust the salad with the hot pepper flakes and serve at once.

Watermelon Salad with Kumquat Dressing

his whimsical salad is the creation of Jan Jorgenson, chef-owner of Janjo's in Coconut Grove. Jan uses both red and yellow watermelons, which make the salad exceptionally colorful. Yellow watermelon can be found at specialty greengrocers; if unavailable, use all red.

SERVES 4

1 cup water

½ cup sugar

1 tablespoon finely chopped fresh ginger

4 fresh kumquats

¼ cup sour cream

Salt and freshly ground black pepper, to taste

2 bunches arugula, stemmed, washed,
*   and patted dry*

1 tablespoon extra-virgin olive oil

1 tablespoon fresh lemon juice

2 cups seeded red watermelon balls

2 cups seeded yellow watermelon balls

1. Combine the water, sugar, and ginger in a saucepan and

bring to a boil over high heat. Add the kumquats and boil until tender, about 5 minutes. Remove the pan from the heat and remove the kumquats from the syrup with a slotted spoon. Let cool completely. Reserve the syrup.

2. Cut the kumquats in half and remove the seeds. Finely chop the kumquats. Whisk enough of the kumquat syrup (2 to 3 tablespoons) into the sour cream to obtain a pourable sauce. Whisk in salt and pepper and chopped kumquat to taste. (You probably won't need all of the kumquat.)

3. Toss the arugula with the olive oil, lemon juice, and salt and pepper to taste. Mound the arugula in the center of 4 salad plates. Arrange the melon balls around the arugula, alternating red and yellow. Drizzle the kumquat cream over the watermelon and greens. Serve at once.

SWAMP LORE

Heart of palm, or swamp cabbage, as it was called at the turn of the century and is still called in backwoods Florida, was a mainstay of the pioneer diet. To this day, it's popular in rural areas. The town of La Belle near Lake Okeechobee in central Florida, for example, holds an annual Swamp Cabbage Festival in February, complete with food booths, craft displays, and a parade with a marching band.

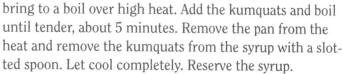

Hearts of Palm Salad in the Style of Cedar Key

Cedar Key is a tiny island off the west coast of Florida, once a booming shipping port and railroad terminus, today a sleepy resort that—for the moment at least—has escaped the developers' greed. Several uniquely Floridian dishes originated here, including the world's strangest hearts of palm salad. Invented several decades ago by an owner of the Island Hotel (built in 1859), this singular salad features an improbable combination of swamp cabbage (Florida heart of palm), pineapple, dates, and a dressing made from peanut butter and ice cream. The result doesn't taste quite as revolting as it sounds, although it definitely takes getting used to. Still, it's a popular item in these parts. The traditional dressing is too sweet for me, but the peanut butter reminds me of Indonesian gado gado and of the peanut sauces of Southeast Asia. This led me to an Asian twist on a Cedar Key classic. For the sake of authenticity, the following recipe includes both the traditional dressing and my own.

SERVES 4

4 cups thinly sliced iceberg or green leaf lettuce
1 cup diced pineapple (preferably fresh)
½ cup diced pitted dates
1 tablespoon minced candied ginger
2 cups thinly sliced hearts of palm, preferably fresh
　(see sidebar)

TRADITIONAL ICE CREAM DRESSING:
⅓ cup vanilla ice cream, softened slightly
⅓ cup mayonnaise
3 tablespoons peanut butter
1 to 2 drops of green food coloring

MY SPICY PEANUT DRESSING:
¼ cup chunky-style peanut butter
¼ cup unsweetened Coconut Milk (see page 331),
　Chicken Stock (page 329), or water
2 tablespoons soy sauce or Thai fish sauce
1 tablespoon fresh lime juice
1 tablespoon sugar
1 teaspoon Thai hot sauce or your favorite hot sauce
1 teaspoon minced fresh ginger
1 teaspoon minced garlic
2 teaspoons minced scallion bulb
1 tablespoon chopped scallion green, for garnish

HEARTS OF PALM

"What's in a name?" mused Shakespeare's Romeo. Plenty, when it comes to vegetables. Few of us would go out of our way to eat something called "swamp cabbage," but serve the dish as "hearts of palm" and epicures' mouths will water.

To most Americans, hearts of palm is a small, white, cylindrical vegetable that is sold canned and served at Continental restaurants. Virtually all of it comes from Brazil. Imagine my surprise on seeing my first Florida heart of palm, a log-shaped behemoth, 3 feet long, 5 inches in diameter, looking more like something you'd put in your fireplace than serve on a plate.

Florida heart of palm has the same delicate flavor and softly crunchy consistency as the more common Brazilian heart of palm. But whereas the latter is loaded with sodium and tends to be mushy after canning, fresh heart of palm is always crunchy, sweet, and mercifully low in sodium.

Swamp cabbage is the core of the stem of Florida's state tree, the sabal palm. Anyone with a sabal palm on his or her property may harvest heart of palm, but the tree cannot be cut down on public lands. Much of the fresh heart of palm served in Florida's restaurants comes from the Seminole Indian Reservation near Lake Okeechobee.

Florida heart of palm is virtually impossible to find outside of the Sunshine State. Even here, its consumption is limited to a handful of upscale restaurants, rural eateries, and private homes. I've never seen it for sale in a market. That's not to say it won't be in the future. Already you can buy fresh hearts of palm (the small variety) from Central America and Brazil.

In the event that you can procure a fresh Florida heart of palm, strip off the tough outside leaves to expose the milk-white core. Cut off any fibrous ends. Using a sharp chef's knife and holding the blade perpendicular to the palm, shave off thin (not more than ¼ inch thick) slices. Store the slices in acidulated water (water with lemon juice) until serving time to keep them from discoloring.

The traditional way to eat swamp cabbage is raw, in salads, or stewed, with salt pork.

1. In a large mixing bowl, toss the lettuce with the pineapple, dates, candied ginger, and half of the hearts of palms. Arrange this mixture on 4 salad plates, in shallow bowls, or on a platter.

2. Prepare the dressing (either version): Combine all of the ingredients (except the garnish) in a blender and blend to a paste. If preparing the peanut dressing, correct the seasonings, adding soy sauce, lime juice, or sugar to taste.

3. Spoon the dressing over the salad and garnish with the remaining hearts of palm. If using the spicy peanut dressing, sprinkle the scallion greens on top.

Citrus Marinated Hearts of Palm Salad

If you can find fresh hearts of palm, this salad will be sensational, but the recipe is eminently tasty made with canned hearts of palm. The recipe comes from Mark Militello of Mark's Place in North Miami.

MARINADE:
½ cup fresh orange juice
¼ cup fresh lime juice
3 tablespoons extra-virgin olive oil (use a mild-flavored brand)
1½ tablespoons honey (Mark uses citrus honey)
1 tablespoon balsamic vinegar
1½ teaspoons Dijon mustard
1½ teaspoons pink peppercorns, lightly crushed
*   with the side of a knife*
1 teaspoon finely chopped fresh tarragon
Plenty of salt and freshly ground black pepper

2 cups thinly sliced hearts of palm, fresh or drained canned
4 to 5 cups mesclun (mixed baby salad greens)
1 tablespoon finely chopped fresh chives

1. Combine the ingredients for the marinade in a nonreactive mixing bowl and whisk until smooth. Add the hearts of palm. If using fresh hearts of palm, marinate for 4 hours. If using canned hearts of palm, marinate for 1 hour. Place a saucer over the hearts of palm to keep them submerged.

2. Drain the hearts of palm, reserving the marinade. Toss the salad greens with 3 to 4 tablespoons of marinade and arrange on salad plates. Arrange the palm hearts on top. Spoon a little more marinade over the palm hearts and sprinkle with finely chopped chives.

Black Bean Salad with Mango and Shrimp

Here's a festive Florida salad with the colors of Halloween. If mango is unavailable, you can use fresh peaches or papaya. I like the smoky flavor grilling imparts to the shrimp, but broiling will work, too. I'm not much of a fan of canned beans (they're too soft and too salty), but there is a new time-saving product on the market: rehydrated black beans. These presoaked beans require only 15 to 20 minutes of cooking. Look for them in the produce section of the supermarket.

SERVES 4

SHRIMP AND MARINADE:

12 jumbo shrimp, peeled with tails intact and deveined

1 tablespoon extra-virgin olive oil

1 tablespoon fresh lime juice

½ teaspoon ground coriander

Salt and freshly ground black pepper, to taste

SALAD:

1 ripe mango

2 cups Firm-Cooked Black Beans (see page 269)

4 tablespoons finely chopped fresh mint leaves or
1 tablespoon dried

4 scallions, trimmed and minced

2 tablespoons extra-virgin olive oil

2 tablespoons fresh lime juice

Salt and freshly ground black pepper,
to taste

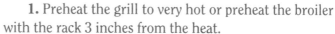

1. Preheat the grill to very hot or preheat the broiler with the rack 3 inches from the heat.

2. Prepare the shrimp and marinade: Combine the shrimp, olive oil, lime juice, coriander, and salt and pepper in a shallow bowl and toss to mix. Cover and marinate in the refrigerator for 30 minutes.

3. Grill or broil the shrimp until cooked, about 1 minute per side, basting with the marinade. Let the shrimp cool.

4. Meanwhile, prepare the salad: Peel and seed the mango as described on page 80 and cut it into ½-inch dice. (The recipe can be prepared ahead to this stage.)

5. Not more than 10 minutes before serving, combine the mango, black beans, 3 tablespoons of the mint leaves, the scallions, olive oil, lime juice, and salt and pepper in a mixing bowl and toss to mix. Correct the seasonings, adding salt or lime juice to taste. The salad should be highly seasoned.

6. Mound the black bean mixture on 4 plates. Arrange 3 shrimp on top of each, tails to the center, raised like a tripod. Sprinkle the shrimp with the remaining mint and serve at once.

HOW TO CUT UP AND EAT A MANGO

Mangos are to Florida what peaches are to Georgia. We're luckier than our northern neighbors, however, as there are literally hundreds of mango varieties to choose from, each with its own distinct flavor. Cutting and eating a mango can be a messy proposition. Old-timers have the right idea when they say there's only one way and one place to eat a ripe mango: naked and in the bathtub!

Actually, there are two convenient methods for removing the fruit from the elongated flat seed. The first is the hedgehog method, so-called because it produces diamond-shape spikes of mango that stick out like the spines of a hedgehog. Slice the top and bottom (flattish sides, not the ends) off the fruit (Step 1), getting as close to the flat seed as possible. Using a sharp knife, score a crosshatch or tic-tac-toe pattern in the flesh, cutting to, but not through, the skin (Step 2). Holding the edges in your hands, press the skin with your thumbs to turn the slice inside out. Bite-size chunks of fruit will extend from the skin, ready to be scooped up with a spoon (Step 3). Don't forget to trim

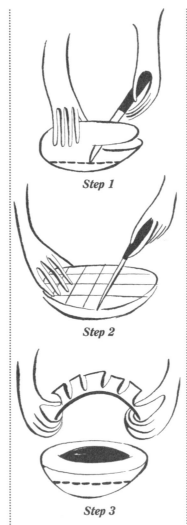

Step 1

Step 2

Step 3

any remaining flesh off the seed with a paring knife.

The second method is ideal for dicing mango for soups and salsas. Pare the skin off the mango with a sharp knife. Whittle the flesh off the

seed by making hooked cuts with a sharp knife.

Whichever method you use, keep in mind that sometimes mango skins exude a sticky sap to which some people are allergic enough to develop a poison ivy-like rash. You may wish to wear rubber gloves when handling or peeling whole mangos.

When buying mangos, look for unblemished fruits free of soft spots. Mangos are usually picked green and will ripen at room temperature (not below 55°F) in a sealed paper bag. Contrary to popular belief, a red or orange skin isn't the only sign of ripeness. The Okrung and Martin varieties, for example, remain green even when ripe. When a mango is ripe, it will be very fragrant and softly yielding when squeezed. Ripe mangos can be stored in the refrigerator. Diced or puréed mango can be frozen for several months.

Mangos not only taste good: They're good for you. Mangos are rich in vitamins A and C and potassium. A medium mango contains about 135 calories and will serve two. A 1-pound mango yields about 1½ cups diced fruit or 1 cup mango purée.

Black-Eyed Pea Salad
with Pepper-Crusted Tuna

The idea for this salad came from a barbecue joint near Orlando. The barbecue itself was of middling quality, but the black-eyed pea salad was sensational. It served as a reminder that, while California and New York have inspired much of the new Floridian cuisine, our roots run deep in Southern cooking. Chicken breasts or scallops can be substituted for the tuna.

SERVES 4

SALAD:

2 cups cooked black-eyed peas (canned are acceptable)

2 ribs celery, cut into fine dice

¼ cup finely diced red onion

¼ cup finely diced red bell pepper

¼ cup finely diced green bell pepper

¼ cup chopped fresh Italian (flat-leaf) parsley,
      plus 4 sprigs for garnish

2 tablespoons red wine vinegar, or to taste

2 tablespoons extra-virgin olive oil

Salt and freshly ground black pepper, to taste

TUNA:

1 pound sushi-quality (very fresh) tuna, cut into
      1-inch-thick steaks

1 tablespoon olive oil

1 teaspoon kosher (coarse) salt

1 tablespoon cracked black peppercorns

1. Preheat the grill to very hot.

2. Combine the ingredients for the salad in a mixing bowl and toss to mix. Correct the seasonings, adding salt or vinegar to taste. The salad should be highly seasoned. (The salad can be made several hours ahead of time, but should be reseasoned and tossed at the last minute.)

3. Rub the tuna with the olive oil. Combine the salt and pepper and thickly coat each side of the tuna with a crust of the salt and peppercorns. Grill the tuna over high heat for 1 minute per side, or until cooked to taste. I like to serve it quite rare in the center. Transfer the tuna to a plate and let cool.

4. Cut the tuna lengthwise into long, thin slices. Fan the slices out on 4 plates or a platter. Mound the salad in the center. Garnish with the parsley sprigs and serve at once.

GRILL-LESS IN THE CITY

Apartment-bound with no backyard and not even a terrace? You can still enjoy this tuna dish. The fish can be quickly seared in a heavy nonstick skillet instead of on the grill.

Red and Yellow Tomato Salad with Crab in Vinaigrette

One of the best things about living in Florida is the availability of gorgeous vine-ripened tomatoes in the winter. Not the pale, hard, cello-packed tomatoes you find in northern supermarkets in the winter. I'm talking about farm stand tomatoes bursting with juice and brimming with flavor. This salad is simplicity itself, but it never fails to delight. If you can't find a yellow tomato, just substitute another red one.

SERVES 4 AS AN APPETIZER,
2 AS A LIGHT ENTREE

SHALLOT VINAIGRETTE:
1 shallot, minced
1 teaspoon Dijon mustard
1 tablespoon rice wine vinegar
1 tablespoon fresh lemon juice
Salt and freshly ground black pepper, to taste
3 to 4 tablespoons light olive oil

8 ounces lump crabmeat
1 large ripe red tomato
1 large ripe yellow tomato
1 bunch of basil leaves, stemmed and washed

1. Prepare the vinaigrette: Combine the shallot, mustard, vinegar, lemon juice, and salt and pepper in a mixing bowl. Whisk until the salt dissolves. Whisk in the oil in a thin stream. Correct the seasonings, adding salt or lemon juice to taste.

2. Pick through the crabmeat, removing any bits of shell or cartilage.

3. Using a very sharp paring knife, cut the peel off the red tomato in a ¾-inch-wide continuous strip. Roll the peel up to make a rose, and set aside. Slice the red and yellow tomatoes as thinly as possible.

4. Arrange the red and yellow tomato slices and whole basil leaves on a round platter, alternating colors and overlapping the slices, working from the outside of the platter to the inside. Spoon half of the vinaigrette over the tomatoes.

5. Toss the crabmeat with the remaining vinaigrette, and mound it in the center. Garnish with the tomato rose and serve.

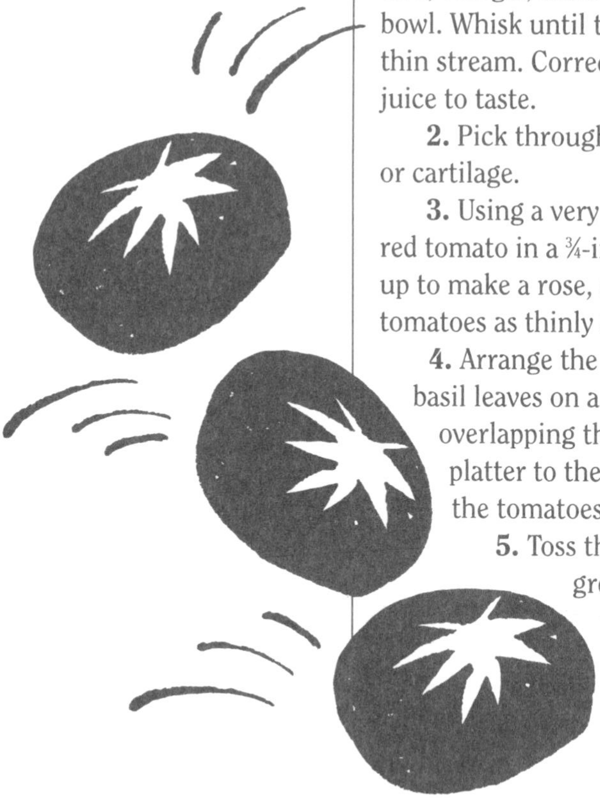

Stone Crab, Melon, and Cucumber Salad

Asia meets Florida in this colorful salad. Stone crab is, perhaps, the greatest of Florida's seafoods, a crustacean whose firm, sweet, meaty claws are eaten in belt-loosening quantities from October to May, when it's in season. If stone crabs are unavailable, you could use blue crab fingers or another type of shellfish.

SERVES 4

DRESSING:

2 tablespoons rice wine vinegar

1 tablespoon fresh tangerine or orange juice

1 tablespoon sugar

1 teaspoon minced fresh ginger

1 teaspoon minced garlic

¼ teaspoon salt, or to taste

2 tablespoons Oriental sesame oil

1 large European-style (seedless) cucumber

1 cup cantaloupe balls

1 cup honeydew melon balls

4 scallions, trimmed and thinly sliced

¼ cup chopped fresh mint or cilantro leaves

4 large stone crab claws, cracked (see Step 1, page 176)
    and shelled

2 tablespoons black sesame seeds

1. Make the dressing: Combine the vinegar, tangerine juice, sugar, ginger, garlic, and salt in a small bowl and whisk until the sugar and salt dissolve. Whisk in the sesame oil.

2. Slice the cucumber as thinly as possible, using a mandoline or food processor fitted with the slicing disk. In a large mixing bowl, toss the cucumber slices with 1½ tablespoons of the dressing. Arrange the slices on 4 salad plates, slightly overlapping, and completely covering the plate.

3. Add the melon balls, scallions, and mint to the bowl and toss with 1½ tablespoons of the dressing. Mound the melon mixture in the center of each plate. Place 1 stone crab claw on each plate on top of the melon. Spoon the remaining dressing over the crab. Sprinkle the salad with the black seseme seeds and serve at once.

Conch Salad

This is a member of a conch triumvirate—which includes cracked conch and conch chowder— eaten from one end of the Florida Keys to the other. If conch is unavailable, you could use scallops or shrimp.

SERVES 4

8 ounces conch

4 to 6 tablespoons fresh sour orange juice or
    lime juice

1 ripe tomato, peeled, seeded, and diced

¼ cup finely diced red onion

1 cucumber, peeled, seeded, and diced

½ red bell pepper, cored, seeded, and diced

½ yellow bell pepper, cored, seeded, and
    diced

½ scotch bonnet chili or 1 to 2 jalapeño
    chilies, seeded and minced

1 to 2 cloves garlic, minced

2 ribs celery, finely diced

½ cup finely chopped fresh Italian (flat-leaf)
    parsley

¼ cup chopped fresh basil or mint leaves

3 tablespoons extra-virgin olive oil

Kosher (coarse) salt, to taste

Cracked black peppercorns, to taste

1 teaspoon Tabasco or other hot sauce

4 romaine lettuce leaves (from the heart of
    the lettuce), for garnish

1. Pound the conch with a meat mallet to tenderize it, as described on page 172. Cut the conch into ¼-inch dice. Place it in a large nonreactive mixing bowl with the sour orange juice. Add all of the vegetables and flavorings to the conch and mix well. Let the salad marinate, covered, in the refrigerator for 30 minutes.

2. Just before serving, correct the seasonings, adding salt, sour orange juice, or hot sauce to taste. Stand a romaine lettuce leaf in each of 4 wine glasses or champagne flutes. Spoon in the conch salad and serve at once.

Breads, Spreads, and Sandwiches

Tangerine Butter

Pecan Corn Bread

Pan Con Leche

Mojo

Idella Parker's Biscuits

Cuban Sandwich

*Y*ou may not have heard of *pan suave* or *media noche*. But to visit Miami without sampling them would be a little like going to Agra and missing the Taj Mahal. *Pan suave* is similar to a dinner roll but with a sweeter flavor—sort of Cuba's equivalent of Jewish challah. *Media noche* is a "midnight" sandwich, a Dagwoodesque commingling of ham, cheese, pickles, and pork that is devoured with gusto day and night by Hispanics and Anglos alike. Both serve as reminders that, although Florida lies within the continental U.S., its culinary horizons stretch to Cuba and Latin America beyond.

The most characteristic bread of south Florida is *pan cubano*, a long, light-crusted loaf that looks like anemic French bread. Softer and less crusty than a *baguette*, Cuban bread is designed to be grilled in a *plancha*, a device that looks like a giant waffle iron. The bread is sliced lengthwise, brushed with butter or margarine, and pressed between the heavy halves of the *plancha*. In the process, it's flattened and toasted into one of the tastiest morsels that ever accompanied a cup of *café con leche*. Cuban sandwiches are toasted in a similar fashion, melting the filling and toasting the bread.

Pan suave (mentioned above) is used to make one of Cuba's most famous sandwiches, a turkey, cream cheese, and strawberry jam sandwich called Elena Ruz. (It tastes better than it sounds.) *Pan de leche* (milk bread) is a white bread with a fine crumb similar to American country-style sandwich bread. There are also a variety of breads and rolls made with puréed tubers, like yuca or boniato. The addition of these starchy root vegetables gives the bread a firm, moist, yet airy texture.

That's not to say that Cubans have a monopoly on Floridian baked goods. Corn bread and biscuits are the breads of choice in northern Florida. Designer pizzas are the fare of the fashion set in the trendy Art Deco

District on Miami Beach. The Jewish bakeries of Miami sell some of the best rye and onion bread in the East.

Florida's cosmopolitan culture encourages a mix-and-match approach to baking, as can be seen in the recipes that follow.

Pan Cubano (Cuban Bread)

Dressed in a white lab coat and hard hat, Gilbert Arriaza looks more like an engineer than a baker. But ask a Cuban restaurateur or housewife where she buys her bread and she'll probably name Gilbert's Bakery. Like thousands of his compatriots, Gilbert fled Cuba in 1962 and began his working life in America as a dishwasher. Today, he owns Miami's foremost Cuban bakery and a wedding cake gallery. "Cuban bread looks like a French baguette, but the texture and flavor are totally different," explains Gilbert. Cubans like their bread to be soft and chewy—ideal for making Cuban sandwiches. Traditionally a palm frond was laid across the loaf during baking; Gilbert uses a wet piece of string. The string helps impede the formation of a hard crust.

Cuban bread owes its distinctive flavor to the use of a starter—made the day before—and to the enrichment of the dough with lard. The latter may trouble health-conscious Americans, but is common not just in the Spanish Caribbean, but throughout Europe. The recipe below calls for lard, but you can substitute vegetable shortening if you wish to.

Serve Cuban bread as an accompaniment to any of the Cuban dishes in this book or use it to make Cuban sandwiches. Another popular way to serve Cuban bread

is thinly sliced lengthwise, buttered, and toasted in a *plancha* (sandwich press) or skillet.

MAKES 4 LOAVES

STARTER:

⅓ *envelope active dry yeast (¾ teaspoon)*

⅓ *cup warm water*

⅓ *cup bread or all-purpose flour*

DOUGH:

2 *envelopes active dry yeast (2¼ teaspoons each) or*
        2 *cakes compressed yeast (0.6 ounces each)*

1 *tablespoon sugar*

1½ *cups warm water*

3 *to 4 tablespoons lard or solid vegetable shortening,*
        at room temperature

½ *batch starter (see above)*

1 *tablespoon salt*

4 *to 5 cups bread or all-purpose flour*

1. Prepare the starter. The day before you plan on baking, dissolve the yeast in the water in a small mixing bowl. Stir in the flour to obtain a thick paste. Cover the bowl with plastic wrap and let the starter ripen for 24 hours in the refrigerator. Leftover starter will keep for several days in the refrigerator and can be frozen.

2. Make the dough: Dissolve the yeast and sugar in 3 tablespoons water in a large mixing bowl. When the mixture is foamy (5 to 10 minutes), stir in the lard, the remaining water, and the ½ batch of starter. Mix well with your fingers or a wooden spoon. Stir in the salt and the flour, 1 cup at a time, to obtain a dough that is stiff enough to pull away from the sides of the bowl, but soft enough to knead. The dough can also be mixed and kneaded in a mixer fitted with a dough hook or in a food processor fitted with the dough blade.

3. Turn the dough onto a lightly floured work surface

and knead until smooth, 6 to 8 minutes, adding flour as necessary. The dough should be pliable, but not sticky.

4. Transfer the dough to a lightly oiled bowl, cover, and let rise in a warm, draft-free spot until doubled in bulk, about 45 minutes. Punch down the dough.

5. Form the loaves: Divide the dough into 4 equal pieces. Roll each out to form a 14-inch long tube. Divide the tubes between 2 baking sheets with 6 inches space between each. Cover the loaves with dampened cotton dish towels and let rise in a warm, draft-free spot until doubled in bulk, about 1 hour. (The dough can be allowed to rise at a lower temperture—even in the refrigerator—but the rising time will be 3 to 4 hours.)

6. Preheat the oven to 350°F.

7. Lay a dampened piece of thick kitchen string or twine (about ⅛ inch thick) on top of each loaf, running the length of the loaf. Bake until the breads are lightly browned on top and sound hollow when lightly tapped, about 30 minutes. Let the loaves cool slightly and remove the strings. Transfer the breads onto a wire rack to cool completely.

Pan Suave (Cuban Sweet Rolls)

Cuba's answer to challah, is *pan suave,* a soft, dense, semi-sweet egg bread that tastes great by itself and makes great French toast and sandwiches. In Miami *pan suave* is usually enjoyed in the form of bullet-shaped rolls, which are used to make *Media Noches* (midnight sandwiches—see page 105). But you can also use the dough to make full size loaves and even braided loaves, like challah. This recipe comes Gilbert's Bakery in Miami.

MAKES TWELVE 5-INCH ROLLS

2 envelopes active dry yeast (2¼ teaspoons each) or
  2 cakes compressed yeast (0.6 ounces each)
¾ cup sugar
1 cup warm water
⅓ cup vegetable oil
2 large eggs, beaten
2 teaspoons salt, plus salt for the egg glaze
4 to 5 cups bread or all-purpose flour, or more as needed
2 tablespoons sesame seeds
1 tablespoon melted unsalted butter (optional)

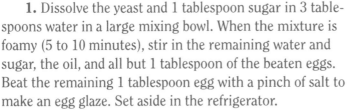

1. Dissolve the yeast and 1 tablespoon sugar in 3 tablespoons water in a large mixing bowl. When the mixture is foamy (5 to 10 minutes), stir in the remaining water and sugar, the oil, and all but 1 tablespoon of the beaten eggs. Beat the remaining 1 tablespoon egg with a pinch of salt to make an egg glaze. Set aside in the refrigerator.

2. Stir the 2 teaspoons salt and the flour, 1 cup at a time, into the liquid ingredients, to obtain a dough that is stiff enough to pull away from the sides of the bowl, but soft enough to knead. The dough can also be mixed and kneaded in a mixer fitted with a dough hook or in a food processor fitted with the dough blade.

3. Turn the dough onto a lightly floured work surface and knead until smooth, 6 to 8 minutes, adding flour as necessary, to obtain a soft dough that is pliable but not sticky. It will be a little moister than regular bread dough.

4. Transfer the dough to a lightly oiled bowl, cover, and let rise in a warm, draft-free spot until doubled in bulk, 1 to 1½ hours. Punch down the dough.

5. Form the rolls: Divide the dough into 12 equal pieces. Roll each on the work surface with the palm of your hand to form a tube 5 inches long with tapered ends. Transfer the rolls to lightly greased baking sheets, leaving 3 inches between each.

6. Cover the rolls with a dampened cotton dish towel and let rise in a warm, draft-free spot until doubled in bulk, about 1 hour. (The rolls can be allowed to rise at a lower temperature—even in the refrigerator—but the rising time will be 3 to 4 hours.)

7. Preheat the oven to 350°F.

8. Brush the rolls with the reserved egg glaze and sprinkle with sesame seeds. Bake the rolls until golden brown and hollow sounding when lightly tapped, 20 to 30 minutes. Remove the rolls from the oven and let cool for 5 minutes. Brush the tops with melted butter, if using. Serve warm or cool to room temperature on a wire rack.

Boniato Bread / Boniato Rolls

This bread is modeled on the yuca bread served at high-class Cuban restaurants. Boniato is a Cuban sweet potato, a purplish-skinned tuber with a mild chestnut flavor but little of the sweetness associated with an American sweet potato. It gives this bread a moist, satisfying consistency. If boniatos are unavailable, the bread could be made with yuca or white potatoes. The Tangerine Butter on page 101 makes a great accompaniment.

MAKES TWO 8-INCH LOAVES OR 18 TO 20 ROLLS

1 pound boniato

1 envelope active dry yeast (2¼ teaspoons)
    or 1 cake compressed yeast (0.6 ounce)

¼ cup warm water

⅓ cup sugar

4 tablespoons (½ stick) unsalted butter

1 tablespoon salt

5½ to 6 cups unbleached all-purpose flour

2 tablespoons milk, for brushing the loaves

1. Peel the boniato and cut it into 1-inch pieces. As you cut, place the pieces in a large saucepan filled with cold water to cover to prevent discoloration. Then bring to a boil, reduce the heat, and simmer, uncovered, until very soft, 15 to 20 minutes.

2. Drain the boniato in a colander, reserving 1½ cups of the cooking liquid. Return the boniato to the pot and mash it with a potato masher or fork.

3. Meanwhile, place the yeast, warm water, and 1 tablespoon of the sugar in a small bowl and stir well. Let stand until the mixture is foamy, about 5 to 10 minutes. Melt the butter in a 1-quart saucepan. Stir in the reserved boniato cooking liquid and warm slightly; the mixture should be warm, not hot.

4. Pour the boniato liquid into a large mixing bowl. Stir in the yeast mixture, salt, and mashed boniato. Stir in the flour, 1 cup at a time, to obtain a dough that is stiff enough to pull away from the sides of the bowl, but soft enough to knead. (It will be stickier than regular bread dough.) Note: The dough can also be mixed and kneaded in a mixer fitted with a dough hook or in a food processor fitted with the dough blade.

5. Turn the dough onto a floured work surface and knead until smooth, 6 to 8 minutes.

6. Wash and lightly oil the mixing bowl. Place the dough in the bowl and press plastic wrap directly on top of it; cover the bowl with a dish towel. Place the dough in a warm, draft-free spot and let rise until doubled in bulk, 1½ to 2 hours. (The dough can be allowed to rise at lower temperatures—even in the refrigerator—but the rising time will be 3 to 4 hours.)

7. To form loaves: Divide the dough in two. Pat each half into an 8-inch-long oval. Plump up each oval in the center and drop, seam side down, into a greased loaf pan. To make rolls: Pinch off twenty 2-inch balls. Place 10 of the balls in a greased 9-inch springform or round cake pan, spacing them ½ inch apart. Place the remaining balls in another pan.

Cover with plastic wrap or a damp dish cloth. Let the loaves/rolls rise until doubled in bulk, about 1 hour.

8. Preheat the oven to 375°F.

9. Brush the top of each loaf with the milk. Using a razor blade or sharp knife, make a series of diagonal slashes, 1 inch apart, cutting ½ inch deep. If making rolls, brush the tops with milk and do not slash.

10. Bake the breads until browned on top and the loaves sound hollow when tapped, 40 to 50 minutes. If making rolls, bake until puffed and golden brown, 20 to 30 minutes. Let the loaves/rolls cool slightly, then turn them onto a wire rack to cool a little more.

Pecan Corn Bread

According to Marjorie Kinnan Rawlings, "'Bread' to the Floridian is corn bread," or so she wrote in her seminal book on Floridian cooking, *Cross Creek Cookery*. The Pulitzer prize-winning author included no fewer than eight corn bread recipes in her book, ranging from humble hoecake to ethereal spoon bread. I'm not sure what Rawlings would have made of this corn bread, which is flavored with vanilla, rum, and pecans. For the best results, use a fine, stone-ground cornmeal—preferably organic. The coarse yellow cornmeal sold in the supermarket produces a very harsh-tasting bread. The Tangerine Butter on page 103 makes a good accompaniment.

MAKES 8 WEDGES, ENOUGH TO SERVE 4 TO 8

4 tablespoons (½ stick) unsalted butter

1 to 1¼ cups buttermilk

1 extra-large egg, beaten

½ teaspoon vanilla extract

1 tablespoon dark rum

¾ cup fine stone-ground cornmeal

1¼ cups all-purpose flour

1 teaspoon baking soda

1 teaspoon baking powder

2 tablespoons sugar

¾ teaspoon salt

½ cup coarsely chopped toasted pecans
 (see page 311)

1. Preheat the oven to 350°F.

2. Melt the butter in an 8-inch cast-iron skillet over high heat. Swirl the pan to coat the sides with butter. Pour the excess butter into a large mixing bowl and let cool. When cool, whisk in the buttermilk, egg, vanilla, and rum.

3. In another mixing bowl, combine the dry ingredients and pecans. Whisk to mix. Add the dry ingredients to the butter mixture and stir with a wooden spoon just to mix. Pour the batter into the skillet.

4. Place the skillet in the oven, and bake the corn bread until firm and golden brown, about 30 minutes. When cooked, an inserted skewer will come out clean. Let the corn bread cool for 3 minutes, then invert it onto a round platter.

CROSS CREEK COOKERY

When most people think of Floridian cooking, they think of the current wave of Caribbean food. But there's another side to Sunshine State cooking, one closer to Savannah than Santiago. For if Florida has one foot in the Caribbean, the other is firmly planted in the culinary traditions of the Deep South.

Marjorie Kinnan Rawlings was keenly aware of Florida's Southern culinary heritage. In 1928, the writer moved to Cross Creek, a remote town in central Florida. Her home was a 72-acre farm with a white clapboard farmhouse built in 1880 and more than 2,000 citrus and pecan trees. It was here she wrote *Cross Creek*, *South Moon Under*, and the Pulitzer Prize-winning *The Yearling*.

If Rawlings was a masterly writer, she was also passionate about food. In 1942, she wrote one of the best books ever on Southern cooking, *Cross Creek Cookery*. In it she describes the genesis of such quintessential southern fare as corn pones, crackling bread, and hush puppies. An avid fisherwoman and hunter, she lovingly explains the preparation of such unique Florida foods as frog legs, donax (a tiny mollusk), and swamp cabbage.

Most of the actual cooking on the farm was done by Rawlings' maid, Idella Parker. Working over a hot, cast-iron wood stove in a kitchen that would seem both claustrophobic and hellish by today's standards, Parker turned out everything from Minorcan gopher stew to sweet potato soufflé. Kumquats, guavas, mangos, and roselles (Florida cranberries) from the farm were transformed into jellies and relishes, which were stored in a tiny pantry.

Today, the Cross Creek farm is a historic site and state landmark. Tours are given in the morning and afternoon, Thursday through Sunday— occasionally by Idella Parker, who is now nearing eighty. Admission is on a first-come basis—only ten people are allowed in the house at a time. For further information, call (904) 466-3672.

Idella Parker's Biscuits

Marjorie Rawlings was the author of *Cross Creek Cookery*, but the creative genius behind much of the book was Rawlings' maid, Idella Parker. Born in Reddick, Florida, in 1914, Idella worked for Rawlings for fourteen years at Cross Creek. She confided in a recent interview that many of the recipes in *Cross Creek Cookery* were actually hers, although she is credited by name for only three. Here are Idella's biscuits, with the cryptic words in Rawlings' version of the recipe, "Mix as usual," explained by Parker herself. Note: these biscuits remain thin—even when baked.

MAKES 28 TO 30 BISCUITS

2 cups all-purpose flour
4 teaspoons baking powder
¾ teaspoon salt
⅓ cup solid vegetable shortening
About ¾ cup milk

1. Preheat the oven to 450°F.

2. Sift the flour, baking powder, and salt into a large mixing bowl. Using 2 knives, cut in the shortening until the mixture feels coarse and sandy.

3. Mix in the milk with the knives, adding just enough to obtain a soft, pliable dough. The dough should be mixed as little as possible.

4. On a lightly floured work surface, roll out the biscuit dough ¼ inch thick. Cut out 1½-inch biscuits, using a round cookie cutter. Combine the scraps and continue rolling and cutting until all of the dough is used up. Transfer the biscuits to a baking sheet, spacing them 1 inch apart.

5. Bake the biscuits until golden brown and wafer crisp, about 12 minutes. Serve with a dab of butter on top.

Bubble Bread

The Bubble Room in Captiva, Florida, is one of the nation's most colorful restaurants, a veritable fantasyland crammed to the rafters with mechanical displays and toys from the 1940s. The waiters wear Boy Scout uniforms and serve belly-bludgeoning portions of Euro-American food. My favorite dish here is a sort of garlic bread called Bubble Bread. The restaurant's owners refuse to disclose their recipe, but here's how I suspect they make it.

SERVES 6 TO 8

1 loaf Italian bread, cut on the diagonal
    into ¾-inch-thick slices
12 tablespoons (1½ sticks) unsalted butter,
    at room temperature
3 to 4 cloves garlic, minced
2 ounces prosciutto, minced
1 cup freshly grated Parmesan cheese
Salt and freshly ground black pepper, to taste
About 6 ounces cream cheese, at room temperature

1. Preheat the broiler.

2. Arrange the bread slices on a baking sheet. Broil until golden brown on both sides, 1 to 2 minutes per side.

3. Cream the butter in a mixing bowl, using a whisk. When light and fluffy, whisk in the garlic, prosciutto, ½ cup of the Parmesan, salt and pepper. You won't need much salt, as the ham and cheese are quite salty.

4. Spread one side of each bread slice with a thin layer of cream cheese. Spread the garlic mixture on top and sprinkle with the remaining ½ cup Parmesan. Arrange the bread slices on a baking sheet.

5. Just before serving, run the bread slices under a hot broiler until the topping is hot and bubbling, 1 to 2 minutes. Alternatively, the bread can be baked in a 400°F oven for 6 to 8 minutes. Serve at once.

FRENCH TOAST

Americans call it French toast and enjoy it at breakfast. The Spanish know it as *torrejas* and serve it for dessert. The French call it *pain perdu* (literally "lost bread") and use it to recycle stale baguettes. Whatever you call it, bread slices dipped in egg batter and fried are a dish of universal appeal.

What makes great French toast? The ingredients couldn't be simpler: bread, eggs, milk or cream, and butter. The secret lies in technique. The bread must be soaked long enough for the batter to reach the center, but not so long that it disintegrates into a soggy mess. The staler the bread or harder the crust, the longer you need to soak it. When you can easily compress the soaked bread with your finger, it's ready for frying.

The flavorings for French toast are limited only by your imagination. Vanilla, cinnamon, and orange liqueur are the traditional standbys. But ginger, cloves, nutmeg, anise, brandy, and other spirits make equally welcomed additions.

Floridian French Toast

A brunch favorite at our house, this French toast was inspired by a dessert popular from one end of Latin America to the other: guava paste with cheese. Guava paste is a dense, sweet jam made from a perfumed fruit whose numerous seeds make out-of-hand-eating impractical. The tang of the cream cheese cuts the cloying sweetness of the paste. Flat tins of guava paste can be found at Hispanic markets and in the ethnic food sections of many supermarkets. If unavailable, you could use raspberry or apricot jam or other preserves. The best sort of bread for this recipe is a long, soft French-or Italian-style bread easily found at a supermarket. A hard-crusted baguette from a bakery is too difficult to slice. One last note: Clarified butter is ideal for frying the toast. When I don't have time to prepare clarified butter, I mix regular unsalted butter with canola oil in equal proportions. The oil helps keep the butter from burning.

1 loaf of French or Cuban bread,
  cut into sixteen 1-inch-thick slices

6 ounces cream cheese

6 ounces guava paste

8 eggs

2 tablespoons sugar

1 cup heavy (or whipping) cream

2 cups half-and-half or milk

3 tablespoons orange liqueur

2 teaspoons vanilla extract

2 teaspoons ground cinnamon

½ cup Clarified Butter (see page 328), for frying

¼ cup confectioners' sugar, for sprinkling

1. Using a serrated knife, cut a deep pocket in each bread slice by cutting the slice almost in half through its thickness. (This is most easily done by laying the bread slice flat on a cutting board. Hold it flat with the palm of your left hand. Keep the knife blade parallel to the cutting board and do the cutting with your right hand. Reverse positions if you're left-handed.)

2. Cut the cream cheese and guava paste into 16 flat slices each. Place a slice of each in the pocket of each bread slice.

3. In a large bowl, whisk the eggs and sugar until smooth. Beat in the heavy cream, half-and-half, orange liqueur, vanilla, and cinnamon.

4. Arrange the bread slices in a large roasting pan and pour the egg mixture over them. Set aside for 5 minutes. Gently turn the bread slices with a spatula and let stand for 5 minutes more or until thoroughly moistened.

5. Just before serving, heat 2 tablespoons of the clarified butter in each of 2 large frying pans over medium heat. Add the bread slices and fry until crusty and brown on one side, about 2 minutes. Divide the remaining butter between the pans and turn the slices. Continue frying until crusty and brown on the bottom, about 2 minutes. Watch closely, as the toast burns easily.

6. Arrange the French toast on a platter. Sprinkle with the confectioners' sugar and serve at once.

Arepas

repas are a popular Colombian snack, a cross between polenta, pancakes, and grilled cheese sandwiches. Thanks to Miami's large Colombian community, *arepas* turn up at carnivals and street fairs, where they're enjoyed by Colombians and non-Colombians alike. The following recipe was inspired by Bogota-born caterer, cooking teacher, and pastry chef Tania Sigal. *Arepa* flour is made from cooked, finely ground corn. Look for it at Hispanic markets. Two popular brands of *arepa* flour are Goya and Pan.

AREPA FLOUR

repa flour is a special flour milled from cooked, dried, ground corn kernels. It's finer than cornmeal but coarser than all-purpose flour. There's really no substitute: The closest in flavor is quick-cook grits.

Arepa flour comes in varieties made from both white and yellow corn. I prefer the white: The resulting pastries are lighter. This flour can be found at Hispanic markets and select supermarkets, where it is sometimes sold by the name *masarepa* or *areparena*. Recommended brands include Goya, Iberia, and Pan. *Arepa* flour is also used to make *tortillas*, *empanadas*, and *buñelos*.

MAKES EIGHT 3-INCH AREPAS; SERVES 4

1 cup arepa flour
Scant ½ teaspoon salt
⅔ cup coarsely grated Monterey jack or
   other mild cheese
3 to 4 tablespoons unsalted butter,
   melted
About 1 cup very hot water

1. Combine the *arepa* flour, salt, and cheese in a large mixing bowl. Stir in 2 tablespoons melted butter and most of the water. Knead the mixture with your hands to obtain a moist, pliable dough. Add more water as necessary: The dough should be the consistancy of mashed potatoes. You may not need all of the water, or you may need a little more.

2. Divide the dough into 8 equal pieces. Wet your hands and roll each piece into a ball, then flatten it to make a patty about 3 inches across and ⅓ inch thick. Continue wetting your hands to prevent the dough from sticking. Alternatively, roll out the dough between two sheets of plastic wrap or waxed paper and cut out 3-inch circles, using a cookie cutter.

3. Heat some of the remaining melted butter in a large skillet or griddle over medium heat. Fry the *arepas* until crusty and golden brown, turning once, about 2 minutes per side. Work in batches, as necessary, to avoid crowding the pan. Add more butter or oil if needed. Serve at once.

Manchego Cheese Butter

Manchego is a firm, full-flavored Spanish sheep's milk cheese made on the plains of La Mancha. Sold at Cuban markets throughout south Florida, it can be found elsewhere in the country at

Hispanic markets and gourmet shops. Romano cheese from Italy makes a tasty, if not strictly identical, substitute.

MAKES ½ CUP

8 tablespoons (1 stick) unsalted butter,
  at room temperature
¼ cup grated Manchego cheese
2 tablespoons minced fresh Italian
  (flat-leaf) parsley
Few drops of fresh lemon juice
Freshly ground black pepper,
  to taste

1. Cream the butter in a mixing bowl, using a whisk. When light and fluffy, whisk in all of the remaining ingredients. Spoon the butter into a ramekin or pretty serving bowl and make a decorative pattern on top. Cover and refrigerate.
2. Serve the Manchego cheese butter on breads and rolls.

Tangerine Butter

A biscuit or roll hot from the oven begs to be slathered with butter. When tangerines are in season, I love to make this honeyed tangerine butter. To make orange butter, substitute the zest and juice of an orange. Lemon, lime, kumquat, and grapefruit butter can be prepared the same way.

MAKES ½ CUP

8 tablespoons (1 stick unsalted butter)
    at room temperature
2 tablespoons honey
1½ teaspoons grated tangerine zest
2 tablespoons fresh tangerine juice

1. Cream the butter in a mixing bowl, using a whisk. When light and fluffy, whisk in the honey, followed by the tangerine zest and juice. Spoon the butter into a ramekin or pretty serving bowl and make a decorative pattern on top. Cover and refrigerate.

2. Serve the tangerine butter on biscuits, muffins, pancakes, waffles, and crêpes.

Elena Ruz
(Turkey Tea Sandwich)

One of the most curious Cuban sandwiches is the Elena Ruz, made with sliced turkey, strawberry jam, and cream cheese on a sweet roll. The combination may seem odd, if not downright revolting, but remember, North Americans enjoy accompanying roast turkey with sweet cranberry sauce. It's not really so very different. Named for a Havana debutante of the 1920s, the Elena Ruz is popular at *merienda* (afternoon tea). It reflects the Cuban fondness for dishes that are both salty and sweet.

CUBAN SANDWICHES

Let Philadelphians have their hoagies, Bostonians their grinders. Miami's Cuban Americans have raised the humble hero sandwich to the level of art. Sandwiches are interwoven into the fabric of Cuban life here, enjoyed by all levels of society at all hours of the day and night.

Visit any Cuban restaurant or *loncheria* (snack bar) in Miami, and you'll find a showcase filled with roast pork, country ham, sliced turkey and cheese, and a dozen other fixings for sandwiches. Baguette-like Cuban bread *(pan cubano)* and shiny sweet dinner rolls *(pan suave)* are piled high in baskets. Whole serrano hams hang overhead. The sandwiches are usually assembled in the morning and cooked to order.

The focal point of the sandwich shop is a hinged grill called a *plancha*. Just before serving, the sandwiches are brushed with butter (or, more often, margarine) and toasted until golden brown. The *plancha* flattens the sandwich, heating the filling, melting the cheese, and crisping the crust. Because they're flattened, you can bite into a Cuban sandwich without unduly straining your jaws.

If you live near a Cuban bakery, you will be able to buy Cuban bread and sweet rolls. Lacking these, the best substitute for *pan cubano* is the long, soft, French- or Italian-style breads you find at the supermarket. (A high-quality bakery baguette is too crusty.) Challah or brioche makes a good substitute for *pan suave*.

In the absence of a *plancha,* the sandwiches can be cooked in a frying pan with a weight (like a bacon press or heavy skillet) on top. You can also use an electric sandwich maker, but you'll have to make smaller sandwiches.

SERVES 1
AND CAN BE MULTIPLIED AS DESIRED

*1 bullet-shaped, slightly sweet roll, 6 to
7 inches long (such as the Pan Suave
on page 91 or a piece of brioche),
or a section of Cuban, French,
or Italian bread the same length*
2 tablespoons cream cheese
2 tablespoons strawberry jam
*3 ounces sliced turkey breast
(preferably from a whole turkey,
not turkey roll)*
*About 1 tablespoon butter, at room
temperature*

1. Slice open the roll lengthwise. Spread the bottom with the cream cheese and the top with the strawberry jam. Place the turkey in the center. Cover with the top of the roll.

2. Lightly butter the entire outside of the sandwich. Place it in a skillet over medium heat. Place a weight, like a bacon press, on top, or flatten the sandwich with a long spatula.

3. Cook the sandwich until crusty and golden brown on both sides, 2 to 3 minutes per side, adding butter as necessary. Slice the sandwich in half on the diagonal and serve at once.

Media Noche
(Midnight Sandwich)

This is the most famous Cuban sandwich—a combination of ham, cheese, and roast pork on a flattened, toasted sweet dinner roll. Traditionally eaten after a movie or a show (which explains the name, midnight), the *media noche* is a relatively small sandwich. It's designed as a late-night snack that won't send you to bed feeling stuffed.

SERVES 1
AND CAN BE MULTIPLIED AS DESIRED

---

1 bullet-shaped, slightly sweet roll, 6 to 7 inches long
(such as the Pan Suave on page 91), or a
section of Cuban, French, or Italian bread the
same length
2 teaspoons mayonnaise
2 teaspoons Dijon mustard
2 ounces thinly sliced cold roast pork
2 ounces thinly sliced cooked ham
1 ounce sliced Swiss cheese
3 thin slices of ripe tomato
1 or 2 iceberg lettuce leaves
3 to 4 thin slices dill pickle
About 1 tablespoon butter or margarine,
at room temperature

1. Slice open the roll lengthwise. Spread the bottom with the mayonnaise, the top with the mustard. Layer the sandwich with the pork, ham, cheese, tomato, lettuce, and pickle. Cover with the top of the roll.

2. Lightly butter the entire outside of the sandwich. Place it in a skillet over medium heat. Place a weight, like a bacon press, on top, or flatten the sandwich with a long spatula.

3. Cook the sandwich until crusty and golden brown on both sides, 2 to 3 minutes per side, adding butter as necessary. Slice the sandwich in half on the diagonal and serve at once.

Note: For an alternative, if slightly unconventional way to make this and other Cuban sandwiches, cut the uncooked sandwiches in halves or quarters and grill in an electric sandwich maker.

MORE CUBAN SANWICHES

Here is a roster of Miami's other popular Cuban sandwiches.

EMPAREDADO (literally "walled in") is the Cuban version of "the works"—an oversized sandwich of cooked ham, country ham, roast pork, cheese, and pickles served on Cuban bread that has been rubbed with garlic. In Oriente in eastern Cuba, *emparedados* are made with chopped roast pork sprinkled with chilies, chopped onions, and garlicky *mojo* (lime juice).

CALLE OCHO (8th Street special) is a belly-bludgeoning blend of ham, turkey, cheese, bacon, lettuce, tomato, and mayonnaise on Cuban bread. This is a specialty of Miami's famous Versailles restauraunt, located on Calle Ocho in the heart of Little Havana.

BOLO is a cooked ham sandwich.

BOLICHE is a Cuban pot roast sandwich.

PALOMILLA is a steak sandwich. The meat is marinated in lime juice, garlic, and cumin, then pan-fried or deep-fried. Fried onions are the requisite accompaniment.

Pan Con Lechón

One of the most popular Cuban sandwiches is *pan con lechón*, freshly roasted pork on Cuban bread, spiced up with thinly sliced onions and *mojo* (garlicky vinaigrette). *Pan con lechón* turns up at street fairs and open-air markets, where the pork is hacked into crisp bits by a sandwich maker wielding a meat cleaver. Technically speaking, the sandwich contains roast suckling pig *(lechón),* but more often than not, it's made with roasted pork shoulder or butt. Like Chinese Peking duck, a good *pan con lechón* will always include a crisp shard of pork skin or cracklings to give crunch to the meat—perhaps not the sort of fare a health-conscious diner would eat daily, but definately tasty as an occasional treat!

SERVES 1
AND CAN BE MULTIPLIED AS DESIRED

1 long section (about 10 inches)
    of Cuban, Italian, or French bread
4 to 6 ounces coarsely chopped or thinly sliced
    warm roast pork (see page 223; be sure to include
    some of the crisp edges and fat)
1 very small onion, thinly sliced
2 to 3 tablespoons Mojo (see page 114)
About 1 tablespoon butter, at room
    temperature

1. Slice open the bread lengthwise. Layer the pork in the center and top with the thinly sliced onion. Spoon the *mojo* on top. Cover with the top of the bread.
2. Lightly butter the entire outside of the sandwich. Place it in a skillet over medium heat. Place a weight, like a

bacon press, on top, or flatten the sandwich with a long spatula.

3. Cook the sandwich until crusty and golden brown on both sides, 2 to 3 minutes per side, adding butter as necessary. Slice the sandwich in half on the diagonal and serve at once.

Mojos, Sauces, and Salsas

Banana-Molasses Ketchup

Tropical Tartar Sauce

Dijon

Cilantro & Corn Vinaigrette

Mango-Mint Vinaigrette

MOJO

When I went to cooking school in Paris, sauce meant a classical demi-glace or béarnaise. I wonder what my old teacher, Chef Chambrette, would make of the new condiments turning up on Floridian tables: fiery tinctures of scotch bonnet chilies and lime juice; rainbow-colored salsas made of mangos, lychees, and other tropical fruits; pastel creams of cilantro or tamarind squirted with Jackson Pollockesque verve from squeeze bottles. Sure, we still make béarnaise sauce, but we're apt to flavor it with cilantro and scotch bonnet chilies.

As with so much of our new cuisine, Florida sauce-making has been profoundly influenced by our Hispanic community. Floridians of all ethnic persuasions douse subs and sandwiches with a garlicky Cuban sour orange sauce called mojo. Supermarkets here carry a full line of bottled mojos, but most Cuban families make their own.

Florida's Nicaraguan-Americans have popularized three Latin American sauces: chimichurri, cebollita, and marinara. The first is a garlicky parsley sauce, the second a pickled onion relish, the third a spicy tomato sauce (quite different than Italian marinara sauce). All three turn up wherever Latin American-style grilled meats are served.

Floridians have certainly done their share to boost salsa consumption, adding star fruit, papayas, lychees, and other tropical fruits to the salsa pot. Salsas are the perfect condiment for the grilled fare of which we're so fond. And unlike the French sauces of my youth, they won't ruin your figure for a bathing suit.

Here is a sampling of some of the new Floridian sauces. So grab your squirt bottles. Escoffier is about to meet Jackson Pollock under the bright Floridian sun!

Key Lime Nuoc Cham

This sauce is a tale of two continents. *Nuoc cham* is a popular Vietnamese dipping sauce that's as essential to the Asian table as ketchup is to our own. This recipe melds the pungent juice of the key lime (regular lime will do in a pinch) and scotch bonnet chilies with the fish sauce so beloved by Southeast Asians. Made from fermented anchovies, fish sauce can be found at Asian markets and many supermarkets. This sauce makes a great dip for clams, oysters, shrimp, and fritters.

MAKES 1 CUP

¼ cup fresh key lime juice or regular lime juice
¼ cup Thai fish sauce (nam pla)
2 tablespoons honey
3 to 4 tablespoons water
3 cloves garlic, minced
2 scallions, trimmed and thinly sliced
2 to 3 paper-thin rings of scotch bonnet chili

1. Combine the lime juice, fish sauce, and honey in a bowl and whisk until the honey dissolves.

2. Stir in all of the remaining ingredients. Correct the seasonings, adding lime juice or honey to taste. Serve within a couple of hours of making.

FISH SAUCE— MALODOROUS MAGIC

Fish sauce is a malodorous condiment made from pickled anchovies. In Southeast Asia this salty brown liquid is used the way soy sauce is used in China and salt is used in the West. Known as *nuoc mam* in Vietnamese and *nam pla* in Thai, fish sauce serves both as a cooking ingredient and a table sauce. Its pungent, cheesy aroma takes some getting used to. (Then again, so does the odor of ripe Gorgonzola or Camembert.) Its tangy flavor reminds me of English Bovril or Marmite.

The best fish sauce in the world is said to come from Phu Quoc Island in Vietnam. Even Thai manufacturers use the words "Phu Quoc" to designate their top grade of fish sauce. The fish sauces sold in glass bottles tend to be better than those sold in plastic. Recommended are the "Flying Lion," "Three Crabs," and "Squid" brands.

Neophytes should try a Thai brand to start with, as Chinese and Filipino fish sauces can taste rather overpowering. Store it away from light at room temperature. Fish sauce keeps forever.

Old Sour

Old Sour is the granddad of Floridian sauces, a piquant mixture of lime juice, chilies, and salt used for seasoning both raw and cooked seafood and grilled meats. An indispensable part of the Key West larder, it was made in large batches when key limes were in season and put up in jars for use throughout the year. It will keep without refrigeration for several months, and it just gets better with age.

MAKES 1 CUP

---

1 to 2 bird peppers, datil peppers, scotch bonnet chilies,
*   or other hot chilies*
1 cup fresh key lime juice or regular
*   lime juice*
2 teaspoons salt

1. Leave chilies whole for a milder sauce, thinly slice for a hotter sauce. Combine all of the ingredients in a sterile jar and cover tightly. Shake well to dissolve the salt.

2. Let the old sour stand for 1 week at room temperature before using. Stir or shake before seasoning meat or seafood.

HOT STUFF!

What's the world's hottest chili pepper? Jalapeño? Pablum! Serrano? Kid's stuff! Tabasco chili? You're not even getting warm! Even Thailand's tongue-blistering bird pepper falls short of the Caribbean scotch bonnet chili. A single scotch bonnet has the firepower of fifty jalapeños!

Lime green, yellow, or orange-red in color, the bonnet chili is shaped vaguely like a Highlander's turban-like headwear—which explains the name scotch bonnet. The walnut-size chili grows throughout the Caribbean, where it's an essential ingredient in Jamaican jerk pork, French West Indian *accras* (salt cod fritters), and in Trinidadian hot sauces, like Matouk's. On the West Coast, scotch bonnets are known by their Mexican name: *chile habañero.* (Some authorities maintain the two are actually slightly different varieties. To me, they taste the same.)

The heat of the scotch bonnet is experienced first in your sinuses and nasal passages. The flavor is floral, aromatic, almost smoky. The tiniest piece tastes like a bite of a high-voltage cable!

Nevertheless, the aromatic flavor of the scotch bonnet quickly becomes addictive. And you definitely build up a tolerance. The first time my cooking students taste a scotch bonnet, they make a frenzied lunge for their water glasses. By the end of the week, they're adding the chili to everything in sight.

When handling scotch bonnet chilies for the first time, I suggest you wear rubber gloves (as you should with any fresh hot pepper). Wash your hands with soap afterward and take care not to touch your eyes or face. If your hands start to sting after touching scotch bonnets, rub them with a little toothpaste! As with all chilies, the seeds are the hottest part.

When buying scotch bonnets, look for firm, springy chilies free of wrinkles, worm holes, or soft spots. They are usually available at Caribbean and Latin American markets. Fresh scotch bonnets will keep for up to a week in an unsealed plastic bag in the refrigerator. Dried habañero chilies are available in upscale supermarkets from the California exotic produce purveyor, Frieda's.

Caribbean Cocktail Sauce

*E*ach day in Florida oceans of cocktail sauce are consumed in the course of enjoying Apalachicola Bay oysters, shrimp from the Gulf of Mexico, and other Florida seafoods. Most of it is an indifferent blend of ketchup and prepared horseradish. This cocktail sauce, spiked with Caribbean hot sauce, is guaranteed to make you stand up and take notice. There are many possibilities for Caribbean hot sauces, including Matouk's from Trinidad, Belinda's from Jamaica, and Inner Beauty Hot Sauce.

MAKES 1 CUP

⅔ cup ketchup
¼ cup freshly grated or prepared horseradish
1 to 2 tablespoons Caribbean hot sauce,
    or to taste
1 tablespoon fresh lime juice

Combine the ingredients in a mixing bowl and whisk until blended. Store the sauce, covered, in the refrigerator until needed. It tastes freshest served within a couple of days but refrigerated it will keep for up to 3 weeks.

Chimichurri

*T*his pungent condiment originated in Argentina, where it's an indispensable accompaniment for grilled meats. But it was the Nicaraguan exiles arriving in Miami after the fall of Somoza who popular-

ized it in Florida. Today it's served at dozens of
Nicaraguan restaurants in Miami, not to mention at
Argentinian steak houses. I like to think of it as Latin
American pesto. Serve *chimichurri* on grilled meats
and chicken. It also makes a great marinade. This
recipe comes from my assistant, Michelle Bernstein,
who was born in Argentina.

MAKES ABOUT 2 CUPS

1 bunch curly parsley, stemmed and minced
    (about 2 cups)
8 to 10 cloves garlic, minced
1 cup olive oil, preferably Spanish
3 tablespoons fresh lemon juice
1 teaspoon red pepper flakes
1 teaspoon salt, or to taste
Freshly ground black pepper

1. Combine the parsley and garlic in a food processor or
mortar and grind to a coarse paste.

2. Work in all of the remaining ingredients. Correct the
seasonings, adding lemon juice or salt to taste. The
chimichurri can be served right away, but it will be better if
you let it ripen for a few days in the refrigerator.

Mojo
(Cuban Garlic-Citrus Sauce)

ojo—pronounced Mo-ho—is Cuba's national
table sauce. To be strictly authentic, you'd use
the acid juice of the sour orange *(naranja agria)*,
a fruit that looks like a green bumpy orange but that

MOJO

Mojo is to Cuban cuisine what vinaigrette is to French. Commercial brands of this tart, tangy, garlicky sauce are available in Hispanic markets and many supermarkets, but the sauce is quick and easy to prepare at home.

Like vinaigrette, *mojo* contains an oil (olive oil), an acid (sour orange juice or lime juice), and an aromatic flavoring (fresh garlic). The difference is that *mojo* is cooked, while vinaigrette is raw. *Mojo* lends itself well to improvisation. you can make wonderful fruit *mojo*s, substituting pineapple juice, passion fruit juice, and other fruit juices for the lime juice in the basic recipe.

tastes more like a lime. Sour oranges can be found at Hispanic markets. Fresh lime juice makes an acceptable substitute. Serve *mojo* on Cuban sandwiches, boiled yuca, grilled seafood and meats, and just about anything else.

MAKES 1 CUP

⅓ cup olive oil
6 to 8 cloves garlic, thinly sliced or minced
⅔ cup fresh sour orange juice or lime juice
½ teaspoon ground cumin
Salt and freshly ground black pepper, to taste

1. Heat the olive oil in a deep saucepan over medium heat. Add the garlic and cook until fragrant and lightly toasted but not brown, about 30 seconds.

2. Add the sour orange juice, cumin, and salt and pepper. Stand back: The sauce may sputter. Bring the sauce to a rolling boil. Correct the seasonings, adding salt and pepper to taste.

3. Cool before serving. *Mojo* tastes best when served within a couple of hours of making, but it will keep for several days, covered, in the refrigerator.

Grapefruit-Rosemary Mojo

Here's what happens when an American cook starts playing around with traditional Cuban recipes. I like to serve this with grilled veal, lamb, or pork.

⅓ cup olive oil

6 to 8 cloves garlic, thinly sliced or minced

1 tablespoon chopped fresh rosemary leaves

⅓ cup fresh grapefruit juice

⅓ cup fresh lime juice

½ teaspoon ground cumin

Salt and freshly ground black pepper, to taste

1. Heat the olive oil in a deep saucepan over medium heat. Add the garlic and rosemary and cook until fragrant and lightly toasted but not brown, about 30 seconds.

2. Add the grapefruit and lime juices, cumin, and salt and pepper. Stand back: The sauce may sputter. Bring the sauce to a rolling boil. Correct the seasonings, adding salt and pepper to taste.

3. Cool before serving. This tastes best when served within a couple of hours of making, but it will keep for several days, covered, in the refrigerator.

Four Tropical Vinaigrettes

Vinaigrette is the perfect sauce for Floridian dishes. Intensely flavored but light, it is equally at home on salads, with vegetables, and as a sauce for grilled meats and seafood. The secret is to use a mild olive oil (extra-virgin tends to be overpowering) and plenty of salt to balance the acidity of the lime juice or vinegar. Each of these vinaigrettes taste best when served the same day it is made. Refrigerate, covered, then rewhisk right before serving.

GINGER-CITRUS VINAIGRETTE

Ꮳ Ꮳ Ꮳ

With its Asian overtones, this vinaigrette goes well with lobster, crabmeat, bean sprouts, and cucumber salad. I also like it on grilled duck.

MAKES ¾ CUP

2 tablespoons fresh lime juice

2 tablespoons fresh orange or tangerine juice

2 tablespoons fresh lemon juice

2 tablespoons rice vinegar

1 tablespoon minced scallion

2 teaspoons minced fresh ginger

½ teaspoon minced garlic

1 tablespoon soy sauce

1 tablespoon Oriental sesame oil

5 tablespoons canola oil

Salt and freshly ground pepper, to taste

1. Combine the lime, orange, and lemon juices in a non-reactive saucepan. Bring the juices to a boil and cook until only 2 tablespoons juice remain. Let cool.

2. Place the citrus reduction in a mixing bowl and whisk in the vinegar, scallion, ginger, garlic, and soy sauce. Gradually whisk in the oils, followed by the salt and pepper. Correct the seasoning, adding vinegar or salt to taste.

BLACK BEAN VINAIGRETTE

Cumin and cilantro give this vinaigrette a Cuban accent; it goes well with grilled chicken and fish, especially salmon.

MAKES 1 CUP

2 tablespoons red wine vinegar
½ teaspoon minced garlic
¼ to ½ teaspoon ground cumin, or to taste
Salt and freshly ground black pepper, to taste
⅓ cup mild olive oil
½ cup Firm-Cooked Black Beans (page 269)
2 tablespoons finely diced red bell pepper
2 tablespoons finely diced green bell pepper
2 tablespoons finely chopped celery
2 tablespoons finely chopped red onion or scallion
¼ cup finely chopped fresh cilantro leaves

1. Combine the vinegar, garlic, cumin, and salt and pepper in a mixing bowl, and whisk until the salt dissolves.
2. Whisk in the oil in a thin stream, followed by the beans, bell peppers, celery, onion, and cilantro. Correct the seasonings, adding salt or vinegar to taste.

CILANTRO AND CORN VINAIGRETTE

The Southwest meets Florida in this flavorful vinaigrette. Serve with any grilled seafood, especially shrimp and snapper.

SEDUCED BY CILANTRO

Cilantro (pronounced see-LAN-tro) may be a relative newcomer to North American cooking, but it has long been a cornerstone of Caribbean and Hispanic cuisines. Once available only at ethnic markets, it has gradually crept into mainstream restaurants and home cooking, turning up in everything from salsas to stir-fries. Sometimes sold by the name of Chinese parsley or fresh coriander, cilantro is the leafy part of the plant that gives us coriander seeds. The delicate, thumbnail-size pungent green leaves have fringed edges and a taste that people either adore or hate.

The flavor of cilantro is impossible to describe. Some people detect a whiff of celery or mint, others the pungent aroma of mothballs. The tiniest bite seems to explode in your mouth with flavor. If the herb tastes soapy to you, you may be one of the small number of people who are allergic to it.

Cilantro is sold by the bunch at most supermarkets and at Hispanic, Caribbean, and Asian markets. Look for bright green leaves, avoiding bunches that are wilted or yellowed. The cilantro you buy in ethnic markets is often quite sandy: wash it in several bowls of cold water, then spin it dry in a salad spinner.

To keep cilantro fresh for extended periods, loosely wrap the whole bunch in a wet paper towel and store in an unsealed plastic bag. It is important to leave the bag open, so the leaves can breathe. Cilantro does not dry well. Use it fresh or not at all.

Fresh mint can be substituted for cilantro in salad and salsa recipes. The flavor is very different, but the aromatic explosion will be the same. Cilantro is generally added to a dish at the end, as cooking darkens the leaves.

Cilantro should not be confused with culentro, a dark green herb with spatula-shaped, sawtooth-edged leaves that occasionally turns up at Hispanic markets. Culentro tastes similar to cilantro, but has a slightly bitter aftertaste. The two can be used interchangeably.

MAKES 1 CUP

½ clove garlic, minced
1 teaspoon Dijon mustard
Salt and freshly ground black pepper, to taste
1 tablespoon fresh lime juice
1 tablespoon red wine vinegar
1 jalapeño chili, seeded and minced
⅓ cup mild olive oil
½ cup Grilled Corn kernels (page 245)
¼ cup minced fresh cilantro leaves

1. Combine the garlic, mustard, and salt and pepper in a mixing bowl, and mash with a fork to a smooth paste.

2. Whisk in the lime juice, vinegar, and chili. Whisk in the oil in a thin stream, followed by the corn and cilantro. Correct the seasonings, adding salt or vinegar to taste.

MANGO-MINT VINAIGRETTE

Half vinaigrette and half salsa, this recipe makes a fine accompaniment for grilled or roasted chicken, game hens, quail, or fish.

MAKES 1 CUP

2 tablespoons fresh lime juice

1 tablespoon rice vinegar

Salt and freshly ground black pepper, to taste

½ cup mild olive oil

*½ cup finely diced ripe mango with
     its juice*

*¼ cup washed and finely chopped
     fresh mint leaves*

½ to 1 teaspoon sugar (optional)

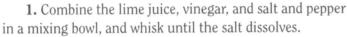

1. Combine the lime juice, vinegar, and salt and pepper in a mixing bowl, and whisk until the salt dissolves.

2. Whisk in the olive oil, mango and its juice, and mint and correct the seasonings, adding salt or lime juice to taste. If the mango is too sour, add a little sugar.

Fresh Carrot Sauce

Florida's ethnic cooking is dominated by our Cuban, Nicaraguan, and Colombian communities. But at least 20,000 Brazilians live in south Florida and the number is growing steadily. The recipe for this carrot sauce comes from a musician friend named Mark Sandman, who spent several years in Brazil. It's especially good with the Yuca Fingers on page 32, and also fried cassava, poached chicken, and grilled fish.

BLENDER-SMOOTH

I find that the blender does a better job of puréeing vegetables than the food processor. When using your blender to make Fresh Carrot Sauce, make sure the bell pepper and onion are totally puréed before adding the carrots. This will ensure a smoother final result.

½ green bell pepper, cored, seeded, and diced
½ cup diced onion
¼ cup canola oil or light olive oil
3 to 4 tablespoons fresh lime juice
8 ounces carrots, peeled and cut into ½-inch slices
4 to 5 cloves garlic
Salt and freshly ground black pepper, to taste
½ teaspoon sugar (optional)
1 to 3 tablespoons water, or as necessary

1. Place the bell pepper, onion, canola oil, and lime juice in a blender or food processor, and blend to a smooth purée. Add the carrots, garlic, salt and pepper, and sugar, and blend again to a smooth purée. Add the water as necessary to obtain a pourable sauce.

2. Correct the seasonings, adding salt, lime juice, or sugar to taste. Carrot sauce will keep for 1 week, covered, in the refrigerator.

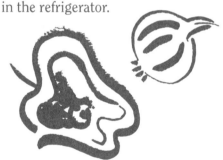

Joe's Stone Crab Mustard Sauce

This creamy condiment is probably the most famous sauce in Florida. Invented by Joe Weiss, founder of the legendary Joe's Stone Crab restaurant on Miami Beach, it's the requisite dip for the meaty claws of *Menippe mercenaria*, the stone crab. If imitation is the highest form of flattery, it's truly a remarkable sauce, as virtually every restaurant in Florida serves its own version of a mustard sauce. Here is Joe's original. It tastes delicious spread on fish sandwiches and also makes a great dipping sauce for shrimp or artichokes.

MAKES 1¼ CUPS

4 teaspoons Colman's dry English mustard
1 cup Hellmann's mayonnaise
2 teaspoons Worcestershire sauce
1 teaspoon A-1 Steak Sauce
2 tablespoons half-and-half
⅛ teaspoon salt
Pinch of cayenne pepper

Combine all of the ingredients in a mixing bowl, and whisk until smooth. Correct the seasonings, adding salt or dry mustard to taste. Cover and refrigerate until serving time. The sauce will keep for 1 week.

Sunshine Aïoli

Aïoli, of course, is garlic mayonnaise from Provence. I give it a Floridian touch by adding annatto oil and lime juice. Annatto oil derives its golden color and unique flavor from a rust-colored Caribbean spice. Traditionally it is used in Spanish Caribbean cooking as a cooking oil. In the new Floridian cuisine, it is drizzled on fish as a condiment. This recipe uses commercially prepared mayonnaise instead of raw egg yolks to eliminate the risk of a salmonella problem. Sunshine aïoli is delicious with fish soups, grilled vegetables and seafood, and even grilled meats.

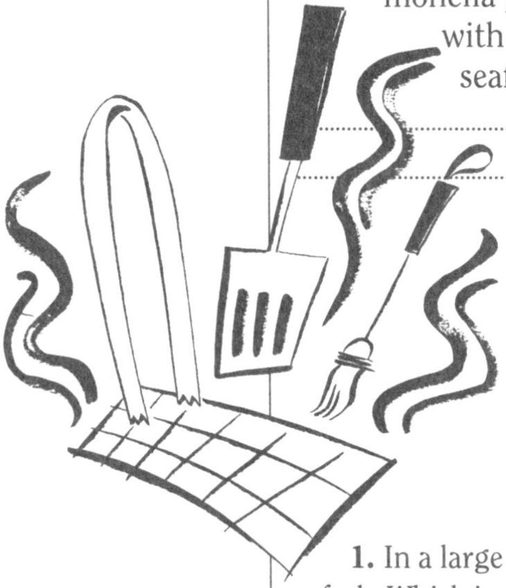

MAKES 1 CUP

6 to 8 cloves garlic, minced
¼ teaspoon salt
Freshly ground black pepper, to taste
Cayenne pepper, to taste
1 cup mayonnaise
2 tablespoons annatto oil
1 to 2 tablespoons fresh lime juice

1. In a large mixing bowl, mash the garlic and salt with a fork. Whisk in the pepper, cayenne, and mayonnaise. Whisk in the annatto oil in a thin stream.

2. Whisk in lime juice. Correct the seasonings, adding salt and lime juice to taste. Cover and refrigerate until serving time. The aïoli will keep for several weeks.

Jalapeño Cream Sauce

This sauce turns up at Miami's numerous Nicaraguan restaurants, where it's served with everything from sautéed shrimp to beef. Pickled jalapeño chilies are sold in jars and can be found in the ethnic foods section of most supermarkets.

MAKES 1 CUP

2 tablespoons unsalted butter
½ cup finely chopped onion
½ cup dry white wine
1 cup heavy (whipping) cream
2 to 3 pickled jalapeño chilies, thinly sliced
1 tablespoon pickling liquid from jalapeños,
    or to taste
¼ cup sour cream
Salt and freshly ground black pepper,
    to taste

1. Melt the butter in a nonreactive saucepan. Add the onion and cook over medium heat until soft but not brown, about 3 minutes.

2. Add the wine and bring to a boil. Boil the wine, uncovered, until reduced to 1 tablespoon, about 4 minutes.

3. Add the cream and sliced chilies. Briskly simmer the mixture, uncovered, until reduced by one-third, about 5 minutes. Stir in the pickling liquid, sour cream, and salt and pepper to taste. Heat through but do not let the mixture boil. Serve this sauce warm.

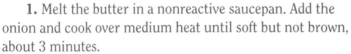

Citrus-Sour Cream Sauce

This sauce is simplicity itself, and it tastes great with any type of grilled or pan-blackened seafood, not to mention with beef, veal, or venison. It's also great squeezed from a squirt bottle to make decorative white squiggles on grilled tuna steaks.

½ cup fresh orange juice
¼ cup fresh lemon juice
¼ cup fresh lime juice
1 cup sour cream
Salt and freshly ground white pepper, to taste
Pinch of cayenne pepper

1. Combine the orange juice, lemon juice, and lime juice in a heavy nonreactive saucepan. Boil the juice mixture until reduced to 2 tablespoons, about 5 minutes. Remove the pan from the heat and let cool.

2. Whisk the sour cream into the juice reduction, followed by the salt and pepper and cayenne. The sauce can be warmed, but don't let it boil or it will curdle. I usually serve it at room temperature.

Tropical Tartar Sauce

Tartar sauce is one of the greatest condiments ever to grace a fried oyster. Unfortunately, most of the tartar sauce served today is loaded with sugar and polysyllabic preservatives. Here's a homemade version that will make any seafood shine. As in the Sunshine Aïoli recipe (page 122), I use commercial mayonnaise instead of raw egg yolks to eliminate the risk of a salmonella problem. The cilantro, lime, and green peppercorns give this tartar sauce a tropical accent.

MAKES 1 CUP

1 cup mayonnaise

1 to 2 jalapeño chilies, seeded and minced

2 tablespoons drained, finely chopped cornichon
pickles

2 tablespoons drained, finely chopped capers

2 tablespoons drained, finely chopped pitted green olives

2 tablespoons finely chopped fresh cilantro

2 tablespoons chopped fresh chives

1 tablespoon drained, coarsely chopped green
peppercorns

1 to 2 tablespoons fresh lime juice, or to taste

¼ teaspoon grated lime zest

Salt and freshly ground black pepper, to taste

Cayenne pepper, to taste

Combine all of the ingredients in a mixing bowl and whisk to mix. Correct the seasonings, adding salt or lime juice to taste. The mixture should be highly seasoned. Cover and refrigerate until serving time. This tartar sauce will keep for 1 week.

Tamarind Cream Sauce

Here's another sauce of embarrassing simplicity, but whenever I serve it, people ask for spoons to eat it straight. Pickapeppa sauce is a tamarind-based condiment from Jamaica. Look for it in the bottled sauce section of the supermarket or gourmet shop. This recipe comes from a popular Coconut Grove restaurant, Café Tu Tu Tango, where it's served with fried alligator. It makes a lively accompaniment paired with any of the fritters in Chapter 2.

MAKES 1 CUP

3 ounces cream cheese, at room temperature
3 tablespoons sour cream
Approximately ½ cup Pickapeppa Sauce

Combine the cream cheese and sour cream in a mixing bowl and whisk until smooth. Stir in enough Pickapeppa Sauce to obtain a creamy, richly flavored dip. Place the sauce in small bowls or ramekins for fritter dipping. Refrigerate, covered, until serving time. Any leftover sauce will keep in the refrigerator for 1 week.

Meyer's Fire

Novelist John D. MacDonald chronicled Florida lowlifes in more than two dozen mystery novels featuring the crusty boat bum, Travis McGee, and his brainy sidekick, Meyer. In the book *Dreadful Lemon Sky*, MacDonald describes Meyer's "Superior Cocktail Dip," a virulent mixture that has been known to make the unsuspecting "leap four feet straight up into the air after scooping up a tiny portion on a potato chip." I've toned it down a little by adding cream cheese and mayonnaise. This dip is good not only for potato chips, but for all manner of fritters and crudités.

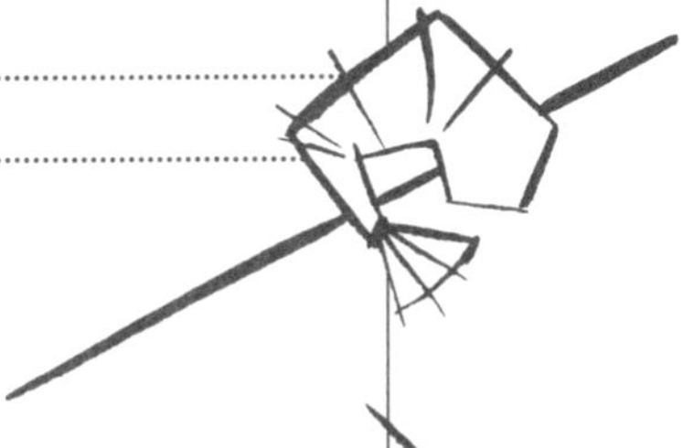

MAKES ¾ CUP

2 tablespoons dry mustard, preferably Chinese
About 2 tablespoons Tabasco sauce
3 ounces cream cheese, at room temperature
3 tablespoons mayonnaise

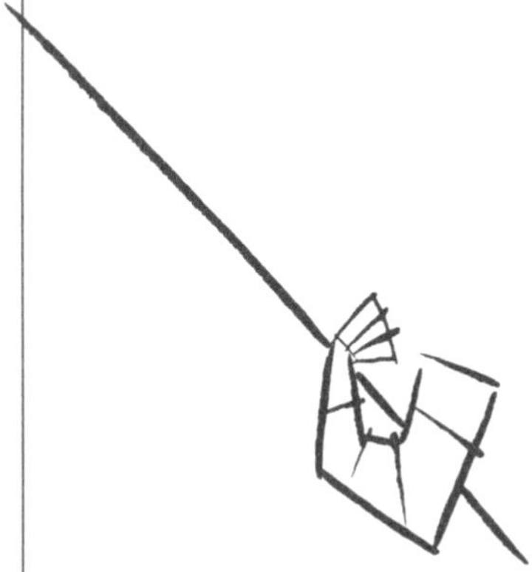

1. Place the mustard powder in a small bowl and stir in enough Tabasco sauce to obtain a thick paste. Let stand for 3 minutes.

2. Combine the cream cheese and mayonnaise in a mixing bowl and whisk until smooth. Whisk in as much mustard mixture as you dare. Refrigerate, covered, until serving time. Any leftover sauce will keep, refrigerated, for 1 week.

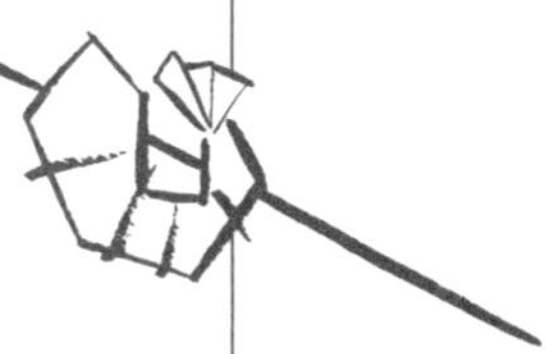

Banana-Molasses Ketchup

To most people, ketchup means a blood red, tomato-based table sauce. In eighteenth century England, however, ketchups were made from a wide variety of fruits and vegetables, including gooseberries, mushrooms, and walnuts. This offbeat banana ketchup makes a delectable dip for fritters, not to mention a great condiment for all sorts of grilled meats and seafoods.

MAKES 3½ TO 4 CUPS

3 ripe bananas, peeled and finely chopped
½ cup finely chopped onion
3 cloves garlic, minced
1 jalapeño chili, seeded and minced
    (for a spicier ketchup, leave the seeds in)
1 cup cider vinegar
1 cup water
⅓ cup molasses
⅓ cup golden raisins
¼ cup honey
¼ cup tomato paste
¼ cup dark rum
1 teaspoon salt, or to taste
½ teaspoon ground cinnamon
½ teaspoon hot pepper flakes
¼ teaspoon ground allspice
¼ teaspoon freshly ground black pepper
⅛ teaspoon freshly ground nutmeg
⅛ teaspoon ground cloves
⅛ teaspoon cayenne pepper

1. Place all of the ingredients in a medium-size, heavy, nonreactive saucepan. Bring to a boil over medium heat, then lower the heat and simmer the ingredients, uncovered, until thick and syrupy, 20 to 30 minutes. Stir frequently while simmering.

2. Purée the mixture in a blender or food processor. Transfer the ketchup to sterile jars and store in the refrigerator. It will keep for several weeks.

Currant Ketchup

This recipe was inspired by one I found in a nineteenth-century English cookbook. It's unlikely that its creator had ever been to Florida. Nonetheless, its sweet-hot-fruity flavor is very much at home in our sunbelt cuisine. Currant ketchup goes particularly well with pork, lamb, and venison.

MAKES 3 CUPS

2 cups dried currants
3 cups water
¼ cup (packed) dark brown sugar
⅔ cup cider vinegar, or to taste
2 shallots, minced
1 tablespoon minced fresh ginger
1 teaspoon yellow mustard seeds
⅛ teaspoon ground cinnamon
⅛ teaspoon cayenne pepper
⅛ teaspoon ground cloves
⅛ teaspoon ground allspice
Salt and freshly ground black pepper,
*   to taste*

1. Combine all of the ingredients in a medium-size, heavy, nonreactive saucepan. Bring to a boil over medium-high heat, then lower the heat, cover, and gently simmer until thickened, 40 minutes. Stir the ketchup occasionally.

2. Correct the seasonings, adding salt, cayenne, vinegar, or brown sugar to taste: The ketchup should be a little sweet, a little sour, and a little hot.

3. Purée the mixture in the blender, adding a little water, if necessary, to obtain a smooth sauce. Transfer the ketchup to sterile jars and store in the refrigerator. It will keep for several weeks.

Papaya and Black Bean Salsa

This colorful salsa combines two of Florida's favorite foods: black beans and papaya. Floridian papaya is larger and softer than Hawaiian or Mexican, with a color that ranges from coral to orange-red. Single fruits can weigh up to 10 pounds, so they're often sold cut up, in large pieces. Florida and Hawaiian papaya can be used interchangeably in this recipe. This salsa makes a good accompaniment to roasted chicken or grilled fish.

SERVES 4

8 ounces ripe papaya, peeled, seeded, and cut
    into ½ inch dice (2 cups)
1 cup Firm-Cooked Black Beans (page 269)
¼ cup finely chopped red onion
½ scotch bonnet chili, or to taste,
    or 2 jalapeño chilies, seeded and minced
2 teaspoons minced fresh ginger
¼ cup chopped fresh cilantro leaves
3 tablespoons fresh lime juice, or to taste
1 tablespoon extra-virgin olive oil
1 tablespoon (packed) light brown sugar (optional)
Salt and fresh black pepper, to taste

Combine all of the ingredients in a mixing bowl, and gently toss to mix. Correct the seasonings, adding salt, lime juice, or sugar to taste. The salsa should be a little sweet and a little sour. This salsa tastes best served within a couple of hours of making. Refrigerate, covered, until serving time.

Banana Salsa

When I was a kid, there was only one kind of banana. Today you can buy a wide range of exotic bananas: apple-flavored manzanos, citrusy raja-puris, even finger-size mysores with their haunting vanilla-pineapple flavor. (For more on bananas, see pages 280 and 282.) Here's a good all-purpose recipe for banana salsa. The flavor will vary with the variety you use. Serve this salsa with grilled chicken, duck, or shrimp.

MAKES 3 CUPS

2 large or 4 finger bananas, peeled and diced
½ cup diced red bell pepper
½ cup diced green bell pepper
½ scotch bonnet chili or 1 to 2 jalapeño chilies,
    seeded and minced
1 tablespoon minced fresh ginger
3 scallions, trimmed and finely chopped
¼ cup chopped fresh mint or cilantro leaves
3 tablespoons fresh lime juice
2 tablespoons packed light brown sugar, or to taste
¼ teaspoon ground cardamom (optional)
1 tablespoon olive oil
Salt and freshly ground black pepper, to taste

FLORIDA'S EXOTIC FRUIT MOGUL

In 1928, Thanksgiving week, a young man with a single employee started a fruit packing business in Home-stead, Florida. His packing house was a tiny tin shed. The first week in business, he shipped one hundred boxes of fresh Florida avocados via rail to New York.

Today, J.R. Brooks & Son is Florida's largest native fruit and vegetable processor. The company processes half the limes grown in the Sunshine State, 60 percent of our avoca-dos, 70 percent of our mangos, and 80 percent of our caramo-las (star fruit). Last year, J.R. Brooks shipped 98 million pounds of tropical produce from its ultra-modern facility in Homestead, which was completely rebuilt after hurri-cane Andrew. It also manages more than 10,000 acres of groves.

J.R. Brooks best sellers include limes, avocados, mangos, and papayas. But the company's product list features a host of lesser known exotics, including canistels, guavas, sapodillas, tam-arind, and yuca.

Combine all of the ingredients in a mixing bowl, and gently toss to mix. Correct the seasonings, adding salt, lime juice, or sugar to taste. The salsa should be a little sweet and a little sour. Banana salsa tastes best when served a couple of hours after making. Refrigerate, covered, until serving time.

Mango Salsa

ucumber adds crunch to this summery mango salsa. When peeling the cucumber, I like to leave a few strips of dark green skin in place for extra color. If you are leaving the skin on, wash the cuke with hot water to remove any wax coating. If mangos are unavailable, the salsa could be made with peaches. Like the preceding salsas, this one goes well with grilled meats and fish of all sorts. It's also a great vegetable side dish.

MAKES 2½ CUPS

2 cups diced ripe mango

1 cucumber, peeled, seeded, and diced

½ poblano chili, seeded and finely diced

1 jalapeño chili, seeded and minced

2 teaspoons minced fresh ginger

¼ cup chopped fresh mint or cilantro leaves

1 tablespoon packed light brown sugar, or to taste

¼ cup fresh lime juice

Salt and freshly ground black pepper, to taste

1. Combine all of the ingredients in a mixing bowl, and gently toss to mix.

2. Correct the seasonings, adding salt, lime juice, or sugar to taste. The salsa should be a little sweet and a little sour. Mango salsa tastes best served a couple of hours after making. Refrigerate, covered, until serving.

A Fisherman's Paradise

Grilled Swordfish with fried garlic sauce

Tangerine Tuna

Shark en Escabeche

Macadamia-Crusted Pompano

y neighborhood fishmonger, Mariner Seafood, is like any of a thousand fish shops in Florida. Fishnets and lobster pots deck the narrow storefront. The display counters are filled with fish so fresh, they're still in rigor mortis. The store is owned by two guys who love to fish and is staffed by several others. Their philosophy is summed up by the sign behind the counter: "Work is for people who don't know how to fish!"

Florida is a fisherman's paradise. More than five hundred species of edible fish swim in our temperate waters. Seventy species of fin-fish and fifteen species of shellfish are fished commercially. Florida is responsible for more than 90 percent of the nation's grouper, pompano, mullet, and Spanish mackerel. The five hundred processing plants in Florida process more than one-third of all the fish caught in the Gulf and South Atlantic regions.

Some further statistics. Floridians spend $400 million annually on fish consumption at home and twice that or more in restaurants. The Florida Department of Marine Resources estimates total economic impact of Florida's seafood industry at $1 billion a year.

Florida has some of the most distinctive fish in the country. Besides pompano, there's cobia, grouper, and wahoo. A dozen different snappers, ranging from the meaty mutton snapper to the buttery schoolmaster. Nine different types of grouper swim in Florida waters, five types of tuna, and three types of jack, mullet, and sea trout. And thanks to Florida's magnificent climate, the boats can go out virtually all year round.

I once worked with a chef who maintained the measure of a great cook is the way he handles seafood. The freshness and diversity of Florida fish makes it hard not to be a great cook.

NUTS ABOUT MACADAMIAS

The macadamia nut is a newcomer to the Sunshine State, and the handsome trees thrive in the semitropical climate of south Florida, where experimental plantings are taking place.

Among the most prized members of the nut family, the macadamia is no ordinary nut. Imagine an orb the size of a large hazelnut, straw colored, softly crunchy, with a mild, sweet-salty, fruity, buttery flavor, and the richness of heavy cream. The macadamia is refined and delicate, but never would you call it bland.

To grind macadamia nuts, use a food processor. Run the machine in short bursts, or you'll reduce the nuts to an oily paste. (It helps to add a small handful of bread crumbs per cup of nuts.) If you don't have a food processor, use a meat grinder. To enhance the flavor, before grinding, toast the nuts on a baking sheet in a 350°F oven until lightly browned, 3 to 5 minutes.

Macadamia-Crusted Pompano

Pompano is the king of Florida's fish, a flat, silver-skinned swimmer with a sweet, delicate flesh. Elsewhere in the country you could prepare the dish using snapper, bass, or even haddock. The Citrus-Sour Cream Sauce on page 124 or the Jalapeño Cream Sauce on page 123 would make a good accompaniment.

SERVES 4

1½ pounds boneless, skinless pompano fillets
Salt and freshly ground black pepper, to taste
1 cup lightly salted macadamia nuts
1 cup fine, dried bread crumbs (preferably homemade)
1 cup all-purpose flour
2 eggs, beaten
3 tablespoons Clarified Butter (see page 328),
    or 1½ tablespoons butter and 1½ tablespoons oil
Lime wedges, for serving

1. Rinse the fish fillets and pat dry. Season the fillets on both sides with salt and pepper. Grind the macadamia nuts and bread crumbs to a fine powder in a food processor, running the machine in short bursts. Do not overgrind, or the mixture will become oily. Place the nut mixture in a shallow bowl, the flour in another, and the eggs in a third.

2. Just before serving, melt the butter in a large non-stick frying pan over medium heat. Dip each piece of fish first in flour, shaking off the excess, then in beaten egg, then finally in the macadamia nut mixture. Pan-fry the fish until crusty and golden brown, about 2 minutes per side. Blot the fish on paper towels and transfer to plates or a platter for serving. Garnish with the lime wedges.

GUIDE TO FLORIDA FISH

Florida juts, like a thumb, into the temperate waters of the Atlantic Ocean and the Gulf of Mexico. Not surprisingly, fish plays a primary role in our cooking. Here's a guide to some of the more exotic species that grace the Floridian table. My thanks to Joey Durante, an avid fisherman and manager of my neighborhood fish shop, Mariner Seafoods in South Miami, for helping me with this guide.

AMBERJACK: A large, firm-fleshed, silvery-green fish with a distinctive brown stripe running from head to tail. A deep-water fish, amberjack has a mild flavor similar to grouper.

CATFISH: A specialty of Lake Okeechobee, where it's sprinkled with cornmeal and fried. More and more Florida catfish come from fish farms.

COBIA: A large warm-water fish that looks a little like a shark. Once classed as a trash fish, cobia is widely appreciated today for its firm, white, mild-flavored flesh. Sometimes it's called ling. Cobia is good for chowders and ceviche.

DOLPHIN: Not Flipper, but a long, slender, mild but rich-fla-vored fish known elsewhere in the country as mahi mahi.

GROUPER: A large, puffy-look-ing fish with a firm, white, mild flesh. Order a fried fish sand-wich in Florida, and it's proba-bly grouper. It's also popular for chowders. Take care not to overcook grouper, or it will be tough. Popular varieties include the red grouper, gag grouper, warsaw grouper, coney grouper, and my favorite, black grouper.

KINGFISH: A long, round-bod-ied, dark-fleshed fish popular with Cubans and Central Americans. When fresh, it's delicious, but because it's oily fish, it acquires a strong fishy flavor after a few days. Kingfish is the traditional fish for mak-ing *escabeche* (Cuban pickled fish).

MULLET: A bullet-shaped fish caught in great quantities off the west coast of Florida. Mullet is not well known else-where in the U.S., but it's the number-one cash fish in Florida. The flesh is rich and oily, making it ideal for smoking.

POMPANO: A flat, silvery fish with mild-flavored fillets that are highly prized among Florida fish lovers. The texture is dry, almost sandy, without being firm or tough. African pompano is a larger and firmer variety.

SNAPPER: Snapper flourishes in the shallow waters off the Florida Keys. The best of the dozen varieties commercially fished here include hog snap-per, mangrove snapper, and the large mutton snapper. Snapper is probably Florida's most pop-ular fish—it's sweet, mild, ten-der, and delicious.

TUNA: Several varieties are fished in Florida, including the huge (500- to 600-pound) yellowfin tuna (recognizable by its pinkish-red flesh) and the smaller (20- to 40-pound) blackfin tuna (distinguished by its dark, blood red meat).

WAHOO: A long, round-bodied game fish that looks like kingfish. The grayish flesh has a firm consistency and flavor reminiscent of kingfish or mack-erel, but it is milder tasting and less oily.

Grilled Yellowtail
with Passion Fruit Beurre Blanc

Of all the snappers available in Florida (more than seventy varieties have been counted, a dozen are fished commercially), yellowtail is my favorite. This handsome fish is recognizable by the yellow-green markings on its *V*-shaped tail. You could substitute any member of the snapper family if yellowtail is unavailable. I like to buy whole small fish (about 1½ pounds) and serve one per person. A 3-pound fish will feed two. The sauce also works well with salmon, although it is very different from yellowtail.

SERVES 4

4 whole small yellowtail snappers, cleaned, gills removed

4 fresh passion fruits or ¼ cup frozen pulp

1 clove garlic, minced

1 teaspoon salt

1 tablespoon fresh lemon juice

2 tablespoons olive oil

Freshly ground black pepper, to taste

PASSION FRUIT BEURRE BLANC:

1 cup acidic white wine, such as sauvignon blanc,
    fumé blanc, or muscadet

¼ cup white wine vinegar

3 tablespoons minced shallots

¼ cup heavy (or whipping) cream

10 tablespoons (1¼ sticks) cold unsalted butter,
    cut into ½-inch pieces

1 tablespoon chopped fresh chives

Salt and freshly ground black pepper, to taste

Cayenne pepper, to taste

1. Prepare a barbecue grill and heat until very hot.

2. Rinse the fish and pat dry. Make a series of parallel slits, 1 inch apart, in the sides of the fish, cutting down to the bone. Place the fish, side by side, in a glass baking dish.

3. Halve the passion fruits and scrape the pulp into a bowl. Mash the garlic and 1 teaspoon salt to a paste in the bottom of a mixing bowl. Stir in the lemon juice, olive oil, and pepper, and half of the passion fruit pulp. Pour this mixture over the fish, stuffing the garlic and passion fruit pulp into the slits. Marinate the fish, covered, in the refrigerator for 30 minutes, turning once.

4. Prepare the beurre blanc: Combine the wine, vinegar, and shallots in a nonreactive heavy saucepan. Boil this mixture until only ¼ cup of liquid remains, 4 to 5 minutes. Add the cream and boil again until only ¼ cup liquid remains, 3 to 4 minutes more.

5. Whisk in the butter, little by little, working over high heat. The sauce should boil while you're adding the butter, but not after all of it is in. Remove the pan from the heat. Whisk in the remaining passion fruit pulp, the chives, and salt and pepper and cayenne to taste. Keep the sauce warm on the stovetop or in a pan of hot water. Do not place the sauce over direct heat or in a double boiler, or it may separate.

6. Just before serving, remove the fish from the marinade and grill over medium heat, basting with the marinade, until cooked, about 5 minutes per side. Transfer the fish to plates and serve the sauce in a sauceboat on the side.

PASSION FRUIT

The flavor of the passion fruit is as enchanting as its name. But woe to the neophyte who tries to bite into it like an apple. The edible part of the fruit is encased in a hard, leathery, bitter-tasting, yellow or purple shell.

The easiest way to eat a passion fruit is to cut it in half with a sharp knife, working over a bowl to catch the juices. Inside the 2-inch sphere you'll find a wet, bright orange pulp comprised of hundreds of small juice sacs embedded with tiny, crunchy black seeds. Passion fruit flesh has the tartness of lime juice, the sweetness of honey, the fragrance of jasmine, and a perfumed flavor reminiscent of guava, lychee, and pineapple. Small wonder it's beloved throughout the Caribbean, Central and Latin America, Africa, and Asia.

Passion fruit was introduced to Florida as early as 1887, but it didn't catch on as a commercial fruit until the early 1980s. The Florida crop is in season from August to January. Brazil and New Zealand assure a steady supply the rest of the year. Here in Florida, passion fruit is often sold by its Spanish name, *maracuja*.

When buying passion fruit, look for large, bright yellow or purple spheres that feel heavy. (They're usually sold by the piece, so choose the largest you can.) You should be able to hear the juice slosh around when you shake them. It's normal for a passion fruit to look creased or partially deflated. In fact, if it's too round, it may not be fully ripe. Passion fruit will keep a week to 10 days in the refrigerator and can be frozen for several months. Scoop out the pulp, transfer it to ice cube trays, and freeze.

A great alternative to the fresh fruit is the frozen passion fruit purée sold at Hispanic markets and gourmet shops. The frozen pulp has the dual advantage of being inexpensive and seedless.

One passion fruit yields about 1 tablespoon intensely flavored pulp. A little goes a long way. The tiny black seeds are edible. Indeed, I rather like their brittle crunch. If you don't like the seeds you can force the flesh through a strainer, but this is somewhat of a hassle.

Whole Fried Snapper with Spicy Tomato Sauce

argo a la tipitapa is Nicaragua's most famous fish dish, named for the town of Tipitapa near Lake Managua. It turns up at Nicaraguan restaurants throughout Miami. The fish of choice is a snapper large enough to serve whole but small enough to be eaten by one person. For ease in eating, I suggest boning the fish before cooking (or have your fishmonger do it). If this seems too complicated, serve the fish whole.

SERVES 4

SPICY TOMATO SAUCE:
3 to 4 tablespoons cider vinegar
½ cup water
Salt and freshly ground black pepper, to taste
3 fresh ripe tomatoes, peeled, seeded, and chopped
2 medium onions, thinly sliced
2 cloves garlic, minced
2 tablespoons tomato paste
4 tablespoons finely chopped fresh Italian (flat-leaf) parsley
1 to 2 jalapeño chilies, seeded and diced

4 whole snappers (1½ pounds each), cleaned, gills
  removed, filleted if desired
Salt and freshly ground black pepper, to taste
2 cups fine cornmeal, for dredging
4 cups vegetable oil, for frying

1. Prepare the sauce: Bring the vinegar, water, and salt and pepper to a boil in a nonreactive large saucepan. Add the tomatoes, onions, garlic, tomato paste, 2 tablespoons of the parsley, and the chilies and gently simmer for 5 minutes. Purée the sauce in a food processor or blender. Correct the seasonings, adding salt and pepper to taste.

2. Just before serving, rinse the fish and pat dry. Sprinkle the fish with salt and pepper. Place the cornmeal in a large bowl. Dredge the fish in the cornmeal, shaking off the excess.

3. Pour the oil to a depth of 2 to 3 inches in a large sauté pan or wok and heat to 350°F. Fry the fish, turning as necessary, until golden brown, 3 to 4 minutes total. You'll probably need to fry the fish in several batches so as not to crowd the pan. (Keep the already fried fish warm in a low— 250°F—oven.) Drain the fish on paper towels.

4. Place the snapper on a platter or plates with the spicy tomato sauce spooned over it. Sprinkle with the remaining 2 tablespoons parsley and serve at once.

Pan-Roasted Mutton Snapper
with Raisins, Capers, and Pine Nuts

Mutton snapper is one of the largest members of the snapper family, with individual fish weighing up to 25 pounds. The flesh is white and meaty, with an elegant, delicate flavor. It's usually sold by the piece or in fillets. But any type of snapper can be substituted for mutton snapper. In other parts of the country you could use bass, cod, haddock, or mahi mahi. This recipe uses a technique called pan-roasting: The fish is lightly browned in butter, then roasted in the oven right in the skillet. This makes the skin exceptionally crisp and tasty.

SERVES 4

4 pieces (6 to 8 ounces each) mutton snapper,
*   with the skin intact*
Salt and freshly ground black pepper, to taste
About ½ cup all-purpose flour, for dredging
1½ tablespoons butter
1½ tablespoons olive oil
3 tablespoons raisins
3 tablespoons drained capers
3 tablespoons chopped fresh Italian (flat-leaf)
*   parsley*
3 tablespoons pine nuts
2 tablespoons Grand Marnier or other
*   orange liqueur*
2 tablespoons fresh lemon juice, or to taste

1. Preheat the oven to 400°F.

2. Rinse the fish fillets and pat dry. Season the fish on both sides with salt and pepper. Place the flour on a paper towel or in a shallow bowl. Dredge both sides of each piece of fish in flour, shaking off the excess.

3. Heat the butter and oil in an ovenproof nonstick frying pan over high heat. Starting with the skinless side, brown the fish pieces on both sides, about 1 minute per side. Place the pan in the oven and bake until the fish is cooked, about 8 minutes. When done, the fish will break into flakes when you press it with your finger.

4. Transfer the fish to warm plates or a platter. Place the frying pan over medium heat, taking care not to burn yourself on the handle. Add the raisins, capers, parsley, and pine nuts. Sauté until the nuts are lightly browned, 1 to 2 minutes.

5. Add the Grand Marnier and lemon juice to the pan and bring to a boil. Correct the seasonings, adding salt and pepper and lemon juice to taste. Spoon this mixture over the fish and serve at once.

Tangerine Tuna

This recipe is simplicity itself, but the combination of flavors is stunning. The marinade is a sort of teriyaki sauce made with fresh tangerine juice. It's delicious not only on tuna, but on all types of seafood, chicken breasts, beef, and lamb. When grilling firm, meaty fish, such as tuna and swordfish, I like to cut the steaks no more than ½ inch thick. This enables you to cook the fish through without drying it out. The steaks can be broiled if grilling is impractical. Note: the easiest way to remove the zest (the oil-rich outer rind) from the tangerine and lemon is to use a vegetable peeler.

SERVES 4

4 tuna steaks (about 1½ pounds total), cut ¼- to ½-inch thick

TANGERINE MARINADE:
¼ cup soy sauce
¼ cup fresh tangerine juice
4 strips (½ inch each) tangerine zest
3 tablespoons honey
2 tablespoons Oriental sesame oil
3 cloves garlic, minced
2 scallions, trimmed and white part
    minced, green part finely chopped
    and reserved for garnish
1 tablespoon minced fresh ginger
3 strips lemon zest (each 1½ inches long)
1 whole star anise (optional)

1 tablespoon Oriental sesame oil, for brushing the tuna
2 tablespoons toasted sesame seeds (preferably a mixture of black
    and white; see sidebar, facing page)

TOASTING SESAME SEEDS

To toast sesame seeds, place them in a dry skillet over medium heat. Cook, shaking the pan, until the seeds are aromatic (white seeds should turn a light brown), 1 to 2 minutes.

1. Preheat a barbecue grill to very hot.

2. Rinse the fish steaks and pat dry.

3. Whisk together all of the ingredients for the marinade in a shallow mixing bowl. Place the tuna steaks in a nonreactive baking dish and pour the marinade on top. Marinate the tuna, covered, in the refrigerator for 30 to 60 minutes, turning the steaks once or twice.

4. Drain the tuna steaks and blot dry. Brush the steaks with the sesame oil. Grill the tuna for 1 minute per side, or until cooked to taste. Sprinkle the tuna with the chopped scallion greens and sesame seeds and serve at once.

Grilled Swordfish with Fried Garlic Sauce

This recipe features two classic Cuban preparations: *adobo* (cumin-lime marinade) and *mojo* (garlic-citrus sauce). It's a great way to prepare any full-flavored fish, from tuna to salmon to mackerel. As in the preceding recipe, I like to cut the fish steaks thin so they cook fully without drying out.

SERVES 4

4 swordfish steaks (about 1½ pounds total), cut ¼ to ½ inch thick

MARINADE:
3 cloves garlic, minced
½ teaspoon salt
¼ cup fresh lime juice
½ teaspoon ground cumin
Freshly ground black pepper, to taste

FRIED GARLIC SAUCE:
¼ cup olive oil
4 cloves garlic, thinly sliced
2 shallots, thinly sliced
¼ cup fresh lime juice
Salt and freshly ground black pepper, to taste

1. Preheat a barbecue grill to very hot.

2. Rinse the fish steaks and pat dry. Trim any bloody spots or gristle off the swordfish.

3. Prepare the marinade: Mash the garlic with the salt in a mixing bowl. Whisk in the lime juice, cumin, and pepper. Arrange the swordfish in a nonreactive baking dish and pour the marinade on top. Marinate the swordfish, covered, in the refrigerator for 30 minutes, turning the steaks once during that time.

4. Prepare the sauce: Heat the olive oil in a small, nonreactive frying pan over high heat. Add the garlic and shallot slices and fry until golden brown, about 1 minute. Stir in the lime juice and salt and pepper, and bring to a boil. Be careful: The mixture may spatter a little. Remove from the heat and correct the seasonings, adding salt and pepper to taste.

5. Remove the swordfish from the marinade and blot dry. Grill for 1 minute per side, or until cooked to taste. Spoon the sauce over the swordfish and serve at once.

FISH MEETS GRILL

Myriad are the methods for cooking fish, but my favorite is grilling.

Almost any type of seafood can be cooked on the grill. Oily fish, like mackerel and kingfish, do well because the oils help baste the fish as it cooks. Whole fish, like yellowtail snapper, are delectable grilled: The skin protects the flesh and becomes a crackling crisp delicacy in its own right. Before grilling whole fish, make diagonal slashes to the bone, and spaced about an inch apart, in the sides of the fish to allow the heat and smoke to penetrate the flesh.

Here are other tips to keep in mind when grilling seafood.

▲ Thoroughly preheat the grill. If using charcoal, wait till the glowing embers are coated with a thin layer of gray ash.

▲ Arrange the coals so that there are hot spots and cool spots on the grill. This way you can control the cooking of individual pieces of fish. Do this by piling up some of the embers and spreading out the others. When working over a gas grill with multiple controls, turn one side on high and the other on medium.

▲ To achieve a smoky flavor, toss mesquite, hickory, or other hardwood chips on the coals just prior to grilling. The chips should be soaked in cold water for a couple of hours beforehand to slow down the rate of combustion.

▲ Useful tools for grilling include a long-handled basting brush, long-handled tongs, and a wide long-bladed spatula with a crooked handle for turning fish fillets and steaks. Cookware shops sell hinged baskets for grilling fish.

▲ Bamboo skewers are great for shrimp and fish kebabs, but soak them in cold water for a couple of hours to prevent them from burning. Protect the ends of the skewers with pieces of aluminum foil.

▲ When cutting large fish fillets into individual portions, slice them on the diagonal into pieces the same weight and, more importantly, the same thickness to ensure even cooking. If this is impossible, make good use of the grill's hot and cool spots, moving the fish around to control the cooking.

▲ Cooking times vary according to the cut and the type of fish. Fish steaks and kebabs can be seared over high heat. Whole fish should be cooked over a moderate heat to avoid burning the skin.

▲ To create an attractive crosshatch of grill marks on fish steaks, place the fish on the grill for 1 to 2 minutes, then, with a spatula, rotate it 60 degrees and grill another 1 to 2 minutes. Repeat on the other side.

▲ Fragile fish, like snapper fillets, can be cooked on a lightly oiled piece of foil that has been perforated with a fork to allow the smoke to reach the fish.

▲ To test the fish for doneness, insert a metal skewer into the thickest part of the fish: The tip of the skewer should feel hot to the touch. Another test for doneness is to press the fish with your finger: If it breaks into firm flakes, it is cooked.

▲ Remember that fish will continue cooking after it is removed from the grill. To avoid overcooking, remove the fish a few seconds before it's completely done.

Shark en Escabeche

To Hispano-Americans pickled fish means *escabeche*. The preparation dates from the pre-refrigeration era, when pickling, salting, and smoking were the only ways to preserve perishable seafood in the tropical heat. *Escabeche* is usually prepared with an oily steak fish, like kingfish, but any firm fish will do. Old timers recall the days when the fish would be pickled raw for five or six weeks before serving. Today, the fish is usually fried before pickling. Kingfish can taste rather strong to some people, so one day I tried *escabeche* with shark: the results were delicious.

SERVES 4 TO 6

*2 pounds mako, lemon, or black tip shark or other firm fish,
    such as kingfish or swordfish, cut into ¾-inch steaks*
Salt and freshly ground black pepper, to taste
About ¼ cup all-purpose flour, for dredging
¼ cup olive oil, for frying

MARINADE:
4 cloves garlic, minced
1 teaspoon cumin seeds
2 bay leaves
⅔ cup dry white wine
⅔ cup red wine vinegar
⅔ cup olive oil

1½ cups thinly sliced white onion
1 green bell pepper, cored, seeded, and thinly sliced
1 red bell pepper, cored, seeded, and thinly sliced
½ cup pimiento-stuffed green olives

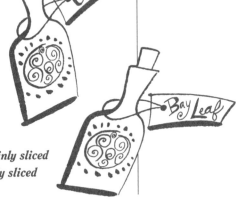

WHAT'S IN A NAME?

Every time I teach a dolphin recipe in cooking class, I get a worried look from at least one of my students. Many people confuse the fish with the friendly telegenic sea mammal. Dolphin fish is a handsome, green-gold fish that makes for some of the best seafood eating in Florida. Even if you've never been to the Sunshine State, you may have tasted it, as dolphin is known and widely distributed elsewhere in the States by its Hawaiian name, mahi mahi.

Dolphin is generally sold in long, slender fillets that are off-white to pinkish gray in color. The meat is firm without being dry and it cooks into beautiful meaty flakes. In the unlikely event your fishmonger has failed to remove the strip of dark red, strong-tasting flesh that runs the length of the fillet, cut it out with a fish knife. Dolphin is great for grilling, baking sautéing, frying, and even smoking.

1. Rinse the fish steaks and pat dry. Salt and pepper the steaks and dredge in the flour, shaking off the excess.

2. Heat the oil in a large skillet over medium heat. Fry the fish until cooked through, 2 to 3 minutes per side.

3. Whisk together the ingredients for the marinade in a nonreactive bowl. Correct the seasoning, adding salt and pepper to taste.

4. In a crock or deep bowl just large enough to hold these ingredients, make a layer of some of the fish, then layer on some of the onion, bell peppers, and finally the olives. Spoon some of the marinade over the layers. Continue layering until all of the ingredients are used up. Pour the remaining marinade over the fish to completely cover it. Marinate the *escabeche,* covered, for at least 24 hours. It's not necessary to refrigerate it, but most cooks will feel more comfortable doing so. The *escabeche* will keep and continue to improve for several weeks.

Dolphin with Fennel and Saffron

No, we're not about to cook Flipper! Dolphin is a type of fish, not a porpoise, with a pink-white, firm-textured, mild-tasting flesh. Elsewhere in the country, the same fish is referred to as mahi mahi. In this recipe the dolphin is braised in a saffron-scented broth to compensate for its tendency to be dry.

SERVES 4

1½ pounds boneless dolphin (mahi mahi) fillets

2 tablespoons extra-virgin olive oil

1 yellow or red bell pepper, cored, seeded, and diced

1 small leek, trimmed, well washed, and thinly sliced

½ bulb fennel, trimmed and diced

2 shallots, thinly sliced

2 cloves garlic, thinly sliced

2 ripe tomatoes, peeled, seeded, and diced

⅛ teaspoon saffron threads, soaked in 1 tablespoon warm water

    Bouquet garni of bay leaf, thyme, and parsley sprigs

      tied together in a piece of cheesecloth

1 cup dry vermouth

1 cup Fish Stock (see page 330), Chicken Stock

    (see page 329), or bottled clam broth

Salt and freshly ground black pepper, to taste

2 tablespoons chopped fresh chives or Italian (flat-leaf) parsley

1. Rinse the fish fillets and pat dry. Cut the dolphin across the grain into ½-inch-thick slices.

2. Preheat the oven to 400°F. Lightly oil a baking dish just large enough to hold the fish.

3. Heat the olive oil in a nonreactive large sauté pan over medium heat. Add the bell pepper and leek and cook for 1 minute. Add the shallots and garlic and continue cooking the vegetables until soft but not brown, 2 to 3 minutes.

4. Add the tomatoes, saffron mixture, bouquet garni, and vermouth and bring to a boil. Add the fish stock, reduce the heat, and simmer the mixture until reduced by half, 6 to 8 minutes. Add salt and pepper to taste.

5. Spoon half of the vegetable mixture into the prepared baking dish. Season the dolphin slices with salt and pepper and place them on top. Spoon the remaining vegetable mixture over the fish.

6. Bake the fish until cooked through, about 10 minutes. When done, it will break into large flakes when pressed. Sprinkle the fish with the chopped chives and serve at once.

Grouper Creole

Grouper is one of the most important fish in the Florida seafood industry. A large, firm, white-fleshed fish, it can weigh up to 80 pounds. The meat is sweet, although not as refined as snapper, and the cost is relatively inexpensive. Grouper's chief drawback is its tendency to become rubbery when over-cooked. Most of the grouper served in Florida is deep-fried, but I like a wet cooking method like the one featured below. Any firm fish, such as halibut, monkfish, or dolphin (mahi mahi), can be prepared in this fashion. Rice makes a good accompaniment.

SERVES 4

1½ pounds boneless, skinless grouper fillets
3 cloves garlic, minced
3 tablespoons fresh lime juice
Salt and freshly ground black pepper, to taste
About ½ cup all-purpose flour, for dredging
About 3 tablespoons olive oil

CREOLE SAUCE:
2 cloves garlic, minced
1 small onion, thinly sliced
1 small green bell pepper, cored, seeded, and
*   thinly sliced*
½ teaspoon ground cumin
1 teaspoon dried oregano
¼ cup tomato paste
1 teaspoon red wine vinegar
About ⅓ cup dry white wine
1 bay leaf
2 tablespoons finely chopped fresh Italian (flat-leaf)
*   parsley*

1. Rinse the grouper fillets and pat dry. Cut the fish into 2-inch squares. Toss the fish with the garlic, lime juice, salt, and pepper in a nonreactive dish and let marinate for 15 minutes.

2. Dredge the fish in the flour, shaking off the excess. Heat the oil in a large skillet over medium heat. Lightly brown the fish pieces on both sides, about 1 minute per side. Transfer the fish to paper towels to drain.

3. Make the sauce: Add oil to the pan if necessary (you should have about 2 tablespoons). Add the garlic, onion, bell pepper, cumin, and oregano and lightly brown over medium heat, 4 to 5 minutes. Stir in the tomato paste and cook for 1 minute. Stir in the vinegar, wine, and bay leaf and mix well.

4. Add the fish and gently simmer for 10 minutes, or until the oil begins to bead on the surface of the sauce. This indicates that the water has evaporated, concentrating the flavor of the sauce. If the fish starts to dry out, add a little more wine. Remove the bay leaf and correct the seasonings, adding salt, pepper, or vinegar to taste. Sprinkle with parsley. Serve the fish over rice with the sauce spooned on top.

Coconut-Curried Wahoo

Wahoo is a prized Florida game fish, a dark fish with a firm bite and robust flavor. If unavailable you could use swordfish, dolphin (mahi mahi), kingfish, or other steak fish. In this recipe the wahoo is simmered in a rich gravy made with curry and fresh coconut milk. The dish takes its inspiration from the curries served in Florida's West Indian restaurants and tastes best served over rice.

WILD ABOUT WAHOO

Writes Hawaiian fish authority Shirley Rizzuto, "The torpedo-shaped ono [wahoo] is one of the fastest swimmers in the ocean. Once cooked, it disappears as fast from your table." That hits the nail right on the head. This tropical fish, whose name in Hawaiian means "sweet," is dulcet, mild, and meaty. Limited supply makes it a luxury fish, so whenever I see it at a restaurant or fishmonger, I buy it.

The wahoo belongs to the mackerel family, but unlike most of its cousins, its flesh is white. It's also more delicately flavored and less oily than other mackerels. Like dolphin, wahoo is usually sold in long slender fillets. The only drawback to wahoo is its tendency to become tough and rubbery when overcooked. Keep the cooking time short and watch the fish like a hawk as it cooks.

FISH AND MARINADE:

1½ pounds wahoo fillets or steaks
2 tablespoons fresh lime juice
2 cloves garlic, minced
Salt and freshly ground black pepper, to taste

SAUCE:

2 tablespoons olive oil
1 onion, finely chopped
3 cloves garlic, minced
3 scallions, trimmed and finely chopped
½ green bell pepper, cored, seeded, and finely chopped
½ red bell pepper, cored, seeded, and finely chopped
1 tablespoon curry powder
2 ripe tomatoes, peeled, seeded, and diced
1 bay leaf
½ cup chopped fresh cilantro or Italian (flat-leaf) parsley
¾ cup Coconut Milk (see page 331), or canned, unsweetened
¾ cup Fish Stock (see page 330), Chicken Stock (see page 329), or bottled clam broth
⅛ teaspoon cayenne pepper, or to taste

1. Rinse the wahoo and pat dry. Cut the fish across the grain into ½-inch-thick slices. In a nonreactive baking dish, toss the fish with the lime juice, garlic, and salt and pepper. Marinate for 20 minutes.

2. Meanwhile, preheat the oven to 400°F.

3. Make the sauce: Heat the olive oil in a nonreactive large sauté pan over medium heat. Cook the onion, garlic, scallions, and bell peppers until soft but not brown, about 5 minutes. Stir in the curry powder and cook for 1 minute. Add the tomatoes, increase the heat to high, and cook for 1 minute.

4. Add the bay leaf, half of the cilantro, the coconut milk, and stock to the pan. Gently simmer the mixture, until thick and well flavored, 10 minutes, Whisk in enough cayenne to give a hint of hotness.

5. Place half of the curry mixture in an attractive baking dish just large enough to hold the fish. Arrange the wahoo on top. Spoon the remaining curry mixture on top. Bake the fish until done, about 10 minutes. When cooked, the fish will break into flakes when pressed with your finger. Sprinkle the dish with the remaining cilantro and serve at once.

From Conch to Stone Crabs

Almond Cracked Conch

Shrimp and Smokies

Stone Crabs a la Nage

Lobster Enchilado

Sofrito Steamed Mussels

From October to May, it's stone crab season in Miami. Traffic will be lined up bumper to bumper on Biscayne Street at the southern tip of Miami Beach, home of Joe's Stone Crab. Crab boats will crisscross the Gulf of Mexico and the Florida Keys, hauling square wooden traps, rushing the catch to processing plants around southern Florida. Roadside stands selling stone crabs will pop up like mushrooms after a rain storm. All this for a food, that eighty years ago, was deemed barely fit for human consumption.

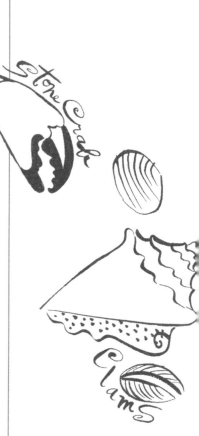

Stone crabs are but one of Florida's popular shellfish. Consider the spiny lobster, also known as Florida lobster or Caribbean lobster. Recognizable by its enormous antennae and lack of claws, the spiny lobster has a wide tail filled with crisp, sweet, pearl-white meat. It's easier to eat than Maine lobster, and its rich flesh can stand up to cumin, curry, and other assertive Caribbean seasonings.

Conch (pronounced KONK) is another important Florida shellfish, although none is actually harvested in Florida today. This giant sea snail, with its flaring pink-white shell, was once so common in the Florida Keys that it gave its name to the inhabitants of Key West. To this day, there are "conch houses" (built with conch shell mortar), a "Conch Train" (that tours the central historic district of Key West), and a high school athletic team called the Fighting Conchs. For the time being, Florida conch grounds are closed to fishermen to allow the stock to be replenished. But conch fritters, conch chowder, and conch salad, made with shellfish imported from the Bahamas, remain an essential part of Floridian cuisine.

Florida's most widely enjoyed shellfish is shrimp. But which shrimp you favor depends on where in the

Sunshine State you live. Key Westers are partial to "pink golds," large, rose-colored, full-flavored shrimp fished from the Gulf of Mexico. Northeastern Floridians dote on "Mayport Whites," white, softly crunchy, delicately flavored shrimp fished from the Atlantic. My own favorite is rock shrimp, once enjoyed only by a handful of diehards who had the patience to extract the sweet crustaceans from their hard shells. Today, thanks to the invention of a special shelling machine, rock shrimp are becoming more widely available.

Other popular Sunshine State shellfish include oysters and clams, the former fished from Apalachicola Bay on the Panhandle and Cedar Key on the west coast; the latter grown in the fertile waters of the Indian River. Blue crabs are also harvested in great abundance here. While Maryland and Louisiana dominate the blue crab market, Florida is one of the few places that has soft-shell crab hatcheries, where blue crabs are induced to shed their shells all year long.

This chapter also includes a recipe for frog's legs. Although not a shellfish, this swamp food is enjoyed at Florida fish houses—especially in the Everglades. Frogs' legs are fished in vast quantities from the prows of airboats skimming the Everglades. If you haven't tried fresh Florida frogs' legs, you're missing out on a very tasty delicacy. It's time to change that.

Oyster Shooter

This recipe takes the work out of eating oysters on the half shell. The various garnishes—lime juice, cocktail sauce, horseradish—are combined with the oysters in a shot glass.

MAKES 1 AND CAN BE MULTIPLIED AS DESIRED

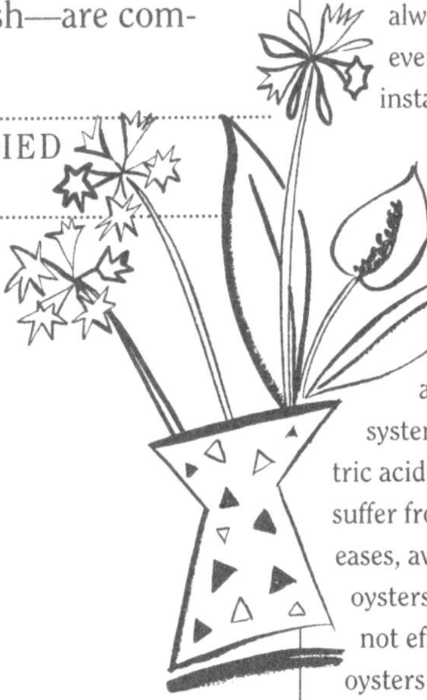

1 lime wedge
1 large oyster in the shell
Splash of Tabasco sauce
Splash of Worcestershire sauce
2 to 3 grinds of fresh black pepper
¼ to ½ teaspoon prepared horseradish
Generous squirt of cocktail sauce
    (preferably the Caribbean Cocktail
    Sauce on page 113)

1. Squeeze the lime juice into a shot glass. Shuck the oyster and slide it, juices and all, into the glass.
2. Add the remaining ingredients in the order listed. Enjoy in a single bite.

RAW FLORIDA OYSTER ALERT

Unfortunately raw Florida oysters are not always safe eating for everyone. In very rare instances, Florida oysters have been found to contain a bacteria that has been known to cause severe illness in people with liver diseases, an impaired immune system, or low levels of gastric acid. If you're elderly or suffer from one of these diseases, avoid eating raw Florida oysters. The bacteria does not effect cooked Florida oysters or raw cold water oysters from the North.

Spice-Fried Oysters

Florida oysters are less well-known on a national level than their New England or Long Island counterparts. But they are no less delicious. The bulk of our oysters come from Apalachicola Bay on the Florida Panhandle. Other sources include the Indian

River on the east coast of Florida and Cedar Key on the west coast. Sunshine Aïoli (see page 122) makes a good accompaniment to these spicy oysters, as does Banana Molasses Ketchup (see page 128).

SERVES 4

24 large oysters (1 pint shucked)
2 eggs
½ cup milk

SPICED FLOUR:
1½ cups all-purpose flour
½ cup fine cornmeal
1 tablespoon salt
1 tablespoon filé powder (ground
sassafras)
1 tablespoon paprika
2 teaspoons garlic powder
2 teaspoons onion powder
1 teaspoon dried thyme
1 teaspoon cayenne pepper
1 teaspoon freshly ground black pepper

About 2 cups oil, for frying

1. Shuck the oysters over a strainer set over a bowl, reserving the liquor. If you use shucked oysters, drain them in a strainer over a bowl, then pick through them, removing any bits of shell.

2. Combine the eggs, milk, and reserved oyster liquor in a mixing bowl and whisk until smooth. Combine all of the spiced flour ingredients in another bowl and mix well.

3. Pour enough oil to reach a depth of 1 inch in a skillet or electric frying pan and heat to 350°F. Using 2 forks, dip the oysters in the milk mixture, then the spiced flour, then the milk mixture again, then the spiced flour again, shaking off the excess.

4. Fry the oysters until golden brown, turning with a wire skimmer, 1 to 2 minutes. Work in several batches so as not to crowd the pan. Drain the oysters on paper towels and serve on doily-lined plates with ramekins of sauce in the center for dipping.

White Water Clams with Chorizo

Indian River, Florida, is famous for its colossal citrus fruit, but there's another crop there that will make your mouth water: shellfish. This shallow intercoastal waterway, stretching from Melbourne to Port St. Lucie, contains some of the richest clam and oyster beds in Florida. According to Dan McLister, president of Manatee Bay Shellfish, Inc., marine biologists developed a hybrid of the rough-shelled southern clam and smooth-shelled but slow-growing northern clam about 10 years ago. The result is one of the sweetest bivalves ever to grace a half shell. Clam nomenclature is a little different in Florida than in the rest of the country. When we say littleneck, we mean a hard-shell clam 1 to 1¼ inches across. A mid-

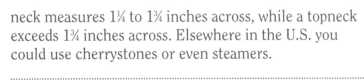

neck measures 1¼ to 1¾ inches across, while a topneck exceeds 1¾ inches across. Elsewhere in the U.S. you could use cherrystones or even steamers.

SERVES 4 AS AN APPETIZER

36 of the tinest clams you can buy
2 tablespoons extra-virgin olive oil
1 chorizo sausage (3 to 4 ounces)
1 onion, diced
3 cloves garlic, thinly sliced
2 tomatoes, peeled, seeded, and coarsely
*   chopped*
½ cup coarsely chopped fresh Italian
*   (flat-leaf) parsley*
1 bay leaf
Freshly ground black pepper, to taste
2 cups dry white wine

1. Thoroughly scrub the clams, discarding any with cracked shells or open shells that fail to close when tapped.

2. Heat the olive oil in a nonreactive large sauté pan or saucepan. Prick the sausage a few times with a toothpick. Fry the sausage over medium heat until cooked, about 5 minutes per side. Transfer the sausage to a cutting board and let cool, then cut into thin slices.

3. Discard all but 2 tablespoons of the fat from the pan. Add the onion and garlic and cook over medium heat until lightly browned, about 3 minutes. Stir in the sausage, tomatoes, parsley, bay leaf, pepper, and wine. Bring the mixture to a boil. Stir in the clams and tightly cover the pot.

4. Cook the clams over high heat until the shells open, about 8 minutes. Shake the pan occasionally to give the shells room to open. Ladle the clams and cooking liquid into large shallow bowls. Discard any that haven't opened. Serve the clams with crusty bread for dipping and extra bowls to hold the empty shells.

Sofrito Steamed Mussels

ofrito is one of the basic seasonings of the Spanish Caribbean, a redolent mixture of onion, garlic, and bell pepper. The ingredients vary from cook to cook and island to island: One might use Cuba's aromatic *cachucha* chili (see page 46), another green bell pepper; another might call for bacon fat in place of olive oil. I prefer small mussels to the jumbos turning up at many fish markets: They're sweeter.

SERVES 4 AS AN APPETIZER

2 pounds mussels in the shells

SOFRITO:
2 tablespoons extra-virgin olive oil
1 bunch scallions, trimmed and finely chopped
1 green bell pepper, cored, seeded, and finely chopped
2 jalapeño chilies, seeded and minced
4 cloves garlic, minced
½ bunch fresh Italian (flat-leaf) parsley leaves,
*   finely chopped*
1 bunch fresh cilantro, finely chopped
Salt and freshly ground black pepper, to taste
1½ cups dry white wine

1. Scrub the mussels under cold running water, discarding any with cracked shells or shells that fail to close when tapped. Right before cooking, remove any threads protruding from the hinges of the mussels. Needlenose pliers work well for this task.

2. Prepare the *sofrito*: Heat the olive oil in a nonreactive large pot over medium heat. Add the scallions, bell peppers, chilies, garlic, and herbs and sauté until soft but not brown, about 4 minutes. Add the salt and pepper.

3. Just before serving, add the wine to the *sofrito* and bring the mixture to a boil. Stir in the mussels and cook, covered, over high heat until the shells open, about 8 minutes. Shake the pan occasionally to give the shells room to open. Ladle the mussels and cooking liquid into large shallow bowls. Serve the mussels with crusty bread for dipping and extra bowls to hold the empty shells.

SHRIMP SIZES

Shrimp are sold by both size (small, medium, large, and so on) and count (the actual number of shrimp to a pound). Here are the common sizes and corresponding counts.

Size	Count/Pound
Colossal	10-15
Extra jumbo	16-20
Jumbo	21-25
Extra large	26-30
Large	31-35
Medium large	36-42
Medium	43-50
Small	51-70

Real Coconut Shrimp

Coconut shrimp is a popular dish at Florida beach clubs. Made with packaged dried coconut, often it is undistinguished bar fare at best. But dip shrimp in egg and coat it with crisp, freshly grated coconut and you will have a morsel worthy of epicurean attention. Instructions for shelling and peeling coconut are on page 292. Coconut shrimp are traditionally served with a sweet sauce, like the Apricot-Horseradish Sauce below or the Caribbean Cocktail Sauce on page 113.

SERVES 6 AS AN APPETIZER, 3 TO 4 AS AN ENTREE

1½ pounds jumbo shrimp
1 tablespoon fresh lime juice
Salt and freshly ground black pepper, to taste
About 1 cup all-purpose flour
2 eggs, beaten
1½ cups freshly grated or very finely chopped
  fresh coconut
3 to 4 tablespoons Clarified Butter (page 328) or
  vegetable oil
Apricot-Horseradish Sauce (recipe follows)
  for dipping

1. Peel and devein the shrimp, leaving the tails intact. Place the shrimp in a mixing bowl and toss with the lime juice and salt and pepper. Let marinate for 5 minutes.

2. Place the flour in a shallow bowl, the eggs in another shallow bowl, and the coconut in a third.

3. Just before serving, melt the butter in a large heavy skillet. Dip each shrimp first in flour, shaking off the excess, then in the egg mixture, then finally in the coconut. Cook the shrimp over medium heat until golden brown, about 1 minute per side. Drain the shrimp on paper towels, and then arrange on doily-lined plates or a platter. Serve the coconut shrimp with the dipping sauce that follows.

APRICOT-HORSERADISH SAUCE

๑๑๑

MAKES 1 CUP

⅔ cup apricot jam
⅓ cup freshly grated or prepared white
horseradish
1 tablespoon fresh lime juice, or to taste
Salt and freshly ground black pepper,
to taste

Combine the jam and horseradish in a mixing bowl and whisk until smooth. Whisk in the lime juice and salt and pepper. If not serving immediately, transfer the sauce to a glass jar with a nonmetallic lid and refrigerate. It will keep for several weeks.

TO PEEL AND DEVEIN SHRIMP

To peel a shrimp by hand, pinch the front legs between your thumb and forefinger. Peel off the upper portion of shell as you would the rind of a tangerine. Next, pinch the tail and slowly wiggle the body out of the lower portion of the shell. The shells can be saved for fish stock.

The vein, or intestine, is the black tube running down the back of the shrimp. Its removal is dictated more by aesthetics than by health concerns, but most people would rather not eat it. I never bother to devein small shrimp. The classic way to devein a shrimp is to cut a *V*-shaped groove down the back and lift out the vein and surrounding meat.

I have a simpler method

for deveining shrimp, one taught to me by a Louisianan. Insert the tine of a fork in the rounded part of the back of the shrimp, just below the vein. Gently pull the fork away from the shrimp and the vein will come with it.

Cookware shops and fish markets sell a simple device that can dramatically facilitate peeling and deveining shrimp. The shrimp peeler looks like a red plastic knife that tapers to a long, slender, flexible tip. To use it, hold the shrimp body straight with your left hand. Insert the slender end of the peeler into the vein at the head end of the shrimp with your right hand and push. (Reverse hands if you're left-handed.) The peeler's wedge-shape blade will cut cleanly through the shell and remove the vein.

Buffalo Shrimp

he Half Shell Raw Bar in Key West isn't what you'd call a temple of high gastronomy, but its open-air harborside dining room, decorated with nautical memorabilia and antique license plates, is heady with the atmosphere of the Florida Keys. One of the house specialties is buffalo shrimp, a tropical twist on an American classic—Buffalo Chicken Wings, which according to *The Dictionary of American Food & Drink* by John Mariani, was invented at the Anchor Bar in Buffalo, New York, in 1964. Expect to get very messy eating this dish and have plenty of beer on hand to extinguish the fires. The Half Shell uses Durkee's hot sauce, but I like the Louisianan brand, Crystal. For the best results, use cracker crumbs made from *galletas* (Hispanic crackers—look for them at Hispanic markets).

SERVES 6 AS AN APPETIZER, 3 TO 4 AS AN ENTREE

1½ pounds jumbo shrimp
1 cup buttermilk
1 cup cracker crumbs
⅓ cup all-purpose flour
Garlic salt, to taste
Freshly ground black pepper, to taste
⅓ cup hot sauce, or to taste
4 tablespoons (½ stick) unsalted butter, melted
About 2 cups vegetable oil, for frying
Roquefort Cheese Sauce (recipe follows), for dipping

1. Peel and devein the shrimp, leaving the tails intact. Place the shrimp in a mixing bowl and toss with the buttermilk.

2. Combine the cracker crumbs, flour, garlic salt, and pepper in a food processor and grind to a fine powder.

3. Combine the hot sauce and melted butter in a mixing bowl and whisk to mix.

4. Just before serving, heat the oil to 350°F in a large heavy skillet or electric frying pan. Drain the shrimp and toss with the breading. Fry the shrimp over medium heat until golden brown, turning with a slotted spoon, 1 to 2 minutes total. Work in several batches so as not to crowd the pan.

5. Transfer the shrimp to paper towels to drain. Toss the shrimp with the hot sauce mixture and serve at once.

ROQUEFORT CHEESE SAUCE

MAKES ABOUT 2 CUPS

⅓ cup Roquefort cheese (3 ounces),
    crumbled and at room temperature
½ cup mayonnaise
½ cup sour cream
1 rib celery, minced
1 tablespoon minced onion
2 teaspoons fresh lime or lemon juice
Salt and freshly ground black pepper,
    to taste

1. Mash the cheese with the back of a fork or wooden spoon in a mixing bowl.

2. Beat in all of the remaining ingredients. Correct the seasonings, adding lime juice or salt.

Grilled Shrimp Mousse on SugarCane Kebabs

This is a dish of Vietnamese origin, but it's very appropriate for Florida. Not only do we lead the nation in sugarcane production; we also harvest the lion's share of shrimp. Sugarcane can be found at Hispanic and Asian markets and in the produce section of many supermarkets. You're not really meant to eat the sugarcane in this dish. The idea is to chew it to release the sugary juices, which counterpoint the saltiness of the shrimp mousse. Serve with the Key Lime Nuoc Cham on page 111.

SERVES 4 AS AN APPETIZER

1 pound shrimp, peeled and deveined

3 cloves garlic, minced

1 scallion, trimmed and minced

*½ scotch bonnet chili or 1 jalapeño, seeded
    and minced*

2 teaspoons soy sauce

1 teaspoon sugar

½ teaspoon Caribbean hot sauce

1 egg white

Salt and freshly ground black pepper, to taste

3 lengths (8 inches each) fresh sugarcane

1 to 2 teaspoons vegetable oil

1. Combine the shrimp, garlic, scallion, and chili in a food processor and purée to a smooth paste. (The ingredients can also be pounded to a paste in a mortar.) Mix in the soy sauce, sugar, hot sauce, egg white, and salt and pepper. Cover and chill the mousse for 1 hour.

2. Peel the sugarcane, using a cleaver or chef's knife

(remove the peel in long, thin strips). Cut each piece of sugar-cane lengthwise into 4 strips.

3. Lightly coat a plate and your fingers with the oil. Take 2 to 3 tablespoons of the shrimp mousse in your hand and mold it around the top half of a strip of the sugarcane. Roll the cane on the oiled plate to smooth and even the layer of mousse. Continue in this fashion until all of the cane sticks are coated. (The recipe can be prepared up to 2 hours ahead to this stage. Store, covered, in the refrigerator.)

4. Preheat a barbecue grill to very hot or the broiler with the broiler tray 3 inches from the heat.

5. Just before serving, grill the kebabs over medium heat until lightly browned, about 1 minute per side. If broiling, cook also for 1 minute per side.

Shrimp and Smokies

No book on Floridian cuisine would be complete without a recipe for U-peel shrimp. This one comes from the Mucky Duck on Captiva Island, a restaurant equally remarkable for its stunning beachfront setting as for its colorful co-owner, Victor Mayeron. He's the guy who strolls through the dining room, squirting red strings from trick ketchup bottles onto the laps of alarmed customers. The Caribbean Cocktail Sauce on page 113 and Joe's Stone Crab Mustard Sauce on page 121 make good accompaniments.

U-PEEL SHRIMP

Floridians are less fastidious than most Americans when it comes to eating shrimp. Indeed, one of our state specialties is a dish called U-peel shrimp. Served at bars and seaside eateries from Pensicola to Key West, U-peel shrimp are simply shellfish that have been boiled in a spice-scented broth and served without ceremony in their shells. Like Maryland's famous steamed crabs and Louisiana's boiled crayfish, you peel and eat them with your fingers, preferably in the company of a pitcher or two of cold beer.

Since the shrimp are cooked in the shell, they are

not cleaned (deveined) before serving. The appearance of a black vein can be disconcerting to some people. The issue is purely aesthetic: Veined shrimp taste every bit as good as the deveined and are just as good for you. Most Floridians eat the shrimp veins and all. If the vein bothers you, scrape it away with the tip of a knife, but few Floridians would bother.

SERVES 4 TO 6

2 pounds large shrimp in their shells
3 bottles of your favorite beer
  (or enough to completely cover the shrimp)
1 pound kielbasa sausage, cut into ½-inch slices
2 bay leaves
1 tablespoon coriander seeds
Salt and freshly ground black pepper, to taste

1. Thoroughly wash the shrimp in cold water.

2. Pour the beer into a large pot. Add the kielbasa, bay leaves, coriander seeds, and salt and pepper. Bring the beer to a boil over high heat. Lower the heat and simmer, uncovered, until well flavored, about 10 minutes.

3. Add the shrimp and boil until firm and pink, 1 to 2 minutes. Drain off the cooking liquid and serve the shrimp and sausage in bowls, with extra bowls for holding the shells. Victor serves the shrimp and smokies hot, but they're also delicious cold. Let each guest peel his own shrimp.

Shrimp with Rum and Mint

This dish could be thought of as the Floridian version of that Italo-American favorite, shrimp scampi. When available, I use "pink golds," the lovely pink shrimp fished from the waters around Key West. Sometimes, I substitute cilantro or Italian (flat-leaf) parsley for the mint. The Coconut Rice on page 261 makes a good accompaniment.

3 tablespoons unsalted butter
1½ pounds shrimp, peeled and deveined
2 cloves garlic, minced
1 to 2 jalapeño or serrano chilies, seeded and minced
¼ cup finely chopped fresh mint, cilantro, or parsley
4 scallions, trimmed and finely chopped
¼ cup dark rum
2 to 3 tablespoons fresh lime juice
Salt and freshly ground black pepper, to taste

1. Melt the butter in a large frying pan over medium heat. Add the shrimp, garlic, and chilies and cook for 1 minute.

2. Stir in the mint, scallions, rum, lime juice, and salt and pepper. Bring the mixture to a boil and cook until the shrimp are done, about 1 minute. Remove the shrimp with a slotted spoon and transfer to a serving dish.

3. Boil the sauce over high heat until thick and syrupy, 2 to 3 minutes. Correct the seasonings, adding salt or lime juice to taste. Pour the sauce over the shrimp and serve at once.

Rock Shrimp Hash with Boniato Pancakes

Rock shrimp are some of the sweetest, most tender, most succulent shrimp in the crustacean kingdom. The only shrimp that come close is the small Northern variety from Maine. So where have they been all these years? Rock shrimp come in rock-hard shells. It wasn't until 1988 that a machine was invented that could shell rock shrimp, making the sweet shellfish available on a commercial level. This recipe comes from Allen Susser, owner of Chef Allen's in North Miami and one of the pioneers of the new Floridian cuisine. If rock shrimp are unavailable, use Maine or even regular shrimp. If boniato (Cuban sweet potato) is unavailable, use regular potatoes.

SERVES 2

PANCAKES:
1 small boniato (about 12 ounces)
3 tablespoons olive oil
Salt and freshly ground black pepper, to taste

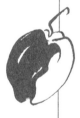

HASH:
1 tablespoon olive oil
12 ounces shelled rock shrimp, cut into ½-inch pieces
½ red tomato, peeled, seeded, and diced
½ yellow tomato, peeled, seeded, and diced
½ teaspoon minced scotch bonnet chili, or to taste
2 tablespoons finely chopped scallions
4 fresh basil leaves (each about 1½ inches long),
     finely chopped
1 tablespoon chopped fresh chervil or Italian
     (flat-leaf) parsley
3 tablespoons dry white wine

1. Make the boniato pancakes: Peel and grate the boniato; you should have about 1 cup. Heat 1 tablespoon of the olive oil in each of two 8-inch nonstick frying pans over medium heat. Add half the boniato to each and flatten with a spatula. Season with the salt and pepper. Cook the pancakes until golden brown on the bottom, 3 to 4 minutes. Flip the pancakes, adding oil if necessary, and brown the other side. Keep the pancakes warm in a low (200°F) oven while you prepare the hash.

2. Heat the oil in a clean nonstick frying pan over medium heat. Add the shrimp, tomatoes, chili, scallions, basil, and chervil. Cook until the shrimp begin to turn white, about 1 minute. Increase the heat to high and add the wine. Cook until the wine evaporates. Correct the seasonings, adding salt or pepper to taste.

3. Slide the pancakes onto plates and spoon the hash on top.

Almond Cracked Conch

Cracked conch is the Floridian name for a breaded, pan-fried conch steak. This recipe owes its distinctive crunch and flavor to the use of almonds instead of the traditional bread crumbs. If you live in Florida, your fishmonger will probably have a machine for tenderizing conch. If not, you can use a ridged mallet. Serve the conch with the Coconut Rice on page 261.

SERVES 4 AS AN APPETIZER,
2 TO 3 AS AN ENTREE

4 medium conchs (about 1 pound total)
Salt and freshly ground black pepper, to taste
1 cup all-purpose flour
2 eggs, well beaten
1 cup thinly sliced almonds, finely chopped
3 tablespoons Clarified Butter (see page 328,
*   or a mixture of 1½ tablespoons butter*
*   and 1½ tablespoons oil), or more*
*   if needed*

HOW TO PREPARE CONCH

Conch has a reputation for being tough, and unless it's prepared properly, it can be as chewy as proverbial shoe leather. The first trick is to tenderize it by pounding, much as you would a veal scallop. The second is to cook it hardly at all or in a pressure cooker for 40 to 60 minutes. Conch cooking is very much like squid cooking: It's best served barely cooked or cooked long enough to pass through the tough stage and back into a second tender stage.

Virtually all of the conch sold in this country arrives frozen in 5-pound blocks. Fortunately, conch freezes better than most seafoods and it doesn't lose its sweetness. Conch can be purchased at many fish shops and West Indian and Hispanic markets. When buying, look for firm white meat tinged with pink, peach, or orange. Avoid conch that is grayish in color or smells fishy or ammoniated. Figure on ⅓ to ½ pound per person.

To prepare conch for cooking, trim off any bits of dark membrane. Place the conch in a Ziploc bag or between two sheets of plastic wrap and pound it with a ridged mallet to a thickness of ³⁄₁₆ inch. For fritters and chowder, the conch should be ground in a meat grinder or food processor or chopped by hand.

SAUCE:
2 cloves garlic, minced
1 scallion, trimmed and finely chopped
½ cup lightly packed fresh Italian (flat-leaf) parsley,
*   finely chopped*
2 tablespoons fresh lemon juice
Salt and freshly ground black pepper, to taste
Lemon or lime wedges, for garnish

1. Trim any tough gristly parts off the conchs. Pound each conch as thin as possible (¼ to ⅛ inch), using a tenderizing mallet to make 4 broad, flat steaks.

2. Season the conch on both sides with salt and pepper. Place the flour in a shallow bowl, the eggs in another shallow bowl, and the almonds in a third.

3. Just before serving, melt the butter in a large heavy skillet over medium heat. Dip each conch steak first in the flour, shaking off the excess, then in the egg mixture, then finally in the almonds. Cook the conch steaks over medium heat until golden brown, about 1 minute per side. Drain the conch steaks on paper towels, and reserve the pan and any remaining butter. There should be about 2 tablespoons left. If there isn't, add enough to make 2 tablespoons. Arrange the conch steaks on plates or a platter.

4. Meanwhile, make the sauce. Add the garlic, scallion, and parsley to the reserved pan. Cook over high heat until fragrant but not brown, about 20 seconds. Whisk in the lemon juice and boil until the pan juices reduce to a thick, syrupy sauce. Season with the salt and pepper and spoon the sauce over the conch. Garnish with wedges of lemon and serve at once.

Conch Chili

Key West meets the Southwest in this unusual chili. Using conch in chili may sound a little weird, but it makes a cholesterol-free, low-fat, and wonderfully tasty version. Chipotles are smoked jalapeño chilies. They're available both canned and dried at Hispanic markets and gourmet shops. If conch is unavailable, make the chili with ground shrimp, scallops, squid, or a mixture of all three.

SERVES 4

2 chipotle chilies, dried or canned

2 tablespoons unsalted butter or olive oil

4 cloves garlic, minced

1 onion, finely chopped

1 green bell pepper, cored, seeded, and finely chopped

1½ pounds conch, coarsely ground

1 teaspoon ground dried bay leaf, or 2 whole bay leaves

1 tablespoon chili powder, or to taste

2 teaspoons ground cumin

2 teaspoons dried oregano

1 cup beer

2 cups tomato juice

1 tablespoon Worcestershire sauce

1 teaspoon Tabasco sauce (optional)

2 tomatoes, peeled, seeded, and diced

Salt and freshly ground black pepper, to taste

1 cup cooked navy or Great Northern beans

1 tablespoon fresh lime juice

¼ cup chopped scallions, for serving

1. If using dried chilies, stem and split them; soak in ½ cup hot water for 30 minutes. Drain and finely chop the chilies, reserving the soaking liquid. If using canned chilies,

THE CONCH REPUBLIC

Conch (pronounced KONK) is a giant edible sea snail. Even if you've never tasted it, you've probably seen its broad, knobbed, flaring, pink-white shell. Conch has been likened to abalone, clams, and scallops. Firm-textured like the first, it hints at the briny flavor of the second and the sweetness of the third. But as any Key Wester will tell you, the flavor of conch is unique.

For millennia, *Strombus gigas,* as conch is called in Latin, has been a cornerstone of the Caribbean diet and culture. The Indians used the shells to make axes, scrapers, fishhooks, jewelry, religious objects, and even musical instruments. Some of the highest elevations in flat Florida are mounds of crushed conch shells discarded by the Indians after conch feasts. Later generations carved conch shells into cameos and crushed them to make terrazzo floors.

The handsome spiraled shellfish is found as far north as Bermuda and as far south as Brazil. Conch was once a staple of the Key West diet—so much so that Key Westers called themselves "Conchs." Unfortunately, overfishing has depleted Floridian stocks to the point where it's illegal to catch this delectable shellfish here. Today, most of the conch served in Florida comes from Costa Rica and the Turks and Caicos islands in the Bahamas.

And much served it is. Popular Florida dishes include conch fritters, conch chowders (both tomato- and cream-based), conch salad, and conch ceviche. Conch stewed with peppers, tomatoes, and ham is a traditional breakfast in Key West's Bahamian community. "Cracked conch," a breaded pan-fried conch steak, is a mainstay at both humble eateries and fancy restaurants alike.

While conch isn't generally considered a health food, it is high in protein and low in fat. But even if healthy eating is not your principle motivation, the next time you visit Florida, make an effort to sample this singular shellfish.

finely chop them and reserve them with 1 to 2 teaspoons of the canning liquid.

2. Melt the butter in a large, heavy, nonreactive pot over medium heat. Add the garlic, onion, and bell pepper and cook until soft and fragrant but not brown, about 4 minutes.

3. Stir in the conch, bay leaf, chili powder, cumin, and oregano. Cook over high heat for 1 minute. Stir in the beer, tomato juice, Worcestershire sauce, Tabasco sauce, tomatoes, chipotles with their soaking liquid, and salt and pepper. Gently simmer the chili, partially covered, for 30 minutes.

4. Stir in the beans and lime juice. Continue cooking the chili until the conch is very tender and most of the cooking liquid has been absorbed, about 20 minutes. If the chili is too soupy, uncover the pan for the last 10 minutes. (The chili can be prepared up to 24 hours ahead to this stage and reheated.)

5. Just before serving, remove the whole bay leaves, if using. Correct the seasonings, adding salt, chili powder, Tabasco sauce, or lime juice to taste. Sprinkle with the chopped scallions and serve at once.

Stone Crabs with Melted Butter and Mustard Sauce

This is the classic way to eat stone crabs, pioneered by Joe Weiss, founder of the legendary Joe's Stone Crab on Miami Beach. Weiss was the first person to serve stone crabs cold, thereby resolving the age-old problem of how to eliminate the iodine flavor of a hot stone crab. Many Floridians would argue that this is the *only* way to eat stone crabs.

6 pounds cooked stone crab claws

4 cups crushed ice

8 lemon or lime wedges

8 ounces (2 sticks) salted butter, melted

Joes's Stone Crab Mustard Sauce (see page 121)

1. Crack the stone crab claws well. Pound them with a wide-headed mallet, lead pipe, or rolling pin, starting at the knuckle, working toward the claw. (I like to cover the claws with a old dish towel when cracking to keep bits of shell from flying all over the kitchen.) If you'd rather not crack the claws yourself, have the fishmonger do it.

2. Mound the ice on a large platter. Arrange the cracked stone crab claws on top. Garnish the platter with the lemon wedges.

3. Provide each guest with small dishes of melted butter and Mustard Sauce, plus a bowl for holding the empty shells. Dip the nuggets of crab in melted butter or mustard sauce. Or, if you're the glutton that I am, dip them first in butter, then in mustard sauce, and then pop them into your mouth!

Stone Crabs à la Nage

Stone crabs are rarely served hot. The reason is simple: The flesh sometimes has an iodine flavor when cooked and served hot. The exception that makes the rule are the stone crabs *à la nage* served at the Brasserie Le Coze in Coconut Grove. *A nage* is an aromatic broth flavored with vegetables and sliced

THE ECOLOGICAL STONE CRAB

Stone crabs are ecologically interesting because their claws are renewable and the crabs themselves are recycled. The fisherman takes only the claws, returning the rest of the rust-colored, stalk-eyed crustacean to the water. New claws grow back in 12 to 18 months. Crabs with a second or third growth of claws are called "retreads."

Stone crab claws are highly perishable so they are

always cooked before selling. They come in three sizes: medium (eight claws to a pound), large (four claws to a pound), and jumbo (one to three claws to a pound). The latter look most impressive and command the highest price. But some connoisseurs prefer mediums, which they claim have a sweeter flesh and a higher ratio of meat to shell.

Stone crab claws are in season from October 15 to April 15. Available at premium fishmongers in most major cities, they can be ordered by overnight mail from Joe's by calling 1-800-780-CRAB or 305-673-9035.

lemon. *Nager* is the French verb "to swim," which is exactly what the crab claws do in this fragrant broth. Here's my version of a Franco-tropical classic.

SERVES 4

BROTH:
1 quart water
1½ cups dry white wine
¼ cup fresh lemon juice
4 strips (each 2 inches long) lemon zest
1 medium onion, coarsely chopped
2 cloves garlic
1 leek, white part only, well-washed,
*   and coarsely chopped*
1 small fennel bulb, trimmed and coarsely chopped
1 rib celery, coarsely chopped
1 tomato, coarsely chopped
1 bouquet garni of 1 bay leaf, 3 sprigs fresh thyme,
*   and 3 sprigs parsley, tied in a piece of cheesecloth*
1½ teaspoons coriander seeds
1½ teaspoons salt
1 teaspoon white peppercorns

CRAB AND VEGETABLES:
24 medium or 16 large stone crabs
1 carrot, cut into julienne
1 leek, white part only, well-washed and cut into julienne
1 rib celery, cut into julienne
1 onion, sliced as thinly as possible
1 lemon, sliced as thinly as possible
¼ cup fresh chervil or cilantro leaves

1. Combine all of the ingredients for the broth in a large nonreactive saucepan. Bring to a boil, reduce the heat, and simmer until well flavored, about 1 hour. Correct the seasonings, adding salt to taste. Strain the broth into another large nonreactive saucepan.

2. Crack the stone crabs as described in Step 1, page 176. Add them to the broth with the carrot, leek, celery, and onion. Poach the claws over low heat for 10 minutes. The vegetables should be tender.

3. Transfer the crab claws to soup dishes with a slotted spoon. Spoon the vegetables on top. Add enough of the broth to partially cover the crab claws. Garnish each bowl with the lemon slices and chervil leaves and serve at once. Be sure to provide crusty bread for dunking, shell crackers, finger bowls, and a bowl for the empty shells.

"Pousse Café" of Stone Crab

When it comes to embellishing stone crabs, I generally adhere to the school of "don't." One exception is this *"pousse café,"* a colorful twist on crab cocktail. A venerable after-dinner drink, *pousse café* is made by layering different-colored liqueurs in a cordial glass. This dish achieves a similar look using a variety of vegetable salsas. The idea comes from Mennan Tekali, chef of Max's Grille in Boca Raton. This is a stunning dish for a party and practical, too, as you can make large quantities ahead of time. If stone crabs are unavailable, substitute blue crab or Maine crab from the Northeast or Dungeness crab on the West Coast.

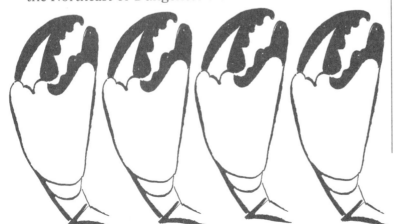

STONE CRABS

Stone crabs have long been eaten in Cuba, but they didn't really catch on in this country until the 1920s. The problem is that the flesh of a freshly cooked stone crab has a watery consistency and a slight iodine aftertaste. Enter one Joe Weiss, a retired waiter from New York, who in 1913 opened a tiny eatery on Alton Beach, as Miami Beach was called in those days. At the urging of a Harvard University marine biologist, who was living and working in Miami at the time, Joe began experimenting with the stone crab. In 1922, he discovered a way to firm up the flesh and eliminate the odd flavor: Serve the coral-colored, thick-shelled claws chilled.

The public tasted the new delicacy. The public was delighted. Joe's grew from a six-table eatery to a sprawling 400-seat restaurant that serves 1,500 people a day. The tourist season on Miami Beach traditionally begins the day Joe's opens in mid-October and is over when Joe's closes in mid-April. At the height of the season, Joe's will serve over 70,000 pounds of stone crabs a week. Joe's success has spawned countless imitators across the state of Florida. In 1991, stone crabbing earned Florida fishermen over $15 million.

The debate still rages over the proper condiment for stone crabs. Joe Weiss favored simple melted butter. But other crab enthusiasts argue for his flavorful mustard sauce. A new generation of Florida chefs is experimenting with new ways to serve this delectable crustacean. In the past year, I've eaten stone crab strudel, stone crab tempura, and even chilies stuffed with stone crab paella.

SERVES 4
AND CAN BE MULTIPLIED AS DESIRED

*2 pounds medium stone crab claws or 1 pound
    lump crabmeat*
1 cup Firm-Cooked Black Beans (see page 269)
1 ripe avocado, peeled, pitted, and diced
*1 cup cooked corn kernels (for instructions
    on grilling corn see page 245)*
1 large tomato, peeled, seeded, and diced
*⅓ cup finely chopped fresh cilantro or Italian
    (flat-leaf) parsley*
2 tablespoons minced shallot
1 to 2 jalapeño chilies, seeded and minced
2 to 3 tablespoons fresh lime juice
Salt and freshly ground black pepper, to taste
1½ cups sour cream
1 to 2 tablespoons Chicken Stock (page 329) or milk

1. Crack the stone crab claws (see Step 1, page 176) or have your fishmonger do it. Reserve 4 of the claw portions. Flake the remaining crabmeat, removing any bits of shell.

2. Place the black beans in a small mixing bowl, the avocado in another, the corn in another, and the tomato in another. Add one-fourth of the cilantro, shallot, chilies, and lime juice to each bowl, plus some salt and pepper. Gently toss each salsa to mix, adding salt or lime juice to taste.

3. Place the sour cream in a small mixing bowl and whisk in salt and pepper and enough stock or milk to obtain a thick but pourable sauce.

4. Set up 4 parfait glasses or champagne flutes. Neatly spoon one-fourth of the black bean salsa into the bottom of each. Spoon a few tablespoons of the sour cream mixture on top. Next, add the flaked crab, followed by the avocado salsa, the corn salsa, more sour cream, and finally the tomato. Work neatly so as to keep the layers separate. Garnish each glass with a final dollop of the sour cream and stand a reserved crab claw upright in the center of each. (The "pousse cafés" can be prepared up to 4 hours ahead and stored, covered, in the refrigerator.) Serve with cocktail forks.

Florida Crab Cakes

When it comes to crab cakes, most people think of Maryland. But a great deal of blue crab comes from Florida waters, and Sunshine Staters are adept at making crab cakes as well. The Tropical Tartar Sauce on page 125 makes a great accompaniment.

SERVES 4

1 pound crabmeat, preferably lump

2 strips bacon, finely chopped

2 tablespoons minced shallots

½ red bell pepper, cored, seeded, and finely chopped

½ green bell pepper, cored, seeded, and finely chopped

1 rib celery, finely chopped

1 clove garlic, minced

¼ cup mixed minced fresh herbs,
 including parsley, cilantro, and or basil

3 to 4 tablespoons fine cracker crumbs

1½ teaspoons Old Bay Seasoning or
 other seafood seasoning

Salt and freshly ground black pepper, to taste

Pinch of cayenne pepper

1 egg, beaten

1 to 2 tablespoons heavy (or whipping) cream

3 tablespoons Clarified Butter (page 328), or equal parts
 melted butter and vegetable oil

FOUR GREAT WAYS TO JAZZ UP CRAB CAKES

Crab cakes lend themselves to a variety of interesting accompaniments. My favorite sauces include the Sunshine Aïoli (page 122); Citrus-Sour Cream Sauce (page 124); Joe's Stone Crab Mustard Sauce (page 121); Banana-Molasses Ketchup (page 128); and Mango Salsa (page 133). Here are some other great ideas:

Make a Cuban crab cake sandwich: Follow the *Media Noche* sandwich recipe on page 105, substituting crab cakes for the pork and ham.

Make crab cake *tostones*: Prepare the *Tostones* with Herbed Salt on page 259. Top each with a miniature crab cake, a spoonful of Gator Guacamole (page 22), and a rosette of sour cream.

Make Floridian eggs benedict: Substitute crab cakes for the Canadian bacon in traditional eggs benedict. Top with the Joe's Stone Crab Mustard Sauce.

1. Pick through the crabmeat, removing any bits of shell.

2. Fry the bacon in a frying pan over medium heat until lightly browned, about 2 minutes. Add the shallots, bell peppers, celery, and garlic and cook until soft but not brown, about 2 minutes more. Transfer the mixture to a mixing bowl and let cool.

3. Stir in the crab, herbs, cracker crumbs, Old Bay Seasoning, salt and pepper, and cayenne. Fold in the egg and enough cream to obtain a moist but firm consistency. If the mixture is too wet, add a few more cracker crumbs. Wet your hands with water and form the crab mixture into 4 large or 8 small patties. Wrap in waxed paper and refrigerate for at least 30 minutes.

4. Just before serving, heat the clarified butter in a non-stick frying pan. Pan-fry the crab cakes until crusty and golden brown, about 3 minutes per side. Alternatively, the crab cakes can be broiled, also for about 3 minutes per side. Drain on paper towels and serve at once.

Grilled Soft-Shell Crabs
with Cilantro and Corn Vinaigrette

Soft-shell crabs are traditionally cooked by sautéing or deep-frying, but they're also delicious grilled. Grilling is ideal for people who are watching their fat intake. Another good sauce for this dish is the Tropical Tartar Sauce on page 125.

SERVES 4

8 soft-shell crabs
3 tablespoons extra-virgin olive oil
2 tablespoons fresh lemon juice
2 tablespoons mixed chopped fresh herbs,
   including basil, chervil, chives, thyme, and/or parsley
Salt and freshly ground black pepper, to taste
Cilantro and Corn Vinaigrette (page 118)

1. Preheat a barbecue grill to very hot.

2. Clean the crabs, as described in the accompanying sidebar or have your fishmonger do it.

3. Combine the olive oil, lemon juice, herbs, and salt and pepper. Marinate the crabs in this mixture for 10 minutes, turning once during this time.

4. Grill the crabs over medium heat, basting with the marinade, until cooked, about 2 minutes per side. When cooked, the shells will turn bright red. Transfer the crabs to plates or a platter and spoon the Cilantro and Corn Vinaigrette on top.

Soft-Shell Crab Tempura

East meets West in this recipe—a favorite at my neighborhood Japanese restaurant, Chiyo, in Coconut Grove. If you think this is good, you should try Chiyo's soft-shell crab sushi, made by rolling slices of tempura-fried crab in sushi rice and seaweed. The Key Lime Nuoc Cham on page 111 or Tropical Tartar Sauce on page 125 would make a good dipping sauce.

SOFT-SHELL CRABS

Soft-shell crab is not a separate species of crab, but a phase in the life of the blue crab. Like all crustaceans, crabs outgrow their shells as they mature. To make room for new growth they periodically shed their shells, a process known as molting. "The back seam of the shell pops open and the crab steps right out," explains Carroll Camp, crab specialist at Clayton's Crab Company in Rockledge, Florida.

The freshly molted crab is an epicure's morsel, but an ephemeral one, as the new shell starts to harden after just four hours. Thus, it's essential to gather the crab just after it has molted.

In most parts of the country, crabs molt only in summertime. Here in Florida, thanks to the efforts of men like Carroll Camp, soft-shells are available all year long. Carroll's kingdom is a laboratory with a dozen shallow, chest-high water tanks. When the fishermen bring in the crab catch, the "peelers" (crabs that are about to molt) are sent to Carroll, who sorts them by closeness to molting time. When the proper time arrives, the crab grabs the tank's chicken wire walls with its claws and scuttles out of the back of its shell.

When shopping for soft-shell crabs, try to buy them live and kicking. Soft-shells range in size from mediums (3½ inches across) to "whales" (5½ inches across or larger). The average restaurant portion is two medium or one large crab per person, but I can eat two whales by myself.

You need to do three things to ready the soft-shell crabs for cooking. This procedure is not for the squeamish: You may wish to have your fishmonger do it.

1. First, make a *V*-shaped cut with a knife or scissors to remove the mouth and eyes. (This dispatches the crab instantly, although it may continue to wriggle.)

2. Second, pry up and remove the "apron," the *V*-shaped tab on the belly.

3. Third, lift the pointed flaps of the top shell and remove the feather-like gills underneath.

SERVES 4

8 large soft-shell crabs
1 cup all-purpose flour
About 1 cup ice water
About 3 cups vegetable oil for frying
1 cup cornstarch

1. Trim the soft-shell crabs as described in the accompanying sidebar or have your fishmonger do it.

2. Combine the flour and 1 cup ice water in a mixing bowl and stir with a fork just to mix. Mix as little as possible: It's okay for the batter to be lumpy. Overmixing will make the batter heavy and tough. The batter should be quite thin (about the consistency of heavy cream). Add water as necessary.

3. Just before serving, in a large frying pan or electric skillet pour in the oil to a depth of at least 1 inch and heat to 350°F. Place the cornstarch in a bowl and dip each crab first in it, shaking off the excess, then in the tempura batter. Lower the crabs into the oil and fry until golden brown, about 2 minutes per side, turning once. Work in two batches if necessary to avoid crowding the pan.

4. Transfer the crabs to a wire rack or paper towels to drain. Serve at once with either of the suggested dipping sauces.

Barbara's Garlic-Broiled Florida Lobster

Florida lobster dries out easily and becomes tough when overcooked. My wife, Barbara, has developed a simple and almost foolproof method for cooking this Florida delicacy.

SERVES 4

4 tablespoons (½ stick) unsalted butter

3 shallots, minced

2 cloves garlic, minced

¼ cup loosely packed, finely chopped fresh Italian (flat-leaf) parsley leaves

1 tablespoon fresh lemon juice

1 teaspoon paprika

Salt and freshly ground black pepper, to taste

4 uncooked Florida (spiny) lobster tails (6 to 8 ounces each), split down the back and deveined

1. Preheat the broiler. Set the broiler tray 3 inches from the heat.

2. Melt the butter in a small saucepan over medium heat. Add the shallots and garlic and cook over medium heat for 1 minute. Add the parsley and cook until the vegetables are soft but not brown, 1 to 2 minutes more.

3. Remove the pan from the heat and stir in the lemon juice, paprika, and salt and pepper.

4. Arrange the lobster tails, cut side up, in a roasting pan. Spoon the butter mixture on top. Broil the lobster tails until the butter starts to bubble and the top is lightly browned, 2 to 3 minutes. Rotate the pan once or twice, if necessary, so the lobster tails brown evenly.

FLORIDA LOBSTER

When most Americans say lobster, they are referring to *Homarus americanus*, the bi-clawed Maine lobster. When Floridians speak of lobster, they generally mean *Palinurus argus*, the spiny lobster, a crustacean with giant antennae and a sharp, barb-covered carapace, but no claws. Not that anyone misses the claws, for spiny lobster has plenty of crisp white meat in its tail.

Spiny lobster is abundant in Florida's waters, especially in the Keys, and is found throughout the Caribbean and as far south as Brazil. As with most Caribbean foods, it is known by a variety of names, including *langosta* in Spanish, *langouste* in French, and rock lobster or Florida lobster in English.

Sharp barbs, spines, and armored plates give the spiny lobster a formidable appearance. Actually, the creature is so docile, it almost can be landed by hand. Large spiny lobsters can weigh up to 15 pounds, but the average is 1 to 2 pounds. They are sold whole and as tails. In either case, ask the fishmonger to split them lengthwise. Figure on 6 to 8 ounces of tail meat per person. There are two to three average Florida lobster tails to a pound.

Spiny lobster can be cooked any way you would a Maine lobster. Whole, they are great for stuffing and baking. Lobster tails can be broiled, baked or shelled and used in stews. The meat tends to dry out quickly, so I favor moist cooking methods, like stewing, poaching, and pan-roasting. Spiny lobster is delectable grilled, but marinate it first and baste it well to keep it from drying out.

The lobsters are relatively easy to shell, but interestingly, the fresher they are, the harder it is to remove the shell. If you're having trouble, try steaming the lobster for a few minutes first.

When preparing spiny lobster, I like to remove the translucent vein that runs the length of the tail. It can give the meat a bitter flavor and it is easy to pull out with your fingers.

In Florida spiny lobster is in season from the end of August to April.

5. Turn the broiler off and leave the lobster tails in the oven for 6 to 8 minutes. The residual heat is sufficient to cook the tails through without overcooking them.

Lobster Enchilado

Among Florida's Cuban-Americans the term *enchilado* refers not to a tortilla dish, but to a seafood stew flavored with onions, bell peppers, and cumin. During lobster season, we eat it once a week. Note: If Florida lobster is unavailable, you can use Maine lobster. Shrimp, crab, or scallop enchilado would be prepared the same way. Serve lobster enchilado with Foolproof Rice (page 260) and *Maduros* (fried sweet plantains, page 257).

SERVES 4

1½ to 2 pounds uncooked Florida (spiny) lobster tails
2 tablespoons olive oil
5 cloves garlic, minced
1 onion, finely chopped
1 small red bell pepper, cored,
    seeded, and finely chopped
½ teaspoon dried oregano
½ teaspoon ground cumin, or to taste
½ cup tomato paste
About ½ cup dry white wine
1 bay leaf
Salt and freshly ground black pepper,
    to taste
3 tablespoons finely chopped fresh Italian (flat-leaf)
    parsley leaves, for garnish

1. Remove the lobster meat from the shells and devein it. Cut the meat into 1-inch pieces.

2. Heat the olive oil in a nonreactive sauté pan or frying pan over medium heat. Add the garlic, onion, bell pepper, oregano, and cumin and cook until the onion is lightly browned, about 4 minutes. Stir in the tomato paste and cook for 1 minute. Stir in the wine and bay leaf and bring to a boil.

3. Stir in the lobster. Lower the heat and gently simmer the stew until the lobster is cooked and the oil begins to bead on top of the sauce, about 5 minutes. If the sauce is too dry, add a little more wine. Remove the bay leaf and season with salt and pepper. Garnish with the parsley and serve at once.

Fra Diavolo of Florida Lobster and Baby Clams

When I was growing up, no dish seemed more authentically Italian than the shellfish in spicy tomato sauce I knew as *fra diavolo*. When my wife, Barbara, and I tried to re-create the dish twenty-five years later, we were astonished not to be able to find a single recipe for this Italo-American classic. Cachuchas are tiny pattypan squash-shaped peppers used in Cuban cooking (see sidebar, page 46). They taste a little like scotch bonnets but without the heat. If cachuchas are unavailable, use green bell peppers.

SERVES 4

---

3 tablespoons extra-virgin olive oil, plus 1 teaspoon for the pasta

1 onion, finely chopped

⅓ cup minced shallots

4 cloves garlic, minced

1 to 2 jalapeño chilies, cored, seeded, and minced

8 cachucha peppers or ½ green bell pepper, cored, seeded, and finely chopped

3 large tomatoes (1½ pounds), peeled, seeded, and finely chopped

3 tablespoons Cognac or other brandy

¼ cup dry white wine

About 1 tablespoon balsamic vinegar

3 tablespoons tomato paste

1 tablespoon chopped anchovy fillets or anchovy paste (optional)

2 bay leaves

½ teaspoon finely chopped fresh or dried thyme

½ cup finely chopped fresh Italian (flat-leaf) parsley

½ teaspoon hot pepper flakes, or to taste

Salt and freshly ground black pepper, to taste

4 uncooked Florida (spiny) lobster tails (6 to 8 ounces each), split down the back and deveined

24 littleneck clams (the smaller, the better), scrubbed

10 ounces dried spaghetti or fettuccine, for serving

1. Heat the olive oil in a large nonreactive sauté pan. Add the onion, shallots, garlic, jalapeños, and peppers. Cook the mixture, uncovered, over medium heat, stirring often, until it just begins to brown, about 5 minutes.

2. Increase the heat to high and stir in the tomatoes. Cook until the tomato liquid begins to evaporate, about 1 minute. Stir in the Cognac and bring to a boil. Stir in the wine and vinegar and bring to a boil.

3. Stir in the tomato paste, anchovies, bay leaves, thyme, half of the parsley, the hot pepper flakes, and salt and pepper. Simmer until thick and well flavored, about 10 minutes. (The recipe can be prepared up to 24 hours ahead to this stage. Let cool to room temperature, then cover and refrigerate.)

4. Add the lobster tails, cut side down. Cook until the meat begins to turn white, about 2 minutes. Turn the lobster tails and stir in the clams. Cover the pan.

5. Gently simmer the mixture until the lobster and clams are cooked: The lobster will be firm and white, the shells of the clams will be open; the whole process will take 6 to 8 minutes. Do not overcook. Discard any clams that haven't opened. Correct the seasonings of the sauce, adding salt, vinegar, or hot pepper flakes to taste. The mixture should be highly seasoned.

6. Meanwhile, cook the pasta in 3 quarts boiling salted water with the 1 teaspoon oil until al dente, about 8 minutes. Drain well.

7. Serve the *fra diavolo* over the cooked pasta. Sprinkle the dish with the remaining parsley and serve at once.

AN EVERGLADES FROG HUNT

Norman Padget gets ready to go to work when most people are just coming home. His "uniform" looks like a cross between safari wear and deep sea fishing garb. He rides to work on an airboat, a uniquely Floridian vessel consisting of a 12 foot skiff propelled by a 6-cylinder airplane engine. Padget is a frog hunter and for the next 6 hours, he'll skim the Everglades on his noisy boat in pursuit of a food that is equally prized by backwoods fishermen and high-falutin chefs.

Padget's hunting grounds are a marsh lying a half hour west of Palm Beach. He works at night (frogs are nocturnal), setting out an hour before nightfall. The frogs are recognizable by their glow-in-the-dark eyes. On a typical night, Padget will land about 60 pounds of frogs (30 pounds of frogs' legs), which he sells to seafood purveyors and restaurants. The frogs' legs are frozen in water-filled Ziploc bags, which prevents them from getting freezer burn.

Even frozen, Padget' frogs' legs are tender, succulent, mild flavored, and incred-

Curry-Fried Frogs' Legs

Coopertown is a tiny town in the Florida Everglades—a post office, restaurant, and air-boat-ride concession clustered together on the Tamiami Trail. The community is so small, you could miss it if you blink at the wrong moment. It was there that I tasted my first Florida frogs' legs. They were enormous by French standards and exceptionally sweet and meaty. The imported frogs' legs pale in comparison. In this recipe, curry lends a West Indian twist to an Everglades classic. If frogs' legs are unavailable, you could substitute chicken wings. Serve the Tamarind Cream Sauce on page 126 for dipping.

ibly sweet. They are so far superior to imported frogs' legs the two shouldn't even be compared. As for the inexpensive Indian and Bangladeshi frogs' legs flooding the market these days, "they have about as much flavor as the cardboard they're packed in," says Padget. "Nothing beats an Everglades frogs' leg." I heartily agree.

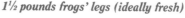

1½ pounds frogs' legs (ideally fresh)
1 cup all-purpose flour
1 tablespoon best-quality curry powder
1 teaspoon cayenne pepper
Salt, to taste
1 egg, beaten
½ cup buttermilk
1 cup fine cracker crumbs
About 2 cups vegetable oil, for frying

1. Wash the frogs' legs and blot dry.

2. Combine the flour, curry, cayenne, and salt in a shallow bowl and whisk to mix. Combine the egg and buttermilk in another bowl and whisk to mix. Place the cracker crumbs in a third bowl.

3. Just before serving, pour in the oil to a depth of at least 1 inch in a heavy frying pan or electric skillet and heat to 350°F. Using 2 forks, dip the frogs' legs first in the flour mixture, then in the egg mixture, and finally in the cracker crumbs, shaking off the excess after each.

4. Fry the frogs' legs until golden brown, turning with a wire skimmer, 1 to 2 minutes total. Work in several batches so as not to crowd the pan. Drain the frogs' legs on paper towels and serve on doily-lined plates with ramekins of Tamarind Cream Sauce in the center for dipping.

Birds of Paradise

Turkey Picadillo

Lychee Salsa

SOY

Miami Wings

Chicken Tropicana

My first Thanksgiving in Florida certainly was a shock. I'd moved to the land of the sun and the palm tree after 15 years in New England. I'd come to assume that Thanksgiving was perforce a cold weather experience, a time of frost on the windows and breath condensing in the air, of mountains of steaming food enjoyed by the warmth of a crackling fire.

So, my first year here, I slavishly re-created a New England Thanksgiving dinner. How strange it was to sit down to turkey with stuffing, cranberry sauce, and pumpkin pie when the temperature was 85 degrees! By the next year, the climate had begun to exercise a tropical influence on my cooking. The candied sweet potatoes of the North became a boniato (Cuban sweet potato) gratin. Fiery datil peppers ignited my traditional cranberry jelly. Northern pumpkin pie gave way to calabaza (West Indian pumpkin) flan.

But the dish that underwent the most dramatic metamorphosis was the Thanksgiving turkey. Our Cuban friend, Elida Proenza, mashed cumin, oregano, and a whole head of garlic to an aromatic paste with a pestle in a mortar. The acidic juice of the *naranja agria* (sour orange) was added to make a classic Cuban marinade called *adobo*. We loosened the skin of the bird and spread the *adobo* underneath. The bird was marinated overnight, then roasted in a cloth bag. What resulted was one of the tastiest turkeys ever to grace my Thanksgiving table.

Turkey isn't the only poultry to undergo a metamorphosis under the tropical sun. West Indian cooks in Florida stuff their chickens with an aromatic paste of garlic, scallions, chives, and scotch bonnet chilies called "seasoning." Cuban cooks turn chicken backs and other undesirable pieces into crackling, crisp *chicharrónes*. The duckling à l'orange of Continental cuisine becomes smoky, grilled duck breast with lychee salsa. Bobwhite quails from central Florida come smothered in shiitake mushroom gravy.

I can't claim that Floridians eat more poultry than elsewhere in the U.S., although the health- and weight-conscious diet of the bathing-suit crowd tends to favor fowl over heavier red meats. But thanks to our incredible ethnic diversity, Floridians enjoy some of the nation's most distinctive poultry dishes.

Miami Wings

Buffalo has nothing on Miami when it comes to savory chicken wings. In place of the traditional Tabasco sauce marinade, I favor a sauce made with fiery datil chili peppers (see the sidebar on page 244). There are two options here—Dat'l Do-It Hot Sauce, a mildly hot, tomato-based sauce and Devil Drops, an incendiary vinegar-based sauce—both made in St. Augustine with Florida's unique datil chili pepper. Available at select gourmet shop, the sauces also can be ordered by mail from Dat'l Do-It, P. O. Box 4019, St. Augustine, FL 32085; (800) HOT-DATL. Another hot sauce can be substituted in a pinch. The wings can be deep-fried, Buffalo-style, or grilled to reduce the overall fat content.

SERVES 4 TO 6

MARINADE:
1 cup Dat'l Do-It Hot Sauce, Devil Drops,
*   or other favorite hot sauce*
½ cup fresh lime juice
½ cup soy sauce or tamari
Plenty of freshly ground black pepper

2 pounds chicken wings, washed, blotted dry, and
*   separated at the joints, tips discarded*

1. Combine the ingredients for the marinade in a large bowl and whisk until smooth.

2. Add the chicken wings and toss to coat with the marinade. Marinate, covered, in the refrigerator for at least 4 hours, but preferably overnight. Turn the wings several times during this time.

3. Preheat a barbecue grill to very hot or preheat the broiler with the broiler tray 3 inches from the heat.

4. Just before serving, drain the wings. Grill or broil until golden brown and cooked, 2 to 3 minutes per side.

Arroz con Pollo
(Chicken and Yellow Rice)

This dish is one of the glories of Hispanic gastronomy. Think of it as a landlubber's paella. Like Spanish paella, *arroz con pollo* is made with short-grain Valencia-style rice. Look for it in Hispanic markets or supermarkets that cater to a Hispanic clientele. Alternatively, you can use arborio rice from Italy. Unlike paella, however, *arroz con pollo* is colored and flavored with annatto oil (see page 333), not saffron.

*1 large chicken (about 4 pounds), cut into
    8 even-size pieces*
1 teaspoon dried oregano
1 teaspoon ground cumin
½ teaspoon freshly ground white pepper
1 tablespoon red wine vinegar

SOFRITO AND BROTH:
2 tablespoons Annatto Oil (see page 333) or olive oil
1 small onion, finely chopped
1 small red bell pepper, cored, seeded, and finely chopped
3 cloves garlic, minced
3 tablespoons finely chopped fresh cilantro
1 small tomato, seeded and diced
3 cups water
1 cup dry white wine
1½ cups beer
½ teaspoon annatto seeds, or ¼ teaspoon saffron
1 tablespoon tomato paste
¼ cup pimiento-stuffed green olives
Salt and freshly ground black pepper, to taste

TO FINISH THE DISH:
1 pound Valencia rice, or other short-grained rice
*½ cup petits pois (tiny green peas), canned or
    frozen, thawed*
2 red pimientos, diced

1. Wash the chicken and blot dry with paper towels. Mix the oregano, cumin, white pepper, and vinegar in a large glass bowl. Add the chicken, turning the pieces to cover with the mixture. Let marinate for 15 minutes.

2. Heat the oil in a large heatproof casserole. Brown the chicken pieces all over, about 2 minutes per side. Transfer the chicken to a platter and pour out all but 2 tablespoons of the fat.

3. Add the onion, bell pepper, garlic, and cilantro and cook over medium heat until soft but not brown, 1 to 2 minutes. Add the tomato and cook for 1 minute more. Return the chicken to the casserole and cook for 1 minute.

4. Add the water, wine, beer, saffron (if using instead of annatto seeds), tomato paste, olives, and salt and pepper. Bring the mixture to a boil. Reduce the heat, cover, and gently simmer the chicken for 30 minutes.

5. While the chicken is cooking, place the annatto seeds in a small saucepan with ¼ cup of the chicken cooking liquid. Gently simmer for 5 minutes. Strain the mixture back into the chicken. (The recipe can be prepared ahead to this stage.)

6. Finish the dish: Thoroughly wash the rice. The easiest way to do this is to place it in a large bowl with cold water to cover by several inches. Swirl the rice with your fingers and pour off the water. Continue adding water and swirling and draining the rice until the water runs clear.

7. Thirty minutes before serving, bring the chicken mixture to a boil. Stir in the rice, reduce the heat, cover the pan, and gently simmer the rice until tender, 20 to 25 minutes. If the rice starts to dry out, add more water. If the mixture looks too soupy, remove the cover during the last 5 minutes of cooking.

8. Just before the rice is finished, stir in half of the petits pois and pimientos. Use the remainder to garnish the top and serve at once.

Chicken Tropicana

Mango, papaya, and pineapple lend this stovetop sauté a tropical accent. If you're in a hurry, you can use the canned coconut milk sold at

Hispanic and Asian markets and at an increasing number of supermarkets. Just be sure to use the unsweetened kind.

SERVES 4

----

1 chicken (about 3½ to 4 pounds), cut into 8 even-size pieces

Salt and freshly ground black pepper, to taste

1 tablespoon vegetable oil

2 tablespoons unsalted butter

¼ cup finely chopped shallots

1 clove garlic, minced

1 tablespoon finely chopped candied ginger or fresh ginger

2 cups Coconut Milk (see page 331), or canned, unsweetened

¼ cup orange marmalade, or to taste

1 cup diced fresh papaya

1 cup diced fresh mango

1 cup diced fresh pineapple

½ cup cashews, lightly toasted (see page 311)

¼ cup toasted coconut (see page 301)

1. Wash the chicken and blot dry with paper towels. Season with the salt and pepper. Heat the oil in a large sauté pan. Brown the chicken on all sides, 3 to 4 minutes. Transfer the chicken to a platter and pour off all the fat.

2. Melt the butter in the pan. Sauté the shallots, garlic, and ginger until soft but not brown, about 2 minutes. Return the chicken to the pan and stir in the coconut milk, marmalade, and salt and pepper.

3. Simmer the chicken, uncovered, until almost cooked, 15 to 20 minutes. Stir in the fresh fruits and the cashews, and cook the chicken through, about 5 minutes more. Correct the seasonings, adding salt and pepper to taste. If the sauce needs sweetness, add a little more orange marmalade.

4. Transfer the chicken to a bowl or platter and spoon the sauce and fruit over it. Sprinkle the toasted coconut on top and serve at once.

Florida Fricassee

Each of Florida's ethnic subcultures has a version of chicken fricassee. Cumin and oregano predominate in the Cuban version, chilies and lime juice in the Haitian. This particular recipe acts as a Miami melting pot and reflects both.

SERVES 4

1 chicken (3½ to 4 pounds), cut into 8 even pieces
3 tablespoons fresh lime juice
2 cloves garlic, minced
1 teaspoon salt
½ teaspoon ground cumin
3 tablespoons olive oil
4 shallots, finely chopped (about ¼ cup)
½ red bell pepper, cored, seeded, and finely
     chopped
½ scotch bonnet chili, seeded and minced
1½ cups dry white wine
1½ cups Chicken Stock (see page 329) or water
¼ cup tomato purée
Spice bundle of 3 annatto seeds, 3 allspice berries,
     and 1 bay leaf tied together in a piece of
     cheese cloth
Freshly ground black pepper
2 baking potatoes, peeled and cut into 1-inch pieces
2 carrots, peeled and cut into 1-inch pieces
¼ cup pimiento-stuffed green olives

1. Wash the chicken and blot dry on paper towels. Mix together the lime juice, garlic, salt, and cumin in a large bowl. Add the chicken pieces and toss to coat with the marinade. Marinate, covered, in the refrigerator for 1 to 2 hours, turning the pieces once or twice during this time.

LITTLE HAITI

Little Haiti lies only a few blocks west of Biscayne Boulevard, one of Miami's major thoroughfares, but the distance could be measured in centuries. Here, in the heart of a major American metropolis, bandana-ed women sell okra and pigeon peas on the street corners. Roosters run free in the streets, while goats graze tethered in vacant lots. Enter a store and you'll find bundles of strange medicinal herbs, religious candles, and yes, tiny dolls for the practice of voodoo. Then take a seat at one of the humble eateries and you'll experience foods you never dreamed existed.

Miami is home to America's largest Haitian population. The official count is 73,000, but the figure is certainly higher.

Unlike Cuban and Nicaraguan cooking, Haitian food is not well known outside the immediate community, but the adventurous eater will find plenty of exotic dishes here to pique his or her palate.

One Haitian specialty is *griots,* pork cubes marinated in garlic and sour orange juice and fried to a crusty brown. Another is *lambi,* conch, which is stewed until meltingly tender with onions, garlic, Caribbean chives, thyme, and fiery chilies. Like most peoples of the Caribbean, Haitians serve some sort of plantain dish and rice and beans at every meal. The bean of choice is the pigeon pea, which tastes like a cross between a green pea and blackeye pea.

These and other dishes are accompanied by a *sauce piment,* a fiery relish made with shredded cabbage, carrots, vinegar, and Haitian chilies. The latter look like elongated scotch bonnets and are every bit as hot. The predominant flavorings in Haitian cooking are sour orange juice, garlic, chives, allspice berries, cinnamon, star anise, and thyme. A less familiar ingredient is the djon-djon, a tiny aromatic black mushroom used as a flavoring for rice. All in all, Haitian food is incredibly flavorful and it deserves to be better known.

2. Heat half the olive oil in a large sauté pan over medium heat. Brown the chicken on all sides, 1 to 2 minutes per side. Transfer the chicken to a platter and pour off the fat from the pan.

3. Add the remaining oil to the pan. Cook the shallots, bell pepper, and chili over medium heat until soft but not brown, about 2 minutes. Return the chicken to the pan and stir in the wine, stock or water, tomato purée, spice bundle, and pepper. Bring the mixture to a boil. Reduce the heat, cover the pan, and gently simmer the chicken until half cooked, 10 to 15 minutes.

4. Stir in the potatoes, carrots, and olives. Continue simmering until the chicken is cooked and vegetables are tender, 10 to 15 minutes more. Remove and discard the spice bundle. Correct the seasoning, adding salt and pepper to taste.

Note: This is a rustic dish, so I serve it without ceremony, but you can garnish the chicken with chopped parsley, cilantro, grated lemon peel, or a mixture of all three.

Chicken Adobo

This recipe was inspired by a dish served at Miami's famous restaurant Yuca, which specializes in *nueva cubana* cooking—Cuban nouvelle cuisine. Chef Douglas Rodriguez serves chicken halves, which he bones before grilling. For ease in preparation, I prefer using boneless, skinless chicken breasts. Note the use of both fresh and dried herbs. "I like the colored speckles of fresh herbs and the flavor of the dried," explains Rodriguez. Serve with the *Mojo* on page 114 or the Boniato Gratin on page 254.

SERVES 4

MARINADE:
3 cloves garlic, coursely chopped
1 shallot, minced
½ teaspoon ground cumin
½ teaspoon dried oregano
½ teaspoon dried thyme
1 tablespoon chopped fresh cilantro
1 tablespoon chopped fresh parsley leaves
3 tablespoons fresh sour orange or lime juice
2 tablespoons extra-virgin olive oil
Plenty of salt and freshly ground black pepper

2 large whole boneless, skinless chicken breasts
      (about 1½ pounds), split in half (4 halves),
      washed, and blotted dry

1. Mash the garlic, shallot, and herbs to a paste in a mortar with a pestle. Work in the remaining ingredients for the marinade. Alternatively, the ingredients for the marinade can be puréed in a blender.

2. Transfer the marinade to a nonreactive baking dish and add the chicken breasts. Turn to coat the breasts with the marinade. Cover the dish and marinate the chicken in the refrigerator for 30 minutes to 1 hour. Turn the chicken breasts once or twice during that time.

3. Preheat a barbecue grill to medium heat or preheat the broiler with the broiler tray 3 inches from the heat.

4. Grill the chicken breasts over medium heat until just cooked, about 2 minutes per side. Broiling time is about the same.

ADOBO:
THE KNIGHTLY MARINADE

Spend any time at all in a Cuban kitchen and you're sure to hear the word *adobo*. This fragrant paste of garlic, salt, cumin, oregano, and sour orange or lime juice is Cuba's national marinade. Fish, shellfish, poultry, and meat all receive a baptism in *adobo* prior to grilling, sautéing, or deep-frying. The preparation is so essential to Cuban culinary well-being, there's even a verb, *adobar*.

According to Maricel Presilla, a professor of Hispanic history, *adobar* is a medieval word that turns up in legal documents from as early as the thirteenth century, when it meant "to join" or "to put together." Presilla hypothesizes that the Spanish term comes from the Old French word *adober,* "to adorn"— the origin of our word "to dub." When a man was dubbed a knight, he was adorned with knightly paraphernalia. In the culinary sense of the word, a meat is enobled by a garlic and lime juice or vinegar marinade.

The first *adobos* were strong salt and vinegar mixtures designed to prevent perishable meats from spoiling. To this day, Galicians in northeastern Spain marinate pork in a mixture of paprika, wine, garlic, and salt to make the curiously named *carnes mortas,* literally, "dead meat." *Adobo* has largely passed out of existence in the rest of Spain, but it flourishes in the former colonies.

The Conquistadors brought *adobo* to the New World, where it was retooled for the indigenous ingredients. In Cuba, for example, the primary flavorings became garlic, cumin, and sour orange juice. Puerto Ricans favored a tangy mixture of vinegar and oregano. In Mexico *adobo* came to refer to a fiery paste of sour orange juice and chipotle (smoked jalapeño) chilies. The preparation even reached the Philippines, where it now describes a chicken stew flavored with coconut milk, vinegar, garlic, and annatto seed. Nowadays, the common elements in any *adobo* are garlic, salt, and some sort of acid.

Supermarkets sell a powdered *adobo*, but it is a sorry substitute for the homemade. To make a good all-purpose adobo, pound 6 cloves garlic, 2 teaspoons salt, and ½ teaspoon each ground cumin and dried oregano to a smooth paste in a mortar with a pestle. Mix in ½ cup fresh sour orange juice or lime juice. Marinate fish in this mixture for 30 minutes to 1 hour, chicken breasts for 1 to 2 hours, and large cuts of meat overnight. Refrigerate all during marination.

Plantain-Stuffed Chicken in a Pecan Crust

Florida doesn't leap to mind with the mention of pecans, but limited quantities of the South's favorite nut are grown in northern Florida. The saltiness of the ham counterpoints the sweetness of the plantain stuffing, which I think is delicious.

SERVES 4

2 large, whole boneless, skinless chicken breasts
     (about 1½ pounds)
1½ cups pecan pieces
3 to 4 tablespoons canola oil
1 ripe plantain, peeled and thinly sliced
Salt and freshly ground black pepper, to taste
4 very thin slices Smithfield ham or prosciutto
About ½ cup all-purpose flour
2 eggs, beaten
3 tablespoons Clarified Butter (see page 328)
     or canola oil, for frying

1. Wash the chicken and blot dry with a paper towel. Remove the "tenders," the long cylindrical strips of meat on the bone side of the breasts. (Save them for stir-frying.) Trim off any bits of sinew or fat. Cut the breasts lengthwise in half. Lay each half flat at the edge of a cutting board and cut a deep pocket in the side, using a thin-bladed knife. Make the pocket as large and deep as you can without piercing the top, bottom or sides. It helps to hold the breast flat with the palm of your other hand when cutting.

2. Grind the pecans to a fine powder in a food processor. Run the machine in spurts. Do not overprocess, or the nuts will become oily.

POUNDING YOUR WAY TO FLAVOR

Like most Americans, I have a kitchen filled with the latest technological gadgetry. My espresso machine churns out frothy cups of cappuccino. An electric bread baker fills my kitchen with the smells of a professional bake shop. But the pride and joy of my cookware collection is a wooden mortar and pestle made in 1890, a gift from my pharmacist grandfather.

A mortar, of course, is a sturdy bowl; the pestle, a club-shaped implement, for pounding. Whenever a Cuban or West Indian starts to cook, chances are he or she will reach for a mortar and pestle. Garlic and salt, chilies and herbs will be pounded to an aromatic paste used to season meats, poultry, and seafood.

Pounding ingredients in a mortar with a pestle produces a different flavor than puréeing the ingredients in a food processor. The pounding action of the pestle extracts more aromatic oils than the whirling of a metal blade. The flavors mesh more evenly to produce a more harmonious end product. This truth is not lost on cultures as diverse as

Mexican, Thai, and Cuban, where the mortar and pestle rank among a cook's most prized possessions. Food processors are great for chopping ingredients, but nothing beats a mortar and pestle for making a spice paste.

In Mexico I've seen lava stone mortars and pestles, in Thailand marble mortars. Here in Florida, as in the Caribbean, the preferred material is wood. When buying a mortar and pestle, choose the largest, deepest mortar you can find. Shallow mortars may make nice shelf decorations, but the ingredients will spatter when you start to pound them. I suggest you avoid porcelain mortars and pestles, which shatter if you use them too vigorously.

3. Heat the oil in a small frying pan over medium heat. Panfry the plantain slices until golden brown, 1 to 2 minutes per side. Transfer the plantains to paper towels to drain and cool.

4. Season the plantain slices with the salt and pepper and place a few in the pocket of each chicken breast. Place 1 ham slice in each chicken breast as well.

5. Season the chicken breasts with the salt and pepper. Place the flour in a shallow bowl or on a paper towel, the eggs in another, and the pecans in another. Just before serving, dredge each chicken breast in the flour, shaking off the excess, then in the egg, then in the pecans.

6. Heat the clarified butter in a heavy frying pan. Panfry the chicken breasts over medium heat until the coating is crusty and brown and the meat is cooked, about 5 minutes per side. If the crust starts to brown too much, turn down the heat. Alternatively, the chicken can be browned in the frying pan and baked in the oven. Insert a metal skewer to test for doneness. It should come out hot to the touch.

7. The chicken breasts can be served whole. For a more attractive presentation, you can slice the breasts crosswise on the diagonal and fan out the slices. Serve at once.

Bajan Roast Game Hens

Florida's ethnic cooking is dominated by our Hispano-American community. But south Florida is also home to one of the nation's largest West Indian communities, a presence witnessed by numerous Jamaican, Bajan (Barbadian), and Trinidadian cook shops. Many Bajan recipes start with "seasoning," a redolent mixture of garlic, shallots, chives, and scotch bonnet chilies. The ingredients can be pounded together in a mortar with a pestle or puréed in a food processor. The Coconut Rice on page 261 makes a good accompaniment.

SERVES 6

3 cloves garlic, coarsely chopped

2 teaspoons minced fresh ginger

2 shallots, chopped

½ scotch bonnet chili or 1 jalapeño, seeded and
     minced

4 scallions, trimmed and chopped

1 cup chopped fresh Italian (flat-leaf) parsley

½ cup chopped fresh cilantro

1 teaspoon fresh thyme leaves

¼ teaspoon ground allspice

About 2 tablespoons fresh lime juice

4 tablespoons (½ stick) softened unsalted
     butter or olive oil

Salt and freshly ground black pepper, to taste

6 game hens

1. Prepare the "seasoning": Mash the garlic, ginger, shallots, chili, scallions, parsley, cilantro, and thyme to a paste in a mortar or purée in a food processor. Work in the allspice, lime juice, butter, and salt and pepper. Correct the seasonings, adding salt, pepper, and lime juice to taste.

2. Preheat the oven to 400°F.

3. Wash the game hens and blot dry with paper towels. Loosen the skin on the hens. To do so, start at the neck of each bird and tunnel your fingers under the skin to separate the skin from the breast meat. Try to loosen the skin over the breast, thighs, and drumsticks. Work carefully so as not to tear the skin.

4. Spread half of the seasoning mixture under the skins of the game hens. The easiest way to do this is to place a spoonful of the mixture under the skin covering the breast.

Rub the skin to force the mixture over the thigh and drumstick meat. Spread the remaining seasoning over the breast skin of the birds.

5. Roast the birds on a rack set in a roasting pan until golden brown, 30 to 40 minutes. When cooked, the juices will run clear. Serve at once.

Roast Duck
with Tamarind-Chipotle Glaze

Tamarind is a tropical seedpod with pulp that tastes like a cross between prunes and lime juice. You've probably tasted it even if you don't realize it: Tamarind is a key flavoring in Worcestershire sauce and Pickapeppa sauce. Fresh tamarind can be found at specialty produce shops and Hispanic markets. Its preparation is explained on page 4. Hispanic markets sell frozen tamarind purée. Both Hispanic and Asian markets sell gummy balls of peeled tamarind pulp, which can be turned into purée by following the instructions also on page 4. Chipotle chilies are smoked jalapeños. They're available both dried and canned at gourmet shops and Hispanic markets. This may seem like a rather involved way to cook duck, but it produces crisp skin and moist, tender meat. The ducks are roasted upside-down for the first 45 minutes to help prevent the breast meat from drying out.

SERVES 4

DUCK AND MARINADE:

2 ducklings (4 to 5 pounds each)

3 cloves garlic, coarsely chopped

2 teaspoons minced fresh ginger

½ teaspoon ground bay leaf

½ teaspoon salt

¼ cup fresh orange juice

GLAZE:

2 chipotle chilies, canned or dried
    (if dried, soak in ½ cup hot water to soften,
    30 minutes)

¼ cup distilled white vinegar

¼ cup (packed) dark brown sugar

¼ cup granulated sugar

1½ cups tamarind purée

¼ cup molasses

¼ cup soy sauce

2 tablespoons tomato paste

1. Preheat the oven to 300°F.

2. Prepare the duck and marinade: Remove any lumps of fat from the ducks. Wash the ducks and blot dry with paper towels. Loosen the skins on the ducks. To do so, start at the neck of each bird and tunnel your fingers under the skin to separate the skin from the breast meat. Try to loosen the skin over the thighs and drumsticks, as well. Work carefully so as not to tear the skin.

3. In a mortar, combine the garlic, ginger, bay leaf, and salt and mash to a smooth paste. Work in the orange juice. Spread this mixture under the skins of the ducks. The easiest way to do this is to place a spoonful of the mixture under the skin covering the breast. Rub the skin to force the mixture over the leg meat. Truss the birds and place them, breast sides down, in a lightly greased roasting pan.

4. Roast the ducks for 45 minutes.

5. Meanwhile, prepare the tamarind-chipotle glaze: Drain and finely chop the chilies. For a mild sauce remove the seeds; for a hotter sauce leave them in.

6. Combine the chipotles, vinegar, and the sugars in a nonreactive heavy saucepan and boil until reduced by half, about 5 minutes. Whisk in all of the remaining ingredients. Simmer the glaze, uncovered, until thick and syrupy, about 10 minutes. Correct the seasonings, adding salt and pepper to taste.

7. Pour the fat out of the roasting pan and invert the ducks. Brush the skin with the tamarind-chipotle glaze. Roast the ducks, brushing the skin with glaze from time to time, for another 45 minutes, or until tender.

8. Transfer the ducks to a cutting board. Cut in half with poultry shears, removing the trussing and backbone. Arrange the duck halves on plates or a platter and brush with the remaining glaze.

Oak-Grilled Duck Breasts with Lychee Salsa

Duckling with lychees is a classic Cantonese dish. The last time I ordered it at a Chinese restaurant, I received a plate of greasy fried duck with sugary, canned lychees and a gluey, unnaturally red gravy. I came away feeling that there must be a better way to combine these marvelous ingredients.

I got the idea for this dish during lychee season last year, when our friends, tropical-fruit growers Mark and Kiki Ellenby, gave us a whole box of fresh lychees. Duck breasts can be purchased at specialty butcher shops. I like to grill the breasts but they can also be cooked in the broiler.

SERVES 4

2 large duck breasts (12 to 16 ounces each),
*   split in half (4 halves), washed and blotted dry*
1 tablespoon Oriental sesame oil
2 tablespoons soy sauce
1 tablespoon honey
½ teaspoon of your favorite hot sauce
Lychee Salsa (recipe follows)
1 cup hickory or other hardwood chips,
*   if grilling, soaked in cold water for 2 hours*

1. Trim off any excess fat or skin from the split duck breasts; there should just be enough skin to cover the top of the breasts. Using a very sharp knife, score the skin on each breast, cutting a fine crosshatch pattern through the skin, just to but not through the meat. Scoring the skin helps the fat melt out during cooking.

2. Combine the sesame oil, soy sauce, honey, and hot sauce in a large shallow bowl and whisk to mix. Add the duck breasts and turn to coat with the marinade. Marinate, covered, in the refrigerator for 1 to 4 hours. Turn the breasts 2 or 3 times during this time.

3. Prepare the Lychee Salsa: Preheat a barbecue grill to medium hot or preheat the broiler with the broiler tray 3 inches from the heat.

4. Just before cooking, place the soaked wood chips, if using, on the coals. Grill the duck breasts, skin sides down, over medium heat until the skin is crisp and golden brown, about 2 minutes. Move the breasts as necessary to avoid flareups from the dripping fat. (Flareups can be controlled

WHERE THERE'S SMOKE

Y ou don't need a degree in restaurateuring to know that America is going up in smoke; That is: fragrant smoke from smoldering oak and hickory; fruit-scented cherry smoke; and tongue-tingling clouds of mesquite. Once the specialty of backwoods smokehouses, smoked foods are turning up at the trendiest restaurants and gourmet shops. It's easy to smoke foods at home. You don't even need any special equipment (see page 52).

Any hardwood can be used for smoking. (Don't use a soft wood, like pine. It contains too much resin.) Hardwood chips can be purchased at most cookware shops and gourmet food stores.

Below are some of the most commonly used woods.

ALDER: A mild, clean, sweet-flavored wood that would best be described as elegant. There is nothing bashful about its flavor, but it isn't overpowering. Alder is well suited to delicate foods, like fish and poultry.

with a few well-aimed squirts of a water pistol.) Turn the breasts and grill on the meat side, about 1 minute more for medium-rare. Broiling time will be about the same.

5. Serve the grilled duck breasts with the salsa on the side.

APPLE: Tangy and sharp-flavored, with a bite like that of Scotch whisky. It's good with meat and game.

CHERRY: Sweet and fruity, with distinct cherry overtones. These chips are good for smoking fish, duck, and pheasant.

HICKORY: This popular wood produces a mild smoky flavor. It goes well with just about everything.

MAPLE: Mellow, mild, and sweet. This is a good choice for people who like a delicate smoke flavor. Use it on poultry, fish, and light meats.

OAK: The best all-purpose wood, with a spicy, well-balanced flavor that goes well with all types of food, especially poultry and meat.

PECAN SHELLS: These produce a robust smoky flavor that goes well with pork and lamb.

LYCHEE SALSA

s there any fruit more lovely, more lasciviously luscious than a fresh lychee? To peel and seed a fresh lychee, cut it in half around the middle, down to the stone. Twist the halves in opposite directions to free one half from the stone; pluck the stone from the remaining half with your fingers. Pinch the skin at the rounded part of each half to pop out the fruit. This salsa goes exceptionally well with duck.

MAKES 2 CUPS

1 pound fresh lychees, halved, seeded, and peeled (2 cups flesh)
½ yellow bell pepper, cored, seeded, and diced
½ red bell pepper, cored, seeded, and diced
1 jalapeño chili, seeded and minced
¼ cup finely chopped fresh mint leaves
3 scallions, trimmed and finely chopped
3 to 4 tablespoons fresh lime juice
1 tablespoon finely chopped candied ginger
1 tablespoon honey (optional)
Salt and freshly ground black pepper, to taste

Combine all of the ingredients in a mixing bowl, and gently toss to mix. Correct the seasonings, adding salt, lime juice, or honey to taste. The salsa should be a little sweet and a little sour.

THE LUSCIOUS LYCHEE

There's very little to recommend summer in south Florida. The humidity turns a freshly pressed shirt into a soggy mess in a manner of minutes. Every mosquito in creation seems to think you're a walking banquet. But perverse as it may sound, I actually look forward to this unseasonably hot season. For June

marks the start of Florida lychee season. And lychees are just about my favorite fruit in the world.

Native to China, lychees measure 1¼ inches across and have a rough, red, knobbly skin. Inside is a succulent white flesh with a single shiny brown seed in the center. The flavor of the lychee hints at honey and muscat grapes, but it is far more luscious than either.

Lychees grew in Florida as early as 1886. But it wasn't until the 1980s that a serious commercial crop was planted in the Redlands, an hour south of Miami. In 1992, the state's lychee production was about 250,000 pounds, up from 75,000 pounds in 1990.

Currently, there are about 200 acres of the majestic trees under cultivation.

Aficionados debate the merits of the Mauritius lychee versus the Brewster (the two main varieties grown in Florida). Mauritius are early ripeners—in season from late-May to mid-June. Enrobed in a pink-yellow skin, the flesh is firm, crisp, and moistly crunchy, with more acidity than the Brewster's. Mauritius lychees are also easier to peel.

Brewsters have the bright red skins one usually associates with lychees. The flesh is sweeter but more watery than the flesh of the Mauritius. Brewsters have more slender seeds, which the locals have nicknamed "chicken tongues." To me the acidic Mauritius has a cleaner, more elegant flavor, but you can't beat a Brewster's velvety texture and sensuous mouth feel. Brewsters are in season from the middle to end of June.

Lychees are generally sold in bunches on snippets of branches, but for a higher price you can buy bags of completely stemmed fruits. They dry out quickly; store lychees in a plastic bag in the refrigerator and use them within a few days. They can also be frozen.

To eat a lychee out of hand, gently bite the fruit in the middle with your incisors to crack the skin. Pull off the top half of the skin and squeeze the bottom half to pop the fruit into your mouth. It is a snap to nibble the fruit off the smooth, shiny seed.

Florida Quail
with Shiitake Gravy

In 1979, I visited Gainesville, Florida, while on tour with the French cooking school, La Varenne. Our hosts served us a northern Floridian specialty, freshly hunted bobwhite quails in mushroom sauce. The birds themselves were delectable, but the sauce turned out to be Campbell's Cream of Mushroom Soup. Nonetheless, the combination left me with a pleasant memory of central Florida. Here's a remake of the dish, using shiitake mushrooms and more than a decade of nostalgia for seasoning. Any exotic mushroom can be substituted for the shiitakes, especially morels and porcini.

SERVES 4

8 small (4 ounces each) or 4 large (8 ounces each) quails

Salt and freshly ground black pepper, to taste

2 tablespoons vegetable oil

3 tablespoons unsalted butter

12 ounces fresh shiitake mushrooms, stemmed

¼ cup finely chopped shallots

1 clove garlic, minced

3 tablespoons Cognac, or other brandy

2 cups Chicken Stock (see page 329)

Bouquet Garni of 1 bay leaf, 2 sprigs fresh thyme (½ teaspoon dried), and 2 to 3 sprigs fresh parsley, tied in a piece of cheesecloth

1½ teaspoons all-purpose flour

½ cup sour cream

2 tablespoons chopped fresh Italian (flat-leaf) parsley, for garnish

1. Wash the quails and blot dry with paper towels. Season the quails inside and out with the salt and pepper. Truss the birds with string. Heat the oil in a sauté pan. Brown the quails on all sides over medium-high heat, about 2 minutes per side. Transfer the quails to a platter. Discard the fat in the pan.

2. Melt half of the butter in the pan. Sauté the shiitake caps until soft, about 2 minutes. Transfer them to the platter with the quails.

3. Melt the remaining butter in the pan. Cook the shallots and garlic over medium heat until soft but not brown, about 3 minutes. Add the Cognac and bring to a boil. Return the quails to the pan. Add the stock and bouquet garni and bring to a boil.

4. Reduce the heat and gently simmer the quail, uncovered, for 10 minutes. Skim off any fat that rises to the surface. Return the shiitakes to the pan and continue simmering until the quails are very tender, 10 minutes. Transfer the quails to a cutting board and remove the trussing strings. Cut the birds in half with poultry shears, removing the backbone. Arrange the quail halves on a platter and keep warm.

5. Boil the cooking liquid until only 1 cup remains, about 5 minutes. Remove and discard the bouquet garni. Whisk the flour into the sour cream in a small bowl. Whisk this mixture into the cooking liquid and simmer for 1 minute, until thickened. Correct the seasonings, adding salt and pepper to taste. Spoon the gravy over the quails and sprinkle the parsley on top.

PORTRAIT OF A GREAT CUBAN COOK

Elida Proenza is one of the finest cooks I've ever had the pleasure to share my kitchen with. But she's not associated with a high-profile restaurant and you won't find her name in any food magazines or cookbooks. I met Elida two years ago, and although she spoke no English and I only a little Spanish, we quickly became fast friends in the kitchen.

Like thousands of Cuban exiles each year, Elida emigrated to Florida to flee the repression of Castro's Cuba. She brought with her a profound knowledge of a style of cooking that is vanishing in Cuba and in Florida. Elida grew up in an age of bounty in Cuba, when meat, seafood, and vegetables were plentiful, when a cook's prowess was limited only by her imagination.

Elida was born in the town of Niquero, in the Oriente province in southeast Cuba, an area famed for its *congrí* (red beans and rice), *ajiaco* (tuber stew), and *casabe* (yuca bread). Her father owned a soft-drink factory. The family's fortunes changed in 1959, when Castro nationalized small businesses. Elida watched her culinary repertory dwindle, as meat, then poultry, then other ingredients became increasingly difficult to purchase. Even seafood, plentiful in Cuba's waters, became impossible to find, as the bulk of the catch became destined for export to bring in hard foreign currency.

As Elida began to help me with my recipe testing, her culinary consciousness awakened, as if from a long slumber. One day, she transformed some leftover black beans into delectable Cuban refries. Another time, I brought home a package of corn husks. That evening we sat down to the lightest, most flavorful *tamales* I've tasted on two continents. Presented with some Florida lobster tails, she regaled us with the exquisite Lobster Enchilado on page 185. Every week, she rediscovers a delicacy and shares another piece of her culture with ours.

Elida paints with a simple palate: a little onion here, a little garlic there, a dab of tomato paste, a splash of lime juice, a pinch of cumin or oregano. She seldom uses more than five or six ingredients, but she creates a bold new world of flavor. Her favorite cooking utensils are the mortar and pestle. Virtually all of her recipes begin with pounding garlic, salt, and cumin to make the classic Cuban marinade, *adobo*. She seldom spends more than 20 minutes preparing a dish.

For Elida, food and health are inextricably interwoven. One day when I had a stomachache, she prepared the Bellyache Soup on page 55. Modern science has confirmed this ancient Cuban folk remedy. Plantains are, indeed, effective antiulcergenics. Elida is forever brewing medicinal herb teas: lemongrass and tangerine tea to relieve a head cold, corn silk tea for urinary tract infections.

For someone whose heritage includes *chicharrónes,* fried pork rinds, as a favorite snack, Elida is remarkably conservative in her use of fat. Her favorite fat is olive oil. She uses only a tablespoon of oil when most of her compatriots would use half a cup of shortening, oil, or lard.

I hope that Elida has the opportunity to return to her homeland, to pass her skills on to a lost generation of Cuban cooks. Knowing her has immeasurably enriched my own cooking.

Cuban Thanksgiving Turkey

Over the years, I've tried many methods for cooking Thanksgiving turkey: stuffed with truffles in the style of the French, smoked over maple wood in the style of New England, blasted with chilies à la Southwest. My favorite is the turkey prepared by our Cuban friend, Elida. The day before, Elida loosens the skin from the bird and rubs the meat with a piquant mixture of garlic, salt, and sour orange juice. (For more on the sour orange, see page 52.) The bird is roasted in a cloth bag or under cheesecloth for the first few hours to keep the breast meat moist. The turkey is cooked at a relatively low temperature to begin with and the heat is increased at the end to crisp the skin. The Pilgrims would have been impressed.

SERVES 12 TO 14

1 turkey (12 to 14 pounds), preferably fresh
Salt and freshly ground black pepper, to taste

MARINADE:
1 head of garlic, broken into cloves and peeled
1 tablespoon salt
1 teaspoon freshly ground black pepper
1½ teaspoons ground cumin
2 teaspoons dried oregano
1 cup sour orange juice or fresh lime juice

8 tablespoons (1 stick) unsalted butter

1. The day before you cook the turkey, remove the giblets and any lumps of fat from the cavities of the turkey. Wash the turkey well and blot dry. Season the inside with salt and pepper. Loosen the turkey skin from the meat. To do so,

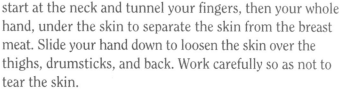

start at the neck and tunnel your fingers, then your whole hand, under the skin to separate the skin from the breast meat. Slide your hand down to loosen the skin over the thighs, drumsticks, and back. Work carefully so as not to tear the skin.

2. Prepare the marinade: Mash the garlic and salt to a paste in a mortar with a pestle. Pound in the pepper, cumin, and oregano and last of all the sour orange juice. If you don't have a mortar and pestle, purée the ingredients in a blender.

3. Add 3 tablespoons marinade to the main cavity and 1 tablespoon to the neck cavity. Place the remaining marinade under the skin. Work over a roasting pan to catch any runoff from the marinade. Place the bird in a large plastic bag with any excess marinade. Marinate the turkey overnight in the refrigerator, turning several times.

4. Preheat the oven to 300°F.

5. Thinly slice the butter and place half of the slices under the turkey skin. Melt the remaining butter. Truss the turkey and place it, breast side up, on a rack in a roasting pan. Brush the skin of the bird with some of the melted butter. Loosely drape a large piece of cheesecloth over the skin, then pour the remaining butter and any leftover marinade over the cheesecloth.

6. Roast the bird for 2 hours. Baste the bird with the juices and melted butter that collect in the bottom of the pan throughout the cooking process. Lift the cheesecloth from time to time to keep it from sticking to the skin. Increase the heat to 350°F and roast for 1 hour.

7. Increase the heat to 400°F and remove the cheesecloth. Roast the turkey, 15 to 30 minutes basting frequently, until done. When cooked, the skin will be golden brown and the leg juices will run clear when pricked with a fork. The internal temperature should read 185°F on an instant-reading thermometer and the drumstick should feel loose when wiggled.

8. Transfer the turkey to a platter or cutting board. Let stand for 15 minutes before carving. Strain the pan juices and serve in a sauceboat on the side.

CUBAN COOKING

Cubans have been the dominant force behind Florida's melting pot culture since the mid-nineteenth century, when the first Cuban cigar workers settled in Ybor City, today part of Tampa. Key West has long had a strong Cuban connection—which isn't surprising, considering that Havana lies only ninety minutes to the south and is a favorite Cuban point of entry into the U.S. The latest polls show that more than a half million Cuban's live in Florida, most of them in Miami and Dade County. But Cuba's culinary influences have spread far beyond the boundaries of the Hispanic community, both in Florida and across the U.S.

The Cuban cuisine enjoyed in Florida today resulted from four centuries of cultural mingling. Long before the arrival of the Spanish, Cuba's Taino and Arawak Indians cultivated corn, peanuts, peppers, and starchy root vegetables, such as yuca, malanga, and boniato. Their primary seasoning was annatto, a rust-colored seed with an earthy, almost iodine flavor. The Tainos left no written recipes, but at least one Taino dish survives more or less intact in modern Cuban cooking: a hardy stew called *ajiaco*.

The arrival of the Spanish in Cuba in 1492 introduced livestock (beef, pork, lamb, chicken) to the island, as well as olive oil, wine, vinegar, European spices, ham, salt cod, and chorizo (Spanish sausage). Metal cooking utensils from Spain greatly improved the kitchen technology in Cuba, allowing for such modern cooking techniques as baking, sautéing, and deep-frying. A marked Spanish influence pervades Cuban cooking, from dishes like *arroz con pollo* (a sort of chicken paella) to sweet desserts, such as *buñuelos* (fritters), *torrejas* (French toast), and flan.

Columbus brought sugar cane to the Caribbean on his second voyage in 1494. By the nineteenth century, millions of slaves had been kidnapped from Africa to work the vast cane plantations that stretched from one end of Cuba to the other. The slaves introduced such native African foods as pigeon peas, okra, and yams and helped popularize another African food that had arrived earlier: plantains. It's hard to imagine a Cuban meal without some sort of plantain dish: *maduros* (fried ripe plantains), *mariquitas* (green plantain chips), *tostones* (mashed fried green plantains), or *fufú* (boiled plantain purée with garlic)—the latter a dish with direct African antecedents.

In order to understand Cuban cooking, you must know about two basic preparations: *sofrito* and *adobo*. The former is a pungent mixture of garlic, onion, and *cachucha* (see page 46) or bell peppers, that are sautéed until soft and fragrant. *Sofrito* is the starting point for a myriad of Cuban soups, stews, and casseroles. *Adobo* is a tangy marinade made with garlic, salt, cumin, oregano, and sour orange juice. Virtually all Cuban meats, poultry, and seafoods are marinated in this mixture prior to cooking.

Cuban cooking is one of the most accessible cuisines in the Caribbean. Its primary flavorings (lime, garlic, onion, and cumin) are familiar to Americans. Cuban food is comfort food: soulful soups, steaming stews, filling starch dishes, and creamy custards. You can make it in large quantities, often ahead of time, so it's well suited to entertaining.

Turkey Picadillo

*P*icadillo (pronounced "pick-a-DE-yo") is a Cuban lunch-counter favorite. Think of it as a cross between hash and chili con carne. The name comes from the Spanish word *picar*, "to cut into small pieces." To be strictly authentic, you would use a not overly lean grade of ground beef. This version, made with ground turkey, is easier on the cardiovascular and digestive systems! *Picadillo* is enjoyed as a dish in its own right and also is used as a filling for fritters and pastries. I like to serve it with the *Yuca con Mojo* on page 255, but it also goes well with the *Maduros* (fried sweet plantains) on page 257, or rice and red or black beans (pages 263 and 265).

SERVES 2 TO 4

1 pound ground turkey

1 teaspoon ground cumin

1 teaspoon salt

1 teaspoon freshly ground black pepper

1 tablespoon olive oil

3 cloves garlic, minced

About ½ cup finely chopped onion

½ red bell pepper, cored, seeded, and finely chopped

1 small tomato, peeled, seeded, and finely chopped

10 pimiento-stuffed green olives, finely chopped

¼ cup raisins

2 tablespoons drained capers, plus 1 tablespoon caper brine

½ cup dry white wine

1 tablespoon tomato paste

1. Combine the turkey, cumin, salt, and pepper in a bowl and mix well with a spoon. Let stand for 5 minutes.

2. Heat the oil in a nonreactive large frying pan over

medium-high heat. Add the garlic, onion, and bell pepper and cook until soft but not brown, about 3 minutes. Stir in the tomato and cook for 2 minutes.

3. Add the turkey mixture and cook, chopping and stirring with a spoon, until it starts to take on a cooked look, about 2 minutes. Stir in the olives, raisins, and capers, and cook for 2 minutes.

4. Stir in the wine, tomato paste, and caper brine, and reduce the heat. Gently simmer the *picadillo* for 6 to 8 minutes, or until the turkey is cooked and most of the liquid has evaporated. The *picadillo* should be moist but not soupy. Correct the seasonings, adding salt, pepper, or cumin to taste, and serve. The *picadillo* will keep for 3 to 4 days, covered, in the refrigerator.

Variation: There are two popular variations on this recipe: *picadillo a la criolla* and *picadillo a la jardineiro*. To make the former, serve the picadillo in a nest of freshly fried potato chips. For the latter, just before serving stir in 1 cup each freshly cooked peas or canned petits pois and diced cooked carrots.

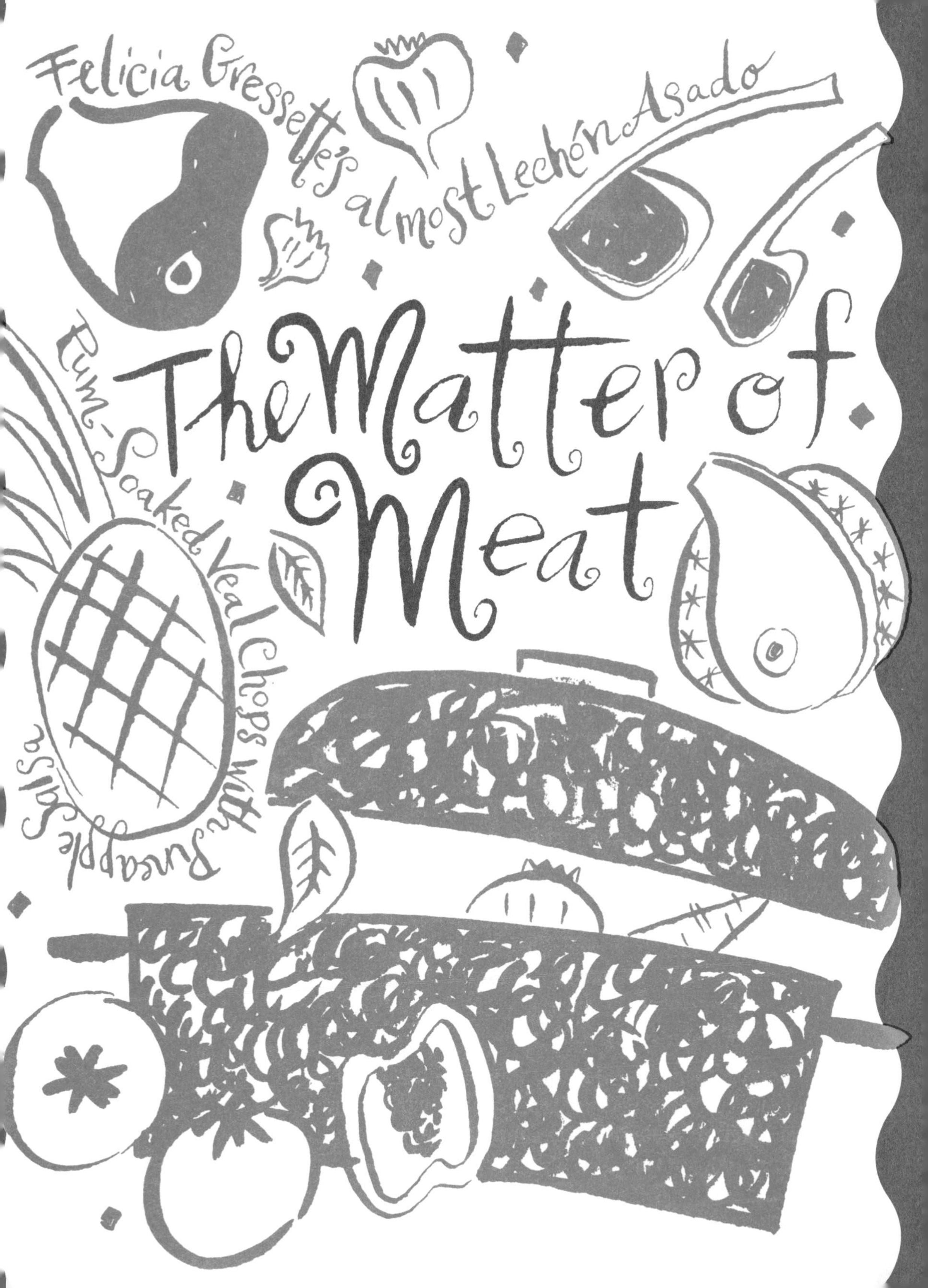

The Matter of Meat

Felicia Gressette's almost Lechón Asado

Rum-Soaked Veal Chops with Pineapple Salsa

Given our warm climate, you might think that Floridians don't eat a great deal of meat. But the Sunshine State has been a carnivore's paradise ever since Ponce de Leon and Hernando de Soto introduced European livestock in the early sixteenth century. After the Civil War, vast cattle ranges were established in the grasslands that stretched from Tampa to Palm Beach County. Once a year, cattlemen would drive their herds along the Cracker Trail, which ran from Fort Pierce to the Kissimmee River, west past Lorida to Tampa and Bradenton. From there the beef was shipped to points as far away as Cuba and New York. The ranches have become horse farms and citrus groves, but our love of beef remains.

Much of that love is kept alive by our Cuban and Nicaraguan communities. The former dote on such colorfully named dishes as *vaca frita*, literally "fried cow" (garlicky shredded fried skirt steak), and *ropa vieja*, literally "old clothes" (skirt steak stewed with onions and bell peppers).

Beef is the dish to eat in our Nicaraguan restaurants. Popular cuts include *churrasco* (thinly sliced, marinated, grilled tenderloin), *punta de filete* (sirloin tips), and *costilla de res* (beef short ribs). *Costilla tatalolo*, a smokily grilled tenderloin with the bone section still attached, is the star attraction at Miami's famous Los Ranchos restaurant, which was founded by members of Nicaragua's former ruling family, the Somozas.

Veal was popularized by the French and Swiss chefs who came to Florida earlier in this century to run the great hotels. It remains a popular meat, but in tropical style, we're just as apt to grill it as sauté it.

Pork plays an equally important role in Floridian cuisine. Each day, thousands of pounds of roast pork are consumed in the form of *pan con lechón*, Cuban roast pork sandwiches. Most ethnic subgroups have a version of fried spiced pork—from Haitian *griots* (garlic- and sour orange juice-marinated pork cubes) to Nicaraguan *cerdo frito* (pork flavored with annato seed and vinegar) to Cuban *masitas de puerco* (pork marinated with cumin, oregano, and garlic). And no Cuban family celebration would be complete without a *lechón asado*, whole roast suckling pig.

Even lamb has an historical antecedent in Florida, popular as it is with the Greek fishermen who settled in Tarpon Springs.

In general, Americans may be eating less and less meat. The following recipes are great reasons for occasionally bucking the trend.

Griots
(Haitian Fried Spice Pork)

Virtually every ethnic subculture in Florida has a version of fried spiced pork. One of my favorites is the *griots* served in Miami's "Little Haiti." These bite-size pork nuggets owe their tangy flavor to a shallot, garlic, and sour orange juice marinade, and their extraordinary tenderness to a two-step cooking method: first boiling, then frying. The Haitian Pickled Slaw on page 241 makes a good accompaniment.

SERVES 6

2 pounds boneless pork shoulder, cut into 1-inch cubes
½ cup fresh sour orange juice or lime juice

MARINADE:
1 cup fresh sour orange juice or lime juice
6 cloves garlic, minced
½ cup minced shallots
1 onion, minced
3 tablespoons minced fresh chives
½ to 1 scotch bonnet pepper or other hot chili,
     seeded and minced (optional)
½ teaspoon fresh or dried thyme
5 whole allspice berries
1 tablespoon salt
Freshly ground black pepper, to taste

½ cup vegetable oil, for frying

1. Toss the pork thoroughly with the ½ cup sour orange juice in a large bowl, then drain in a colander.

2. Combine all of the marinade ingredients in a nonreactive bowl. Add the pork and toss to cover with the marinade. Cover and refrigerate for at least 2 hours or as long as overnight. Toss the pork occasionally during that time.

3. Transfer the pork and marinade to a large, heavy, nonreactive casserole. Add enough water to cover the pork. Bring the mixture to a boil, reduce the heat, and simmer the pork, uncovered, until very tender, about 1 hour. Add water as necessary to keep the pork from burning.

4. Drain the pork. (The cooking liquid can be saved for soups or stews.) Wash out the casserole.

5. Just before serving, heat the oil in the casserole. Fry the pork and spices over medium-high heat, stirring well, until the meat is crusty and brown on all sides, about 5 minutes. Using a slotted spoon, transfer the pork to paper towels to drain. Serve at once.

FOIL TENTS

When making a foil tent, it is best to use wide, heavy-duty aluminum foil. Tear off a sheet 1½ times the width of your roasting pan and fold it in half to make a crease. Open up the sheet and place it over your roasting pan so that it forms a tent-like cover. Tightly crimp the edges of the foil under the lip of the pan to form a seal.

Felicia Gressette's Almost Lechón Asado

The mere mention of *lechón asado* is enough to make a Cuban-American's mouth water. Whole roast suckling pig is as indispensable to a traditional *Nochebuena* (Cuban Christmas Eve supper) as turkey is to an American Thanksgiving. Caterers provide most of the *lechón asado* enjoyed in Florida at Christmastime, as few people have the facilities to cook a 30-pound pig in their oven—although purists still use a pit in their backyard. *Miami Herald* food editor Felicia Gressette whittles the problem down to size by cooking half a fresh ham (pork leg) in the same manner. The traditional accompaniment is the *Mojo* on page 114.

SERVES 10

½ fresh ham (pork leg; about 8 pounds)

MARINADE:
1 head of garlic, broken into cloves, peeled and minced
1 tablespoon salt
1½ teaspoons dried oregano
1½ teaspoons ground cumin
½ teaspoon freshly ground black pepper
¼ teaspoon ground bay leaf
1 tablespoon olive oil
1 cup fresh sour orange juice or lime juice
¼ cup dry sherry
2 large onions, thinly sliced

1. The day before you plan to serve this dish, trim the excess fat off the pork leg. Make shallow slits all over the pork, using the tip of a knife.

2. Mash the garlic, salt, oregano, cumin, pepper, bay leaf, and olive oil to a paste in a mortar. Rub this mixture all over the roast, forcing it into the slits. Combine the sour orange juice, sherry, and onions in a bowl. Place the roast in a large, heavy plastic bag. Add the sour orange juice mixture, moving the roast around so all of it gets covered with the mixture. Refrigerate and marinate the roast in the bag overnight, turning occasionally during that time.

3. Preheat the oven to 350°F.

4. Drain the roast and pat dry, reserving the marinade. Place the roast in a lightly oiled, nonreactive, heavy, roasting pan. Cook the roast for 1 hour, turning once or twice to brown it on all sides.

5. Reduce the heat to 325°F. Pour the marinade and onions over the pork. Tent the pan with aluminum foil (see the sidebar page 223). Continue roasting the pork, basting from time to time with the pan juices, until almost cooked, about 1 hour. Add a little water or sherry if the pan dries out.

6. Uncover the roast and continue cooking until the internal temperature reads at least 150°F on a meat thermometer, about 30 minutes more. Most Cubans like their pork really well done, to about 180°F.

7. Let the roast stand for 10 minutes before carving.

Baby Back Ribs
with Guava Barbecue Sauce

he Deep South meets the New South in this recipe—a Caribbean twist on a Southern favorite. Guava paste is a sweet, dark-red jelly made from the perfumed tropical fruit, guava. It's sold in flat 21-ounce cans at Hispanic markets and in the

canned fruit or ethnic foods section of many supermarkets. Leftover guava paste keeps for months when wrapped in plastic and refrigerated. This recipe makes a little more sauce than you actually need for the ribs, but it keeps well and can be used with poultry, pork, and even lamb. Serve the ribs with the Pecan Corn Bread on page 95.

SERVES 4

---

3 pounds baby back ribs
1 onion, quartered
2 cloves garlic
2 bay leaves
1 teaspoon ground cumin

GUAVA BARBECUE SAUCE:
1 cup guava paste
6 tablespoons cider vinegar
¼ cup dark rum
¼ cup tomato paste
¼ cup fresh lime juice
1 tablespoon soy sauce
2 teaspoons ketchup
2 teaspoons Worcestershire sauce
2 tablespoons minced fresh onion
1 tablespoon minced fresh ginger
2 cloves garlic, minced
¼ to ½ scotch bonnet pepper or other hot chili, seeded
    and minced
Salt and freshly ground black pepper,
    to taste

1 onion, thinly sliced
1 teaspoon vegetable oil
3 tablespoons fresh lime juice
Salt and freshly ground black pepper,
    to taste

1. In a large pot, combine the ribs with the onion, garlic, bay leaves, and cumin. Add water to cover and bring to a boil over high heat. Boil for 5 minutes. Drain the ribs and rinse well.

2. Meanwhile, combine all the ingredients for the barbecue sauce in a nonreactive heavy saucepan. Simmer until the sauce is slightly thickened and richly flavored, about 5 minutes. Correct the seasonings, adding salt or pepper to taste.

3. Preheat the oven to 250°F.

4. Place the sliced onion in the bottom of a nonreactive roasting pan. Add water to a depth of 1 inch. Place a roasting rack on top and brush the rack with the oil. Sprinkle the ribs with the lime juice, and salt and pepper, and brush on both sides with half of the barbecue sauce. Tightly tent the pan with aluminum foil (see page 223). Bake the ribs until very tender, about 2 hours. (The recipe can be prepared several hours ahead to this stage.)

5. Preheat a barbecue grill to very hot or preheat the broiler with the tray 3 inches from the heat.

6. Just before serving, grill or broil the ribs until crusty and brown, 2 to 3 minutes per side, brushing with the remaining guava barbecue sauce.

Note: For extra flavor, if grilling, add hardwood chips, as described in Jamaican Jerk Rack of Lamb (below).

Jamaican Jerk Rack of Lamb

Jerk—meat marinated in a fiery blend of onions, rum, allspice, and scotch bonnet chilies and cooked over a smoky fire—is one of the national dishes of Jamaica. Jerk pork, chicken, and beef turn up at

Jamaican eateries throughout Florida. The preparation originated with runaway slaves in Jamaica, so the story goes, who used it to preserve wild boar and other game without refrigeration. My version calls for tame rack of lamb, which is smokily grilled over coals. A small rack of lamb is easier to grill than a large one. Scotch bonnet chilies are insanely hot, so I've given a range to suit all levels of heat tolerance.

SERVES 4 TO 6

2 small racks of lamb (each 1¼ to 1½ pounds trimmed)

JERK MIXTURE:
2 tablespoons olive oil
1 large onion, finely chopped
4 scallions, trimmed and finely chopped
4 cloves garlic, minced
1 to 4 scotch bonnet peppers or other hot chilies,
    seeded and minced
2 bay leaves
½ teaspoon ground allspice, or to taste
½ teaspoon dried thyme
⅛ teaspoon ground cloves
2 teaspoons salt, or to taste
¼ cup dark rum
2 tablespoons fresh lime juice, or to taste

1 cup hardwood chips, for grilling (optional)

1. The day before you plan to serve this dish, trim most of the fat off the lamb, leaving a thin layer intact. Make shallow slits all over the lamb, using the tip of a knife.

2. Prepare the jerk mixture: Heat the oil in a large saucepan over medium heat. Add the onion, scallions, garlic, chilies, and herbs and spices, and sauté, stirring often, until the mixture turns a deep golden brown, 4 to 6 minutes.

3. Increase the heat and stir in the salt, rum, and lime juice. Simmer the mixture until all of the liquid is absorbed. Correct the seasonings, adding salt or lime juice to taste. Let the mixture cool. (The jerk mixture can be prepared several days ahead to this stage.)

4. Rub the marinade all over the lamb, forcing it into the slits. Let the lamb marinate, covered, in the refrigerator for at least 4 hours, or preferably overnight, turning occasionally during this time.

5. Soak 1 cup mesquite, hickory, or other hardwood chips in cold water for 1 hour.

6. Preheat a barbecue grill to medium hot or preheat a broiler with the tray 3 inches from the heat.

7. Drain the wood chips, and scatter them over the coals. Grill or broil the racks of lamb, turning once, until cooked to taste, 3 to 4 minutes per side for medium-rare; 4 to 6 minutes for medium. If grilling, stand the racks upright on each end for 1 minute to sear the ends. Let the racks rest for 5 minutes before carving. Carve into ribs and serve.

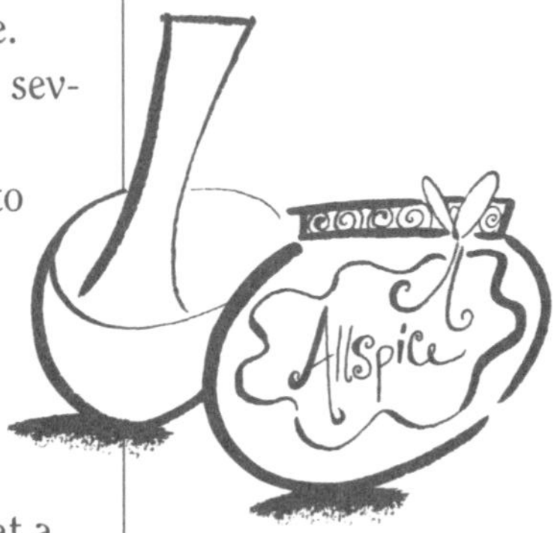

Rum-Soaked Veal Chops with Pineapple Salsa

ineapple ranks among the most popular fruits native to the New World. Columbus first encountered it in Guadeloupe in 1493. He called it *piña de Indes*, "West Indian pine cone," on account of its pine cone-like appearance. Pineapples were once grown commercially in Florida, and they're still a popular ingredient.

4 veal chops (8 to 12 ounces each)
1 cup dark rum
¼ cup fresh pineapple juice (see below)
3 tablespoons olive oil
3 cloves garlic, minced
3 tablespoons fresh lime juice
Salt and freshly ground black pepper, to taste

PINEAPPLE SALSA:
2 cups diced fresh pineapple (save the juices for
marinating the veal chops)
¼ cup diced red onion
¼ red bell pepper, cored, seeded, and diced
½ scotch bonnet chili or 1 jalapeño chili, seeded and minced
½ cup (loosely packed) chopped fresh mint or cilantro leaves
3 tablespoons fresh lime juice, or to taste
1 tablespoon dark brown sugar (optional)
Salt and freshly ground black pepper, to taste

1. Place the veal chops in a nonreactive baking dish. Mix the rum, pineapple juice, 2 tablespoons of the olive oil, the garlic, lime juice, and salt and pepper in a small bowl and pour over the meat. Turn the chops to cover completely. Marinate the chops, covered, in the refrigerator for 1 to 2 hours, turning occasionally during this time.

2. Not more than 1 hour before serving, combine all of the pineapple salsa ingredients in a large bowl and mix well. Correct the seasonings, adding salt, sugar, or lime juice to taste. The salsa should be both a little sweet and a little sour.

3. Preheat a barbecue grill to medium or preheat a broiler with the tray 3 inches from the heat.

4. Drain the chops and blot dry with paper towels. Brush each chop with the remaining tablespoon olive oil and season with salt and pepper. Grill or broil the chops until cooked through, 3 to 4 minutes per side. Serve with the salsa spooned on top or served on the side.

Whole Grilled Beef Tenderloin with Fire and Spice

This dish makes a dramatic centerpiece for a poolside feast or backyard buffet. It has the added advantage of being quick to prepare and easy to cook. Have your butcher trim off all the fat and silverskin from the tenderloin. The beef is marinated in the morning, then grilled at the last minute.

SERVES 10 TO 12

1 beef tenderloin (3½ to 4 pounds), fat and silverskin trimmed off

FIRE AND SPICE:

8 cloves garlic, minced

1 tablespoon minced fresh ginger

1 bunch scallions, trimmed and finely chopped

½ cup chopped Italian (flat-leaf) parsley leaves

½ cup finely chopped cilantro leaves

½ scotch bonnet pepper or 1 jalapeño chili, or to taste, seeded and minced

2 teaspoons salt, or to taste

2 teaspoons ground cumin

2 teaspoons ground coriander

2 teaspoons ground turmeric

1 teaspoon freshly ground black pepper

¼ cup extra-virgin olive oil

2 tablespoons fresh lemon juice, or to taste

1. Fold the tail (the skinny flap-like end) back over the body of the tenderloin and tie it in place with butcher's string.

2. Prepare the fire and spice: Pound the garlic, ginger,

scallions, parsley, cilantro, chilies, salt, and herbs and spices to a coarse paste in a mortar or grind in a food processor. Work in the olive oil and lemon juice. Correct the seasonings, adding salt or lemon juice to taste.

3. Using the tip of a paring knife, cut slits ½ inch deep and wide in the tenderloin, spacing them about 1 inch apart. Stuff half of the spice mixture into the slits, enlarging them with your fingertips as you stuff. Spread the remaining spice mixture over the surface of the tenderloin. Place the meat in a nonreactive roasting pan and let marinate, covered, in the refrigerator for 6 to 8 hours, turning occasionally during this time.

4. Thirty minutes before cooking, preheat a barbecue grill to very hot or preheat a broiler with the tray 3 inches from the heat.

5. Grill or broil the tenderloin, turning several times and basting with any leftover marinade, about 20 minutes for medium-rare (125°F on a meat thermometer); 20 to 25 minutes for medium (140°F on a meat thermometer); and 25 to 30 minutes for well done (160°F on a meat thermometer). Let the tenderloin rest for about 5 minutes before carving. The beef can be served either hot or chilled.

NICARAGUAN BEEF

Nicaraguans are avid beef eaters, preferring lean, grass-fed beef to the corn-fed, well-marbled cattle found in the United States. Los Ranchos, a chain of Nicaraguan restaurants, imports grass-fed beef from Costa Rica and Honduras. It has a bit more chew than the beef most Americans are accustomed to, but I find it richly flavored. *Churrasco,* however, is delicious prepared with American beef as well.

Churrasco (Nicaraguan-Style Grilled Beef Tenderloin)

Churrasco is the Argentinian word for grilled beef. But it was Nicaraguan immigrants of the Sandinista era who popularized the dish in Miami. Today, we have dozens of Nicaraguan steak houses, ranging from ranch house-style restaurants decorated with wrought iron and cowhide to bucolic haciendas.

Nicaraguan *churrasco* is always served with a trio of sauces: *Chimichurri* (page 113), Spicy Tomato Sauce (page 141), and a spicy pickled onion relish called *Cebollita* (page 242). Other classic accompaniments include *Gallo Pinto* (red beans and rice, page 263) and *Maduros* (fried sweet plantains, page 257).

SERVES 4 TO 6

1 piece beef tenderloin (2½ pounds),
 fat and silverskin trimmed off

MARINADE:
½ cup chopped Italian (flat-leaf) parsley leaves
3 cloves garlic, minced
¼ cup Spanish olive oil
¼ cup dry sherry
3 tablespoons sherry vinegar or wine vinegar
1 teaspoon freshly ground white pepper
1 teaspoon salt

Nicaraguan table sauces, for serving (see above)

1. Cut the tenderloin lengthwise, with the grain, into 4 flat, even strips. Place the strips between sheets of plastic wrap and gently pound with the side of a cleaver to form steaks 10 inches long and ½ inch thick.

2. Combine all of the marinade ingredients in a nonreactive dish or bowl. Add the beef and marinate, covered, in the refrigerator for 1 to 2 hours, turning occasionally during that time.

3. Preheat a barbecue grill to very hot or preheat the broiler with the tray 3 inches from the heat.

4. Drain the beef and blot dry with paper towels. Grill or broil the beef for 1 minute per side for rare; 1 to 1½ minutes per side for medium; and 2 minutes per side for well done. Serve the beef with the trio of Nicaraguan table sauces on the side.

NOT AGAINST THE GRAIN

Although you are probably accustomed to slicing meat across the grain, note that the instructions for making *churrasco* call for the beef to be sliced *with* the grain. Once cut, the slices are then pounded into broad flat sheets.

MANAGUA MEETS MIAMI: NICARAGUAN CUISINE

They came for a variety of reasons: to flee the Contras or the Sandinistas, to continue a way of life they enjoyed under the Somoza regime, or to seek opportunities no longer available at home. Like any immigrant group, Nicaraguans brought with them a longing for the foods they left behind. They set up *fritangas,* "fry shops," where they could nibble *repochetas* (fried cheese turnovers), while conversing with friends from the "old country." They opened homey neighborhood eateries and million dollar restaurant chains. They're Miami's Nicaraguan community of more than 100,000 people, and they've captivated the tastes of south Florida.

"In 1980, you could count the number of Nicaraguan restaurants on one hand," recalls Julio Somoza, nephew of former Nicaraguan ruler Anastasio Somoza and owner of a chain of restaurants called Los Ranchos. "Today, there are over fifty." When Somoza opened his first restaurant a decade ago, 98 percent of his customers were Nicaraguan. These days, the proportion of Anglos to Nicaraguans is half and half.

Nicaraguan food differs strikingly from the cuisines of its Central American neighbors. "We don't use as much deep-frying as Cubans and Puerto Ricans," explains Somoza. "Unlike Mexicans, we don't go in for the heavy use of spices, chilies, and lard." A great deal of Nicaraguan food is marinated, grilled, and served with salsa-like condiments instead of calorie-laden sauces.

Somoza goes so far as to call his country's cooking "Latin American health food." That's stretching things a bit, considering the Nicaraguan love of beef, fried plantains, and sweets. But there are elements of Nicaraguan cooking that appeal to health-conscious North Americans. Beans figure prominently in the Nicaraguan diet, as do rice and corn products. Seafood is popular and many foods are, indeed, cooked by grilling.

As elsewhere in Latin America, corn, rice, and beans are the cornerstones of the Nicaraguan diet. Nicaraguan tortillas are softer and thicker than their Mexican cousins; they remind me of freshly baked pita bread. When fried, they are called *enchiladas* and are served with *chile criolla*, a piquant salsa made with vinegared onions and chilies.

No Nicaraguan meal would be complete without *gallo pinto*, red beans and rice. The name literally means "multicolored rooster" in Spanish. The other mainstay of the Nicaraguan diet is the plantain, which appears in three incarnations. Green plantains are cut lengthwise into paper-thin slices and deep-fried to make crunchy chips called *tajadas. Maduros* are meaty chunks of fried ripe plantain that are banana-sweet and meltingly tender. To make *tostones,* green plantains are fried, mashed, and fried again.

Nicaraguans are among Latin America's most accomplished bakers. Their most famous dessert, *tres leches,* "three milks" cake, has been adopted in Miami by restaurants of all ethnic persuasions. Another popular dessert is Pio Quinto, a rum- and custard-soaked sponge cake named for Pope Pius V. To wash them down, like most Hispano-Americans, Nicaraguans drink tiny cups of strong, sugary, black espresso.

Ropa Vieja

his and the *Vaca Frita* on page 235 are mainstays of the Cuban-American diet. Both are made with skirt steak, a stringy cut of meat with the poetic name of *fajita* ("girdle") in Spanish. Skirt steak can be found at Hispanic markets, Jewish butcher shops, and at an increasing number of supermarkets. Flank steak makes an acceptable substitute. Both recipes call for the meat to be boiled with aromatic vegetables. The resulting broth makes a fabulous soup—simply add cooked noodles or rice. *Ropa vieja*—literally means "old clothes," and is an apt description of the shredded appearance of the meat. It is traditionally served with white rice and fried plantains.

SERVES 4

1½ pounds skirt steak
1 small onion, quartered
1 tomato, quartered
1 carrot, cut into 1-inch pieces
2 cloves garlic, peeled

TO FINISH THE DISH:
2 tablespoons olive oil
2 cloves garlic, minced
1 small onion, thinly sliced
½ green bell pepper, cored, seeded, and thinly sliced
½ red bell pepper, cored, seeded, and thinly sliced
½ teaspoon ground cumin, or to taste
⅓ cup tomato purée
3 tablespoons dry white wine
Salt and freshly ground black pepper, to taste

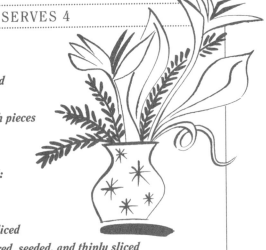

1. Combine the beef, quartered onion, tomato, carrot, and garlic cloves with 6 cups of water in a large pot. Bring to a boil over a high heat. Skim off the scum that rises to the surface. Reduce the heat and simmer the beef, uncovered, skimming often, until tender, 30 to 40 minutes.

2. Strain the meat, reserving the broth for soup. Let the meat cool. Tear it, along the grain, into pencil-thick strips.

3. Heat the oil in a large nonreactive frying pan over medium heat. Add the minced garlic, sliced onion, and bell peppers and cook until soft but not brown, 3 to 4 minutes. Stir in the meat, cumin, tomato purée, wine, and salt and pepper. Cook until the meat is well coated with the sauce and the sauce is reduced and flavorful, about 5 minutes. Correct the seasonings, adding salt and pepper to taste.

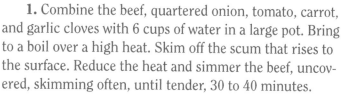

Vaca Frita

Another curiously named dish, *vaca frita* (literally "fried cow") demonstrates the Cuban resourcefulness with inexpensive cuts of meat. Boiled skirt steak is shredded into thin filaments. These, in turn, are marinated in garlic and lime juice, and then fried until crusty and crisp. Warning: Some Cuban restaurants will serve you a whole deep-fried skirt steak and call it *vaca frita*. Unless it's shredded before frying, it isn't the real McCoy. Serve *vaca frita* with white rice and black beans.

SERVES 4

1½ pounds skirt steak
1 small onion, quartered
1 tomato, quartered
1 carrot, cut into 1-inch pieces
2 cloves garlic, peeled

TO FINISH THE DISH:
3 cloves garlic, minced
½ teaspoon salt
3 tablespoons fresh lime juice or sour orange juice
2 tablespoons olive oil
1 small onion, sliced as thinly as possible

1. Combine the beef, quartered onion, tomato, carrot, and garlic cloves with 6 cups of water in a large pot. Bring to a boil over high heat. Skim off the scum that rises to the surface. Reduce the heat and simmer the beef, uncovered, skimming often, until tender, 30 to 40 minutes.

2. Strain the meat, reserving the broth for soup. Let the meat cool. Using the tip of a knife or your fingertips, tear the meat, along the grain, into the thinnest possible shreds. Toss the meat with the minced garlic, salt, and lime juice in a mixing bowl. Let marinate, covered, in the refrigerator for at least 15 minutes, or as long as overnight.

3. About 5 minutes before serving, heat the oil in a non-stick frying pan until smoking. Add the meat and sauté over medium-high heat until crisp, 3 to 4 minutes. Transfer the meat to plates or a platter with a slotted spoon or tongs. Add the sliced onion to the pan and fry until lightly browned, about 2 minutes. Top the *vaca frita* with the fried onion and serve at once.

On the Side: An Exotic Array

Grilled Corn & garlic flan

Stuffed Chayotes

Maduros

El Palacio de los Jugos ("The Juice Palace") is located at a busy intersection in a commercial district of West Miami. But step inside and you could be at a street market in Cuba or Central America. Before you are bins of unfamiliar tropical fruits and vegetables, shocks of sugar cane, mountains of plantains—a whole flora and fauna of West Indian produce. Florida may well be the third most populous state in the Union, but it often makes me feel as if I'm living in a foreign country.

You don't have to go to an ethnic market to experience this otherworldliness. My local Publix supermarket sells yuca, malanga, and boniato (Caribbean tubers), calabaza (West Indian pumpkin), chayotes, papayas, and mangos. The nearby produce stand carries carambolas (star fruit), lychees, key limes, atemoyas, sapotes, mameys, and fresh tamarind. Florida is a proving ground where the fruits and vegetables of tomorrow are being grown, marketed, and integrated into American cuisine today.

If Florida had an official state dish, it might well be rice and beans. Cubans would be lost without their *congrí*, Nicaraguans without their *gallo pinto* (both rice and red bean dishes). Haitians and Bahamians share a common passion for pigeon peas and rice. Indeed, our Caribbean-inspired rice dishes are so popular that several fast food chains have incorporated them into the menus of their Miami outlets.

Rice has deep roots in Florida history. The grain was introduced here in the seventeenth century by the Spanish settlers of St. Augustine. Today, rice-loving Floridians buy it by the 50-pound sack at the supermarket. Floridian cooks use two basic types of rice:

long grain and short grain or Valencia-style. The former—typified by Uncle Ben's—is the rice used for everyday eating with beans or as a vegetable side dish. Valencia-style rice is a short-grain, starchy rice similar to Italy's arborio. Short-grain rice cooks to a sticky consistency that is ideal for holding together *arroz con pollo* and paella.

Wherever you find rice, you're sure to find some sort of bean. There's a modern scientific explanation for this age-old combination. Both grains and beans are rich in amino acids, but neither contains a complete set. Combining them gives you all the amino acids necessary for a usable form of protein. *Moros* (the nickname for Cuban black beans and rice) and *gallo pinto* (Nicaraguan red beans and rice) are classic examples of complementary proteins.

The Cuban-American community has made the black bean *(frijole negro*—also known as turtle bean) Florida's most popular bean. Other local favorites include the red kidney bean *(frijole colorado)*, pigeon pea *(gandule)*, and—in northern Florida—the black-eyed pea. Butter beans (baby lima beans) are popular in central and northern Florida, where they're traditionally boiled in water and butter. Fresh butter beans are in season in late spring.

Here's a look at some of Florida's vegetable and rice and bean dishes. They're great as side dishes and some as meals in themselves.

Florida Slaw

Coleslaw may have Dutch origins (*cole* is the Dutch word for cabbage, *sla* for salad), but this summery side dish has become an American institution. Star fruit, scotch bonnet chilies, and mango lend this coleslaw a Floridian touch. Black sesame seeds can be found in Asian markets and some health food stores.

SERVES 8

DRESSING:
⅓ cup mayonnaise
3 tablespoons sour cream
¼ cup Orange Syrup (page 332) or
    orange juice concentrate
2 tablespoons rice wine vinegar
2 tablespoons fresh lime juice
2 tablespoons black sesame seeds
Salt and freshly ground black pepper, to taste

½ green cabbage, cored and thinly shredded
    (5 to 6 cups)
½ red bell pepper, cored, seeded, and thinly sliced
½ yellow bell pepper, cored, seeded, and thinly sliced
1 poblano chili or ½ green bell pepper,
    cored, seeded, and thinly sliced
½ scotch bonnet pepper or 1 jalapeño chili, seeded
    and minced
1 ripe mango, diced
2 star fruits, thinly sliced
2 carrots, cut into julienne
1 bunch of scallions, trimmed and finely chopped
¼ cup chopped fresh cilantro leaves

STAR FRUIT

Nature's love of symmetry is apparent everywhere you look. Consider the graceful swirl of the nautilus shell or the intricacy of a snowflake. For me, the ultimate aesthetic treat is the star-shaped carambola.

Also known as the star fruit, the carambola (pronounced ca-ram-BO-la) is an oval, yellow fruit, 2 to 6 inches long, with 5 deep longitudinal wings. Sliced crosswise, it produces perfect five-point stars. Carambola has the crispness of a cucumber and the succulence of a grape.

The star fruit originated in Southeast Asia, where it has been cultivated for centuries. (*Carambola* is the Hindu word for the fruit.) Experts believe that the star fruit was brought by sandalwood traders to Hawaii, then to South America and the Caribbean. There are written accounts of carambolas being grown in Key West as early as 1840.

But it wasn't until the 1980s that the fruit achieved the status of culinary superstar. Championed by the pioneers of nouvelle cuisine, it began to turn up at chic restaurants and specialty green grocers. The development of sweeter varieties and the lowering of its price enhanced its popularity.

When buying carambolas, look for crisp, heavy fruits with firm, fat ribs. Light blemishes at the edges of the ribs (called wind scarring) aren't the end of the world, but avoid fruits that are battered, browned, limp, soft, or oozing. Ripe fruits will be pale to bright yellow or orange. Green fruits can be ripened at home at room temperature. When ripe, the fruit will smell perfumy and fragrant. Ripe carambolas will keep for up to 2 weeks in the refrigerator.

Florida's star fruits are in season from August to March. Munch on them as you would an apple (discard the small oval seeds). The most common way to prepare the fruit is to cut it, crosswise, into ¼-inch slices, which will form five-point stars.

1. Prepare the dressing: Whisk the mayonnaise and sour cream in a large mixing bowl until smooth. Whisk in the orange syrup, vinegar, lime juice, sesame seeds, and salt and pepper. Correct the seasonings, adding lime juice or salt to taste.

2. Stir in all of the remaining ingredients, reserving one of the sliced starfruits for garnish. Correct the seasonings, adding salt, pepper, or vinegar to taste. Decorate the salad with the reserved starfruit slices and serve at once.

Haitian Pickled Slaw

This fiery slaw is served as a condiment at the restaurants in Miami's Little Haiti. The firepower comes from Haitian peppers, which look like elongated scotch bonnets. Scotch bonnets work fine. Use the slaw sparingly the first time. Soon you'll be eating it by the bowlful.

MAKES 1 QUART; 8 TO 12 SERVINGS

2 cups distilled white vinegar

⅔ cup water

1 tablespoon salt, or to taste

½ teaspoon sugar (optional)

½ green cabbage, cored and thinly sliced (5 to 6 cups)

2 medium onions, thinly sliced

3 cloves garlic, minced

2 carrots, peeled and shredded

1 to 4 scotch bonnet peppers or other hot chilies, seeded and thinly sliced (for a hotter slaw leave the seeds in)

1. Whisk the vinegar, water, and salt and sugar, if using, together in a nonreactive large mixing bowl until all of the salt (and sugar) dissolves.

2. Stir in all of the remaining ingredients. Let the cabbage pickle, covered, in the refrigerator overnight. Stir it occasionally during that time.

3. Transfer the slaw to a clean 1-quart jar or 2 pint jars. The slaw will keep for several weeks in the refrigerator.

Cebollita
(Nicaraguan Pickled Onions)

*C*ebollita, pickled onions, is one of the three table condiments served with *churrasco* and other Nicaraguan beef dishes. You can make it as spicy as you desire by increasing the amount of jalapeño chilies.

MAKES 1½ CUPS

1 large white onion (about 2 cups sliced)
1 fresh jalapeño chili, or to taste
1 cup distilled white vinegar
⅓ cup water
½ teaspoon salt, or to taste
½ teaspoon sugar

1. Cut the onion top to bottom into ¼-inch wedges. Slice the chili as thinly as possible.

2. Combine the vinegar, water, salt, and sugar in a large jar with a tight-fitting lid. Shake until the salt and sugar dissolve. Add the onion and chili. Let the onions pickle in this

mixture at room temperature or in the refrigerator for 2 to 3 days, stirring occasionally. *Cebollita* will keep for several weeks in the refrigerator.

Candied Kumquats

Kumquats are the smallest member of the citrus family, elongated orange fruits—roughly the size and shape of large olives—with an aromatic, pleasantly bitter flavor. You eat them skin and all. Many people like them raw, but I prefer them poached in a sweet-sour syrup. Candied kumquats can be enjoyed by themselves as pickles or relish, and they go well with the Watermelon Salad on page 74.

MAKES 1 QUART

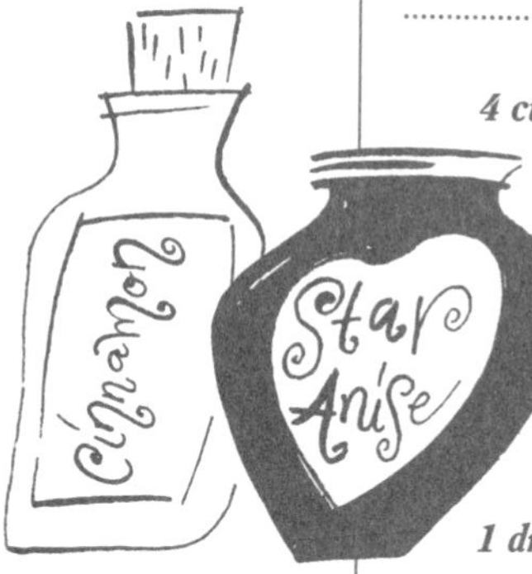

4 cups kumquats

2 cups sugar

1 cup cider vinegar

½ cup water

2 cinnamon sticks (each 3 inches long)

10 whole cloves

2 whole star anise pods

1 dried chili pepper (optional)

1. Thoroughly wash the kumquats, discarding any stems. Place the kumquats in a nonreactive large pot with water to cover and bring to a boil. Reduce the heat and simmer the kumquats until tender, about 5 minutes. Drain in a colander and refresh under cold water.

2. Place all of the remaining ingredients in a large, heavy, nonreactive saucepan and bring to a boil. Add the kumquats. Reduce the heat to low and poach the kumquats until very tender and well flavored, about 8 minutes. With a slotted spoon, transfer the fruit to clean jars. Let the syrup cool to room temperature. Pour the syrup over the kumquats. The kumquats will keep for several months in the refrigerator

Datil Pepper and Cranberry Jelly

ere's a distinctly Floridian way to spice up Thanksgiving. Datil peppers taste like scotch bonnets and are every bit as fiery. This recipe comes from the Ritz-Carlton Hotel in Amelia Island.

MAKES 6 CUPS

1 to 1½ tablespoons seeded, minced datil peppers,
  scotch bonnet chilies, or other hot peppers
  (1 to 2 whole chilies)
¼ cup minced yellow bell pepper (about ¼ pepper)
About 1 cup red wine vinegar
5 cups sugar
2 cups cranberry juice
3 ounces liquid pectin (the Ritz chef uses Certo)

1. Combine the datil pepper, yellow pepper, and ¼ cup vinegar in a nonreactive bowl and let stand for 5 minutes.

2. Combine the sugar (5 cups sounds like a lot but is correct) and cranberry juice in a large, heavy, nonreactive saucepan and stir to mix. Cook the mixture over medium

FIRE FROM ST. AUGUSTINE: DATIL PEPPERS

et the Mexicans have their *habañeros*, the Jamaicans their scotch bonnets. Floridians living around St. Augustine have a native chili that's every bit as fiery: the scorching datil pepper. Closely related to the scotch bonnet, the datil (pronounced DAT-l) is smooth, elongated, tapered, and lime green. The datil may be skinnier than the scotch bonnet, but the smoky aroma and the atomic heat are the same.

Popular lore holds that the datil was brought to St. Augustine by Minorcan settlers, who arrived in Florida's oldest city in the mid 1700s. The problem with this theory is that there has never been mention of the datil in Minorcan history. In all likelihood, Spanish traders brought the pepper to Florida from the Caribbean or Central America. Jacksonville, Florida journalist Jonathan Rogers believes the datil pepper came from Santiago, Chile, in the 1880s.

Today, datil peppers are grown chiefly around St. Augustine and Jacksonville, and in limited quantities elsewhere in Florida. Unless you live in these areas, you probably won't be able to find fresh datil peppers. But an enterprising St. Augustine restaurateur, Chris Way, has created a line of datil pepper products. "Dat'l Do-It Hot Sauce" is a sweet tomato-based hot sauce. "Hellish Relish" is a sweet pickle relish full of datil pepper firepower. "Devil Drops" is a fiery sauce in the tradition of Tabasco.

For further information and mail order call 1-800-HOT-DATL or write Dat'l Do-It, P.O. Box 4019, St. Augustine, FL 32085. The products are also sold at the Hot Shop in St. Augustine.

heat, stirring steadily, until the sugar is completely dissolved, about 5 minutes. Skim off any foam that rises to the surface.

3. Stir in the pepper mixture and remaining vinegar. Add more vinegar if a tarter flavor is desired. Bring the mixture to a boil over medium heat and cook until syrupy, 6 to 8 minutes. Continue to skim off any foam that rises to the surface.

4. Stir in the pectin and boil for 3 minutes, skimming well. Pour the mixture into 6 sterilized ½-pint canning jars and tightly seal. Let cool to room temperature. Refrigerate before serving.

Grilled Corn

Grilling is a year-round pastime in Florida, and it's one of my favorite ways of cooking fresh corn on the cob. The smoky flavor from the grill complements the sweetness of the corn perfectly. Many recipes call for the corn to be husked, soaked in cold water, buttered, rewrapped in the husk, then grilled—a procedure that not only is time-consuming, but keeps the smoke flavor away from the corn. I like to cook shucked ears of corn directly over the coals. It takes only a few minutes and the flavor is terrific. Grilled corn is great eaten off the cob and it's an ingredient in many of the recipes in this book.

SERVES 4

8 ears fresh sweet corn
¼ to ½ cup melted unsalted butter or olive oil
Salt and freshly ground black pepper, to taste

1. Preheat a barbecue grill to medium hot.

2. Meanwhile, shuck the corn. Generously brush each ear of corn with some of the butter and sprinkle with salt and pepper.

3. Grill the corn, basting the corn with the butter to keep it moist and turning the ears to brown the kernels evenly, until cooked, about 5 minutes. Serve at once with salt, pepper, and the remaining butter on the side.

Grilled Corn and Roasted Garlic Flan

Sweet flan is a Spanish dessert, of course, but savory flans make a wonderful accompaniment to grilled meats and seafood. This one combines the sweetness of roasted garlic and the smoky flavor of grilled fresh corn. If you don't have time for grilling, tasty results can be obtained by using frozen corn kernels.

SERVES 6

2 tablespoons melted unsalted butter
1 head of garlic
1½ cups Grilled Corn kernels (from 2 to 3 ears; see page 245)
 or frozen corn kernels
1½ cups half-and-half or milk
2 whole eggs
2 egg yolks
Salt and freshly ground white pepper, to taste
Freshly grated nutmeg
Pinch of cayenne pepper
Splash of your favorite hot sauce (optional)
½ teaspoon sugar, or to taste
4 sprigs Italian (flat-leaf) parsley, for garnish

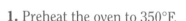

1. Preheat the oven to 350°F.

2. Brush six 4-ounce ramekins with some of the melted butter. Chill the ramekins in the freezer until the butter sets, about 5 minutes. Brush the bottom and sides of the ramekins a second time with melted butter and chill again. Alternatively, the ramekins can be sprayed or coated with oil.

3. Roast the head of garlic in its skin in a small roasting pan until soft, about 45 minutes. Let cool. Leave the oven on.

4. Cut the garlic crosswise in half and squeeze the sweet pulp out of the skins. Place the pulp in a mixing bowl and mash with a fork.

5. Whisk in the corn, half-and-half, eggs, egg yolks, salt and pepper, nutmeg, cayenne, and hot sauce. If the corn isn't particularly sweet, add the sugar. Spoon the mixture into the ramekins.

6. Bring 1 quart water to a boil. Place the ramekins in a small roasting pan. Pour in the boiling water to a depth of ½ inch. Loosely cover the pan with aluminum foil. Bake the flans until set and a skewer inserted comes out clean, 25 to 35 minutes.

7. Remove the ramekins from the water

and let the flans stand for 3 minutes before unmolding. Run a sharp knife tip around the inside of each ramekin. Place a plate on top and invert. Gently shake the dish: The flan should slip out easily. Garnish each flan with a parsley sprig and serve at once.

Stuffed Chayotes

Chayote is an avocado-shaped, squash-like vegetable native to Central America. Here in Florida it goes by many names: *chayote* in Spanish, *cho-cho* in Jamaican English, *christophine* in Creole. Elsewhere in the country, you may know it by its Cajun name, mirliton. Whatever you call it, chayote has a delicate flavor similar to cooked cucumber or zucchini and its rounded shape is ideal for stuffing.

SERVES 8 AS AN APPETIZER OR SIDE DISH, 4 AS A LIGHT ENTREE

4 chayotes (1½ pounds total)
Salt
1 cup fresh bread crumbs
½ cup slivered almonds, coarsely chopped
3 tablespoons unsalted butter or olive oil
1 onion, finely chopped
1 to 2 cloves garlic, minced
1 cup freshly grated Parmesan cheese
¼ cup minced Italian (flat-leaf) parsley
¼ cup finely chopped scallions
1 teaspoon fresh lemon juice
½ teaspoon grated fresh lemon zest
Freshly ground black pepper

Parsley

CHAYOTES AKA MIRLITONS

Newcomers to Florida produce markets may be perplexed by the chayote (pronounced shy-O-tay). It looks like a pale-skinned, slightly flattened avocado. But try eating it in its uncooked state and you could risk cracking a tooth. Also known as vegetable pear, chayote is squash-like and popular throughout the Caribbean and Latin America.

Chayotes can grow quite large, ranging from 3 to 6 inches long, weighing 6 ounces to a couple of pounds. Depending on the variety, the rind can be tan, brown, or green; smooth-skinned, furrowed, or covered with Velcrolike prickles. The variety most commonly found in the U.S. is pale green, thin-skinned, and about the size of a pear.

The chayote is sold at West Indian and Hispanic markets and at an increasing number of supermarkets. Choose ones that are firm and unblemished. (Unlike tomatoes or avocados, the harder the chayote the better.) Figure on 8 ounces per person. Chayotes will keep for 2 to 3 weeks in the refrigerator. By themselves, they are low in fat and calories—only 40 calories for a 1-cup serving.

Chayotes usually are cooked by boiling or steaming. It takes longer than you would think, considering the small size of the vegetable, for the flesh to become tender: 25 to 30 minutes. (The cooking time can be shortened by using a pressure cooker.) Cooked chayotes can be added to salads, mashed like potatoes, batter-fried like zucchini, and stuffed like eggplants. The squash's delicate flavor goes well with shrimp, lemon, parsley, nuts, and cheese.

One of the most interesting techniques for cooking chayote comes from Mark Militello, chef-owner of Mark's Place in North Miami. Mark cuts the squash into wafer-thin slices on a meat slicer. The slices are then brushed with olive oil and grilled over live coals until tender but not soft.

1. Cut each chayote lengthwise in half to obtain 2 flattish halves. Remove the seed with a spoon. Cook the chayotes in 2 quarts boiling salted water until tender, about 30 minutes. When cooked, the chayotes should be easy to pierce with a skewer. Refresh the chayotes under cold water and drain.

2. Preheat the oven to 350°F. Lightly oil a large round or rectangular baking dish.

3. Using a melon baller or spoon, scrape most of the flesh out of the chayotes, taking care not to pierce the skins. Set the shells, rounded sides up, on a wire rack to drain. Coarsely chop the flesh and place it in a strainer to drain.

4. Lightly toast the bread crumbs on a baking sheet in the oven, about 7 minutes. Toast the almonds on a baking sheet until a light golden brown, about 5 minutes. Increase the oven temperature to 400°F.

5. Melt 1½ tablespoons of the butter in a small frying pan over medium heat. Add the onion and garlic and cook until soft but not brown, about 3 minutes. Remove the pan from the heat.

6. Combine the chayote pulp, bread crumbs, almonds, onion and garlic mixture, cheese, parsley, scallions, lemon juice, lemon zest, and salt and pepper to taste in a mixing bowl and gently toss to mix. Correct the seasonings, adding salt or lemon juice to taste. Stuff this mixture into the chayote shells, mounding it in the center. Arrange the chayotes, stuffed sides up, in the prepared baking dish and dot with the remaining 1½ tablespoons butter. (The chayotes can be prepared up to 6 hours ahead to this stage and kept, covered, in the refrigerator.)

7. Just before serving, bake the chayotes at 400°F until golden brown on top and thoroughly heated, about 15 minutes. Serve at once.

Variation: Sometimes I substitute 8 ounces of crab meat or diced chicken or shrimp for the almonds. You could also add a little minced scotch bonnet or jalapeño chili for spice.

Baked Tomatoes
with Tropical Pesto

Fresh cilantro and macadamia nuts lend a tropical touch to pesto. For the best results, use ripe tomatoes—the sort that squish, not bounce, when you drop them.

SERVES 6

6 large ripe tomatoes
⅓ cup lightly toasted macadamia nuts (see page 311)
2 cloves garlic, finely chopped
1 jalapeño chili, seeded and minced
1 cup coarsely chopped cilantro leaves
⅓ cup goat cheese
3 tablespoons extra-virgin olive oil, plus additional oil
    for the baking dish and drizzling
1 tablespoon fresh lime juice, or to taste
Salt and freshly ground black pepper, to taste
3 to 4 tablespoons fine dried bread crumbs

1. Preheat the oven to 400°F.

2. Cut the tomatoes crosswise in half. Gently squeeze each half to wring out most of the liquid and seeds. Arrange the tomato halves, cut sides up, in a lightly oiled baking dish.

3. Purée the macadamia nuts, garlic, and chili in a food processor. Add the cilantro and process until finely chopped. Add the goat cheese and process to a smooth paste. Grind in the olive oil, lime juice, and salt and pepper.

4. Place a heaping spoonful of pesto on each tomato half. Sprinkle the tomato halves with the bread crumbs and drizzle the tops with a little olive oil.

5. Bake until the tomatoes are soft and the topping is golden brown, about 15 minutes. Serve immediately.

Hearts of Palm
with Pancetta and Cream

Swamp cabbage cooked with white bacon (salt pork) was a favorite pioneer dish and it's still enjoyed in parts of rural Florida today. My version calls for pancetta (Italian bacon) instead of the salt pork and cream instead of the traditional evaporated milk. If making the recipe with canned hearts of palm, omit Step 1.

SERVES 4

2 cups thinly sliced fresh hearts of palm,
　　or drained, canned
Salt

　　4 thin slices pancetta or bacon, cut into
　　　¼-inch slivers
2 cloves garlic, peeled
¾ cup heavy (or whipping) cream
Freshly ground white pepper

1. If using fresh hearts of palm, thinly slice it as described on page 76. Cook it in boiling salted water until tender, but still quite crisp, 4 to 6 minutes. Taste the water after 3 minutes: If it tastes bitter, add fresh water. Drain the heart of palm well in a colander.

2. Lightly brown the pancetta and garlic in a sauté pan or heavy skillet over medium heat. Discard the garlic cloves and most of the rendered fat.

3. Stir in the hearts of palm and the cream. Simmer, uncovered, until most of the cream is absorbed by the hearts of palm, 5 to 10 minutes. Season with salt and white pepper to taste. Serve at once.

Sweet Potato Latkes

*L*atkes, potato pancakes, are a specialty of the Jewish restaurants on Miami Beach, where they're eaten not only at Hanukkah, but all year long. Sweet potatoes give the recipe a Southern twist.

MAKES 8 TO 10

1 large sweet potato (about 1 pound), peeled

1 very small onion

1 egg, beaten

½ teaspoon baking powder

2 to 3 tablespoons all-purpose flour
or matzoh meal

About 2 cups vegetable oil, for frying

Confectioners' sugar, applesauce, and/or sour cream,
for serving

1. Shred the sweet potato and onion on the julienne disk of a food processor or on the coarse side of a hand grater.

2. Toss together the potato, onion, egg, and baking powder in a mixing bowl. Stir in enough of the flour to hold the mixture together.

3. Just before serving, pour the oil to a depth of at least 1 inch in a frying pan or electric skillet and heat to 350°F. Using 2 spoons, form the sweet potato mixture into 3-inch pancakes. Lower these into the fat. Fry the latkes, 4 at a time, turning with a slotted spoon or wire skimmer, until golden brown on both sides, about 2 minutes total.

4. Using a skimmer or slotted spoon, transfer the latkes to paper towels to drain. Sprinkle with confectioners' sugar and serve with applesauce and/or sour cream.

Yam Bake

To most Americans, a yam is just another name for sweet potato. True yam is a large African root vegetable with pale yellow or white flesh and no discernible sweetness. It tastes rather like a potato with a hint of chestnut, but the flavor is really unique. True yams can be found at Hispanic and West Indian markets. If whole yams are too large, ask the produce manager to cut off a piece the size you need. This recipe can be prepared with any Caribbean root vegetable, not to mention with potatoes or North American sweet potatoes. Use a pan that's heavy enough to spread the heat evenly, but attractive enough to serve at table: Cast iron is ideal.

SERVES 8

3 tablespoons unsalted butter or olive oil
2 onions, thinly sliced (about 2 cups)
2 pounds yam, peeled and cut into ½-inch slices
Salt and freshly ground black pepper, to taste
½ cup heavy (or whipping) cream
3 to 4 cups Chicken Stock (page 329) or canned broth
¼ cup coarse fresh bread crumbs

1. Melt half of the butter in a large cast-iron skillet over medium heat. Add the onions and cook, stirring often, until golden brown, 4 to 6 minutes.

2. Stir the yam into the onions and season with salt and pepper. Stir in the cream and enough stock to cover the vegetables. Bring the mixture to a boil.

3. Reduce the heat to medium and simmer the yams, stirring occasionally, until tender, 20 to 30 minutes. Add a little stock if necessary, but not too much; the mixture shouldn't be soupy. Correct the seasonings, adding salt and pepper to taste.

4. Preheat the oven to 400°F.

5. Sprinkle the bread crumbs over the yam mixture and dot the top with the remaining 1½ tablespoons butter. Bake the yams until the topping is crusty and brown, 5 to 10 minutes. Serve the yam bake in the pan in which it was cooked.

Boniato Gratin

The name boniato (a Cuban sweet potato) comes from the Spanish word for "good" or "harmless." The early explorers of the Caribbean encountered a bewildering array of new plants—many of them poisonous. In a world of strange and sometimes toxic foods, the nourishing boniato must have made a welcome addition to the settlers' diet. The coffee liqueur brings out the sweetness of the boniato.

SERVES 6

2 pounds boniatos, peeled and cut into ½-inch dice

Salt

½ cup heavy (or whipping) cream

½ cup Chicken Stock (see page 329)
*   or canned broth*

1 tablespoon coffee liqueur

Freshly ground black pepper

Pinch of grated nutmeg

¼ cup coarse fresh bread crumbs

2 tablespoons butter

BONIATO: THE OTHER SWEET POTATO

Say the word sweet potato and most Americans think of a sweet, bright orange-fleshed root vegetable. In Hispanic and West Indian communities in Florida, not to mention throughout the Caribbean, sweet potato means a turnip-shaped tuber with patchy purplish skin and cream-colored flesh: the boniato.

A beauty it's not, which may explain the boniato's slow acceptance in North America. This is a shame, for the tuber has a far more interesting flavor and texture than our sweet potato. It's less sweet than the latter, tasting like freshly roasted chestnuts. It's also harder and drier than an American sweet potato, with a starchy consistency similar to that of a baked potato.

When buying boniatos, look for hard, firm tubers free of mold, tiny worm holes, or soft spots. It's normal for the skin to look patchy, but it shouldn't be shriveled or wet. Boniatos range from the size of a lemon to that of a coconut, but the size doesn't alter the flavor. Store them in a loosely sealed paper bag at room temperature and try to use within 2 or 3 days of purchase.

Boniatos can be cooked any way you would a potato or sweet potato, including baking, boiling, steaming, frying, sautéing, or puréeing. I find that a paring knife works better than a vegetable peeler for peeling them. Keep the peeled boniato in water to cover until cooking time: the pale flesh discolors when exposed to air. Baked or boiled boniato should be served immediately, as it becomes a little starchy if it sits for too long.

1. Boil the boniato in salted water to cover (at least 2 quarts) until very tender, 6 to 8 minutes. Drain the boniato and return to the pan.

2. Mash the boniato to a coarse purée with a potato masher or fork. Work in the cream, stock, coffee liqueur, salt, pepper, and nutmeg. The mixture should be highly seasoned and moist. If necessary, add a little more stock.

3. Spoon the boniato mixture into a lightly buttered 8-inch gratin dish. Sprinkle with the bread crumbs and dot with the butter. (The recipe can be prepared several hours ahead to this stage.)

4. Preheat the oven to 400°F.

5. Just before serving, bake the gratin until crusty and golden brown, 15 to 20 minutes.

Yuca con Mojo

*Y*uca con mojo is the Cuban equivalent of boiled potatoes. Yuca (cassava) is a starchy root vegetable with a mild, buttery flavor. *Mojo* (pronounced MO-ho) is a light sauce made with garlic and sour orange juice or lime juice. The addition of cold water while the yuca is boiling helps spread open the vegetable's fibers. This is real Hispanic comfort food!

SERVES 4 TO 6

2 pounds yuca
Salt

MOJO:
3 tablespoons olive oil
2 to 3 cloves garlic, minced
¼ cup fresh lime juice or sour orange juice
Salt and freshly ground black pepper, to taste

½ small white onion, sliced as thinly as possible, for garnish
2 tablespoons chopped fresh Italian (flat-leaf) parsley, for garnish

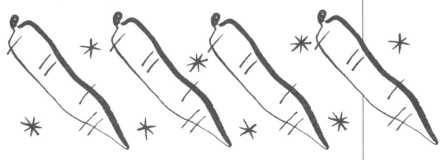

1. Cut the yuca crosswise into 2-inch pieces and peel with a paring knife. Cut the large pieces in quarters or halves so that all are of uniform size.

2. Bring at least 2 quarts of salted water to a boil. Add the yuca and cook until the ends of the pieces begin to split, about 10 minutes. Add 1 cup cold water. Bring the yuca back to a boil and cook until very soft, 5 to 10 minutes.

3. Meanwhile, prepare the *mojo*: Heat the oil in a nonreactive small saucepan over medium heat. Add the garlic and fry until soft but not brown, about 1 minute. Add the lime juice and salt and pepper and bring to a boil. Correct the seasonings, adding salt and pepper to taste.

4. Drain the yuca and scrape out any fibers with a fork. Arrange the yuca on a platter or on plates, and pour the hot *mojo* on top. Garnish with the onion and parsley and serve at once.

Maduros
(Fried Ripe Plantains)

C andy sweet and as golden as pieces of eight are *maduros*, literally "ripe ones," fried ripe plantains. *Maduros* are the obligatory accompaniment to Cuban fried spiced pork (*masitas de puerco*), Nicaraguan *churrasco*, and just about any other dish in the Hispano-American repertory. The key to great *maduros* is to use plantains so ripe, they look like you should throw them out. The skin should be completely black. Here in Florida, ethnic markets sell already ripe plantains. If you live in an area that doesn't have a large Hispanic community, you may need to buy green plantains and let them ripen at room temperature. There's a trick for bringing out the sweetness of less than fully ripe plantains: Start frying them in warm (300°F) oil and gradually increase the heat.

SERVES 4

2 very ripe plantains (about 1 pound total)
About 1 cup canola oil or other vegetable oil

1. Cut the plantains crosswise into 2½-inch pieces. Make a lengthwise cut in each and peel off the skin as described on page 28. Cut the plantain on the diagonal into ½-inch slices.

2. Pour the oil to a depth of ½ inch in a heavy frying pan and heat to 350°F. Add the plantain slices and fry until crusty and golden brown, about 1 minute per side, turning once.

3. Transfer the plantains to paper towels to drain. Serve at once.

Plantain Mash

Another popular plantain dish found throughout the Caribbean, this recipe derives from an ancient Dominican dish called *mofongo*. Traditionally, the plantains would be mashed with pork cracklings and pork fat. To lighten up the recipe, I use a little bacon for flavor and chicken stock to moisten the mash. For the best results, use semi-ripe plantains, called *pinton* in Spanish, recognizable by a yellow skin mottled with black.

SERVES 4

2 semi-ripe plantains (about 1 pound)
2 cups Chicken Stock (see page 329), canned
    broth, or water
2 strips bacon, cut into thin slivers
2 tablespoons butter
2 cloves garlic, minced
Salt and freshly ground black pepper, to taste

1. Cut the plantains crosswise into 2½-inch pieces. Make a lengthwise cut in each and peel off the skin as described on page 28. Cut the plantains into ½-inch slices. Combine the plantains and chicken stock in a large saucepan and boil until soft, about 10 minutes. Drain the plantains, reserving the liquid.

2. Meanwhile, lightly brown the bacon in a medium-size frying pan. Transfer the bacon with a slotted spoon to a paper towel to drain. Discard the bacon fat from the pan.

3. Melt the butter in the pan over medium heat. Add the garlic and cook until fragrant but not brown, about 1 minute. Remove from the heat and add the boiled plantains and bacon. Mash with a potato masher or wooden spoon, adding stock as necessary to obtain a thick but moist purée. Add salt and pepper and cook until thoroughly heated through, 2 to 3 minutes. I normally serve plantain mash like mashed potatoes. For a fancier presentation, you can spoon the mixture into buttered molds and invert them onto plates or a platter.

Tostones with Herbed Salt

The third of the popular Caribbean plantain trio, *tostones* are fried, mashed, green plantains. Frying the *tostones* in olive oil gives them a Mediterranean accent, but canola or any vegetable oil can be used.

SERVES 4

2 green plantains (1 pound total)
About 2 cups olive oil

HERBED SALT:
½ teaspoon dried oregano
½ teaspoon dried thyme
½ teaspoon garlic powder
½ teaspoon salt

1. Cut the plantains crosswise into 2½-inch pieces. Make a lengthwise cut in each and peel off the skin as described on page 28. Cut the plantains on the diagonal into ½-inch slices.

FRYING TOSTONES

The recipe for *tostones* calls for two fryings—the first in medium (325°F) oil to cook them through, the second in very hot (375°F) oil to crisp them. Between fryings, the plantains are flattened in a device that looks like a hinged tortilla press. Hispanic markets sell inexpensive *tostone* makers. Alternatively, the *tostones* can be flattened in a tortilla press or with a meat pounder or heavy skillet.

2. Pour the oil to a depth of ½ inch in a heavy frying pan and heat to 325°F. Add the plantain slices and fry until soft, about 2 minutes per side, turning once. Transfer the plantains with a slotted spoon to paper towels to drain.

3. Mix the ingredients for the herb salt in a small mixing bowl.

4. Just before serving, heat the oil to 375°F. Using a *tostone* maker, tortilla press, meat pounder, or other heavy object, flatten each plantain slice until ⅛ to ¼ inch thick. The thinner the *tostone*, the crisper it will be.

5. Fry the *tostones* until crisp and golden brown, about 1 minute per side. Drain on paper towels. Sprinkle the *tostones* with the herbed salt and serve at once.

Foolproof Rice

Here's how a Cuban grandmother would prepare white rice. The method is virtually foolproof and it produces fluffy white grains that are never sticky or dried out. The secret is to rinse the rice before cooking.

MAKES 3 CUPS; SERVES 4

1½ cups long-grain white rice, preferably Uncle Ben's
About 2½ cups water
½ teaspoon salt
1 tablespoon butter or vegetable oil

1. To wash the rice, place it in a large bowl with cold water to cover by 2 inches. Swirl it around with your fingers; the water will become cloudy. Pour it off and add more water. Continue rinsing the rice until the water is clear.

2. Place the rice in a large heavy saucepan. Add enough

of the water to cover the rice by ¾ inch. Stir in the salt and butter and bring the rice to a boil.

3. Tightly cover the pan, reduce the heat to low, and cook the rice until tender, about 18 minutes. Check the rice after 15 minutes: If it's too moist, set the cover ajar to allow some of the steam to escape. If too dry, add a little water.

4. Remove the pan from the heat and let the rice stand, covered, for 2 minutes. Fluff with a fork and serve at once.

Coconut Rice

Coconut milk and ginger give this rice a Caribbean accent. Instructions for making your own fresh coconut milk are found on page 331. In a pinch you could use canned coconut milk—just make sure it's unsweetened.

MAKES 3 CUPS; SERVES 4

2 tablespoons oil or butter
2 cloves garlic, minced
2 teaspoons minced fresh ginger
1½ cups long-grain white rice, preferably Uncle Ben's
1 cup Coconut Milk (see page 331)
1½ cups water
Salt

1. Heat the oil in a heavy saucepan over medium heat. Add the garlic and ginger and cook until fragrant but not brown, about 1 minute. Add the rice and sauté until the individual grains are shiny, about 1 minute.

2. Add the coconut milk, water, and salt and bring to a boil. Reduce the heat, cover the pan, and cook the rice until all of the liquid is absorbed and the grains are tender, 18 to 20 minutes.

3. Remove the pan from the heat and let the rice stand, covered, for 1 minute. Fluff with a fork and serve at once.

Sofrito and Corn Risotto

I taly meets Florida in this recipe, a tropical remake of classic risotto. Valencia-style rice is the Hispanic equivalent of Italian arborio. Both have the ability to thicken the cooking liquid into a creamy sauce while retaining the pasta-like firmness of the individual rice grains. Available at Hispanic markets and many supermarkets, Valencia-style rice has the added advantage of costing a fraction of the price of arborio. The two rices can be used interchangeably. I like to make this dish with Grilled Corn but any type of corn will do.

SERVES 4 TO 6

2 tablespoons annatto oil (see page 333) or olive oil

1 onion, finely chopped

1 red bell pepper, cored, seeded, and diced

1 cup Grilled (or cooked) Corn kernels (see page 245)

2 cloves garlic, minced

1½ cups Valenciana-style or arborio rice

½ cup dry white wine

5 to 5½ cups Chicken Stock (see page 329),
*   or canned broth, heated to simmering*

½ cup freshly grated Parmesan cheese

¼ cup finely chopped Italian (flat-leaf) parsley leaves

Salt and freshly ground black pepper, to taste

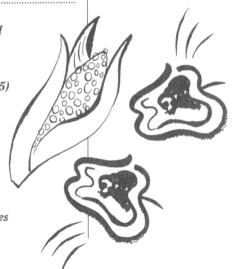

1. Heat the oil in a large saucepan over medium heat. Add the onion, bell pepper, and corn and sauté for 3 minutes. Add the garlic and sauté until soft and fragrant but not brown, about 2 minutes. Stir in the rice and cook until all of the grains are shiny, about 1 minute.

2. Add the wine and bring the mixture to a boil, stirring constantly. When most of the wine is absorbed, 1 to 2 minutes, stir in ½ cup of the stock. Cook the rice, at a brisk simmer, stirring frequently, until most of the liquid is absorbed, another 1 to 2 minutes. Stir in another ½ cup stock and continue cooking and stirring until absorbed.

3. Continue adding the stock, ½ cup at a time, until 5 cups have been incorporated. Wait until each batch of broth is absorbed before adding the next. If the rice is still firm after 20 minutes, add the remaining ½ cup stock. When ready, the risotto will have a creamy consistency, but the individual grains of rice will still be discernible and al dente. Remove the pan from the heat.

4. Stir in the cheese, parsley, and salt and pepper. The cheese is quite salty, so you may not need additional salt. Guests may wait for risotto, but risotto does not wait for anyone. Serve it at once.

Gallo Pinto
(Nicaraguan Red Beans and Rice)

It's hard to imagine a Nicaraguan meal without *gallo pinto*, red beans and rice. The beans and rice are cooked separately, then fried together in onion-flavored lard or olive oil. The longer the mixture fries, the more flavorful it becomes. "Thus, it's best to order *gallo pinto* late in the meal," quips Julio Somoza, owner of Miami's Nicaraguan steak house, Los Ranchos. Nicaraguan markets sell a special *gallo pinto* bean, which looks like a small kidney bean.

SERVES 6 TO 8

1 cup gallo pinto beans or small red kidney beans,
*   picked through and washed*
1 bay leaf
1 small onion, peeled
1 whole clove
2 cloves garlic, peeled
Salt
1½ cups long-grain white rice,
*   preferably Uncle Ben's*
3 tablespoons olive oil
1 onion, finely chopped
Freshly ground black pepper

1. Soak the beans in cold water to cover by 3 inches for at least 4 hours, or overnight.

2. Drain the beans and place in a large pot with 2 quarts water. Pin the bay leaf to the onion with the clove, and add to the beans. Add the garlic. Gradually bring the beans to a boil. Skim off any foam that rises to the surface.

3. Reduce the heat and gently simmer the beans, uncovered, until tender, 1 to 1½ hours, adding salt to taste during the last 10 minutes. Drain the beans in a colander and refresh under cold water. Discard the onion.

4. Bring 2½ cups of water and 1 teaspoon of salt to a boil in a large heavy saucepan. Add the rice and bring to a boil. Reduce the heat, cover, and gently simmer the rice until tender, about 18 minutes. Let the rice sit, covered, for 5 minutes. Fluff the rice with a fork. (The recipe can be prepared several hours ahead to this stage and stored in the refrigerator.)

5. Heat the oil in a large frying pan. Add the chopped

MIAMI'S CALLE OCHO

Let New York have Little Italy, San Francisco its Chinatown. Miami boasts an ethnic neighborhood equally steeped in tradition and local color: "Little Havana." For three decades, exiles from Castro's Cuba have gathered there to munch *media noches* (Cuban sandwiches), smoke locally made cigars, and play marathon domino games at the outdoor tables in Antonio Maceo Park, better known as Domino Park.

The main artery of Little Havana is Southwest Eighth Street, or *Calle Ocho* in Spanish (pronounced "KAH ye OH-cho). The streets are lined with *loncherias* (Cuban snack bars) and *botanicas* (herb shops specializing in medicinal and religious plants used in ceremonies of Cuba's Afro-Caribbean religion, Santeria). Record stores pulsate with mambo and merengue music. The *bodegas* (food markets) overflow with Hispanic provender: exotic root vegetables, like yuca and malanga;

exotic fruits, like mamey sapote (a coconut-shaped fruit that tastes like sweet potato); fresh sugarcane; guava paste; salt cod; and plantains.

The favorite pastime on *Calle Ocho* is eating. Miamians of all ethnic persuasions flock to cavernous restaurants, such as Versailles and La Carreta, for mammoth servings of *arroz con pollo* (chicken with yellow rice) and *ropa vieja* (braised, shredded skirt steak). Anytime, day or night, you'll find a large crowd gathered at the carryout window of Versailles for a quick snack of *croquetas* (ham croquets) or *empanadas* (guave paste- and cheese-filled turnovers). Tiny cups of sugary, black Cuban coffee keep the energy level high.

Calle Ocho is the culminating site of *Carnaval* Miami, a week-long festival that takes place in March. The event concludes with a 23-block-long street party featuring food, dance, and music, with more than one million revelers taking part.

onion and thoroughly brown over medium heat, about 5 minutes.

6. Add the beans and rice and cook over medium heat until the rice is lightly browned and the mixture is very aromatic, about 5 minutes. Correct the seasonings, adding salt and pepper to taste.

Moros y Cristianos

Serve up *moros* and you're serving up a cornerstone of the Cuban diet. The name is short for *moros y cristianos*, literally "Moors and Christians," a poetic description of the colorful combination of black beans and white rice. The traditional way to serve this dish is to ladle the black bean stew over the rice. But you can also cook the black beans dry and panfry them with the rice, as described in the *Gallo Pinto* recipe on page 263.

SERVES 4

3 cups cooked Foolproof Rice (page 260)
2 cups Soupy Black Beans (page 270)
2 tablespoons finely chopped scallion greens

Mound the rice on plates or a platter. Ladle the bean mixture on top and sprinkle with the scallion greens.

BEAN CUISINE

Beans have always played an important role in Floridian cooking.

Few foods are more versatile, flavorful, and inexpensive.

Beans are also good for you: They're rich in protein and fiber and low in fat.

Home cooked dried beans are superior to canned. The latter contain unnecessarily high levels of sodium and tend to be mushy. Many people are intimidated by the prospect of preparing dried beans, but nothing could be easier. True, it takes several hours to cook dried beans, but the actual work time is just a few minutes.

1. Spread the beans on a baking sheet and pick through them, removing any pebbles or bits of stem.

2. Rinse the beans thoroughly in a strainer under cold water.

3. Place the beans in a bowl and add enough cold water to come at least 3 inches above the beans. Set aside to soak for at least 4 hours, or as long as overnight in the refrigerator. Soaking the beans shortens the cooking time and draining the soaking liquid helps

remove some of the polyoligo-saccharides, long carbohydrate molecules that tend to cause flatulence. The exception to this rule is black beans, which are cooked with the soaking liquid to maintain the black color. Of course, soaking isn't absolutely necessary, but the cooking time will be longer if you don't.

4. Drain the beans and transfer them to a large pot. Add enough water to cover by at least 3 inches. Add flavorings, such as onion, garlic, celery, bay leaf, or other herbs, at the beginning. Don't add salt or acidic ingredients, such as tomatoes, vinegar, or wine, until the end of cooking. Salt and acids will

toughen the bean skins if added at the beginning.

5. Bring the beans to a boil. Reduce the heat and gently simmer until cooked, 1 to 2 hours, depending on the size of the beans and how soft you like them. To test for doneness, pinch a single bean between your thumb and forefinger. It should crush easily. There's nothing worse than eating undercooked beans. Unsoaked beans require 2 to 3 hours boiling.

For beans with a soft consistency for soups and sauces, cover the pan while cooking. For beans with a firmer exterior, cook uncovered.

A pressure cooker can cut the cooking time for beans by half or even two-thirds. Follow the manufacturer's instructions.

New to the market are hydrated dried beans, which don't need soaking. Look for hydrated beans in the produce section of the supermarket. One popular manufacturer is Frieda's, Inc., of California.

One cup of dried beans makes 2 to 2½ cups cooked, enough to serve 4 people as a side dish.

Florida Refries

What happens if you make refried beans with that Florida staple, black beans, instead of Tex-Mex-style pinto beans? Miami's Cuban-Americans know the answer to that question: a dish that is part pancake and part hash called *frijoles guisados,* "stewed beans." I like to finish the dish with sour cream. You could also serve the refries like hash, crowned with a couple of fried eggs. Other variations include making the refries with garbanzo beans (chick-peas)—mash them with a potato masher before frying— or enriching the beans with diced chorizo or bacon.

SERVES 4 AS AN APPETIZER, 2 AS A LIGHT MAIN COURSE

2 tablespoons olive oil
¼ cup very finely chopped red bell pepper
¼ cup very finely chopped onion
2½ cups Firm-Cooked Black Beans (page 269),
    cooked until soft
3 cloves garlic, minced
2 scallions, trimmed and finely chopped
½ teaspoon ground cumin
½ teaspoon dried oregano
Salt and freshly ground black pepper,
    to taste
¼ cup sour cream
Cilantro or parsley sprigs, for garnish

1. Heat the oil in a 10-inch nonstick frying pan over medium heat. Add the bell pepper and onion and cook until soft and fragrant but not brown, 3 to 4 minutes.

2. Stir in the beans, garlic, scallions, cumin, oregano, and salt and pepper. Cook over medium heat for about 5 minutes, gently patting the top and sides of the beans with a spatula to form a compact cake. Mash some of the beans with the back of the spatula to form a paste that will hold the pancake together.

3. Reduce the heat and continue cooking the beans until very soft, very tender, and quite dry, 10 to 15 minutes. The refries should be crusty on the bottom and should form a thick pancake. Taste for seasonings, adding salt and pepper as necessary.

4. To serve, place a platter over the pan and invert the refries onto it. Garnish with dollops of the sour cream and the sprigs of cilantro.

Black Beans Cooked Two Ways

Here are two ways to prepare black beans, which are so essential to Floridian cooking. The first produces firm black beans that retain their individuality. The second produces soupy beans, which are great spooned over rice. Firm black beans can be added to rice (substitute them for the red beans in the *Gallo Pinto* recipe, page 263) and they're also good for adding to salsas and salads. The secret to keeping the beans black is to cook them in the soaking water. (Normally bean soaking water is discarded.)

EACH RECIPE MAKES 4 TO 5 CUPS;
SERVES 8 TO 10

FIRM-COOKED BLACK BEANS

1 pound dried black beans, picked through and washed
1 small onion, cut in half
2 ribs celery, cut into 2-inch pieces
2 carrots, cut into 2-inch pieces
½ green bell pepper, cored and seeded
3 cloves garlic, peeled
1 bouquet garni of 1 bay leaf, 3 sprigs fresh thyme or ½ teaspoon
*   dried, and 3 sprigs fresh parsley tied in a piece of cheesecloth*
½ teaspoon ground cumin
½ teaspoon dried oregano
Salt and freshly ground black pepper, to taste

1. In a large heavy pot, soak the beans in cold water to cover by at least 3 inches for no less than 4 hours, or overnight. (If omitting this step, add approximately 1 hour to the cooking time.)

2. Add the vegetables, garlic, bouquet garni, cumin, and oregano to the pot of beans and soaking water. Bring to a boil over high heat. Skim off any foam that rises to the surface.

3. Reduce the heat and gently simmer the beans, uncovered, stirring occasionally, until tender, 1 to 1¼ hours. Add water as necessary to keep the beans submerged.

4. Season the beans with salt and pepper during the last 10 minutes of cooking. Drain the beans in a colander and rinse with cold water. Remove and discard the vegetables and bouquet garni. The beans are now ready for adding to salads or salsas. Store, covered, in the refrigerator for up to 3 days. The beans can also be reheated in a skillet or saucepan.

SOUPY BLACK BEANS

1 pound dried black beans, picked through and washed
1 small onion, cut in half
4 cloves garlic, peeled
2 bay leaves
½ green bell pepper, cored and seeded
About 1 teaspoon ground cumin
About 1 teaspoon dried oregano

SOFRITO:
2 strips bacon, cut into ¼-inch slivers (optional)
1 tablespoon olive oil
½ small onion, finely chopped
2 cloves garlic, minced
½ green bell pepper, cored, seeded, and finely chopped
3 scallions, trimmed and finely chopped

SEASONINGS:
2 tablespoons dry white wine
1 tablespoon red wine vinegar, or to taste
½ teaspoon sugar
Salt and freshly ground black pepper, to taste

1. In a large heavy pot, soak the beans in cold water to cover by at least 3 inches for no less than 4 hours, or overnight. (If omitting this step, add about 1 hour to the cooking time.)

2. Add the halved onion, garlic cloves, bay leaves, bell pepper, cumin, and oregano to the pot of beans and soaking water. Bring to a boil over high heat. Skim off any foam that rises to the surface.

3. Reduce the heat, cover, and gently simmer the beans, stirring occasionally, for 1 hour. Add water as necessary to keep the beans submerged. Remove the onion, garlic, bay leaves, and bell pepper with a slotted spoon and discard.

4. Meanwhile, prepare the *sofrito*: If using bacon, brown it in a heavy frying pan over medium heat. Pour off the fat.

5. Add the olive oil and the remaining *sofrito* ingredients. (If not using bacon, heat the olive oil in a frying pan, add the *sofrito* ingredients, and continue with the recipe.) Cook over medium heat until just beginning to brown, about 3 minutes. Stir the *sofrito* into the beans along with the wine, vinegar, sugar, and salt and pepper. Cover and continue simmering the beans, until very soft, about 20 minutes.

6. Just before serving, correct the seasonings, adding salt, pepper, cumin, oregano, or vinegar. The mixture should be highly seasoned. Spoon the soupy black beans over rice.

GRITS: FLORIDA'S SOUTHERN HERITAGE

The first time I encountered them, I was truly perplexed. There on my breakfast plate, next to the eggs and bacon, where the hash browns should have been, was a pile of steaming white mush. "Grits," explained the waitress, a touch of condescension in her voice, as though the identity of this strange breakfast food should be self-evident to any self-respecting Floridian. It was the first of many reminders that while much contemporary Floridian cooking has been inspired by Californian and Caribbean cuisine, our roots go equally deep in the South.

Grits
with Tomato Gravy

Grits with tomato gravy is the traditional accompaniment to fried freshwater fish in central and northern Florida. The mere mention of the dish is enough to make a rural Floridian's mouth water. This recipe comes from Floribel Clement, who lives in Lake Placid, Florida. Traditionally, the tasty gravy is made with canned tomatoes and bacon fat. For the sake of authenticity, I've included the recipe. But I've also included a lighter version that uses fresh tomatoes.

SERVES 4 TO 6

2 cups water

2 cups milk or light cream

Salt and freshly ground black pepper, to taste

1 cup quick-cooking grits

Old-Fashioned Tomato Gravy or Fresh Tomato Gravy
  (recipes follow)

Fresh basil sprigs, for garnish (optional)

1. Bring the water, milk, and a little salt and pepper to a boil in a large heavy saucepan. Add the grits in a thin stream, stirring constantly. Bring the mixture back to a boil. Reduce the heat and simmer the grits, uncovered, stirring occasionally, until cooked, 3 to 4 minutes. Correct the seasonings, adding salt and pepper to taste.

2. Spoon the grits onto plates and make a depression in the center. Pour either gravy over the grits, garnish, if desired, and serve at once.

OLD-FASHIONED TOMATO GRAVY

4 strips bacon, cut into ¼-inch slivers
3 tablespoons all-purpose flour
1 can (28 ounces) whole plum tomatoes,
    coarsely chopped, with their liquid
Salt and freshly ground black pepper, to taste

1. Fry the bacon in a nonreactive heavy skillet over medium heat until golden brown, about 2 minutes. Pour off all but 3 tablespoons of the fat.

2. Stir in the flour and cook, stirring constantly, until it turns brown, about 3 minutes. Remove the pan from the heat and stir in the chopped tomatoes with their juices. Return the pan to medium heat and bring the mixture to a boil, stirring constantly. Simmer the sauce until thick and well-flavored, about 3 minutes. Add salt and pepper.

A GRITS GAZETEER

Simply defined, grits are dried, hulled, coarsely ground white corn kernels. The corn is treated with wood ash (lye) to facilitate hulling—a trick discovered by Native Americans. This alkaline processing has the added advantage of increasing the calcium content in grits and improving the balance of the amino acids. The corn is then ground to pieces just smaller than sesame seeds and just larger than grains of sand.

Boiled grits are a mandatory part of a Southern breakfast, where they are served, not as a breakfast cereal, as is often but erroneously written, but as a starchy side dish. "We use them in place of potatoes… never as a cereal," wrote Pulitzer Prize-winning author Marjorie Rawlings, who served grits often at her farmhouse in Cross Creek in central Florida.

But breakfast is just a starting point. Grits, grunts, and johnnycake (grunts are a type of fish, johnnycake a cornmeal pancake) make a traditional Florida Keys supper. Grits with tomato gravy is a classic accompaniment to fried fish not only in rural Florida, but throughout the South.

Other grits delicacies include grits pudding, grits spoon bread, grits soufflés, and even crusty slabs of fried grits. Rawlings had the right idea when she observed that "a day without grits [is] a day wasted."

Other grits delicacies include grits pudding, grits spoon bread, grits soufflés, and even crusty slabs of fried grits. Rawlings had the right idea when she observed that "a day without grits [is] a day wasted."

Grits are available in three forms: traditional, instant, and quick. The first require soaking for several hours prior to boiling for 30 to 40 minutes.

Quick grits are probably the most practical form: Simply add them to boiling water, milk, or stock, and simmer, stirring, for 4 to 6 minutes. The most widely available brands of quick grits are from Quaker and Aunt Jemima.

Instant grits are cooked and dried before packaging. I'm not particularly fond of them, as they lack the creamy consistency of the slower, longer cooked products.

For truly spectacular results use stone-ground grits, such as Adams Old-Fashioned Whole Heart Grits (Adams Milling Company, Route 6, Box 148A, Napier Field Station, Dolthan, AL 36303) or Callaway Gardens Speckled Heart Grits (Callaway Gardens Country Store, Pine Mountain, GA 31822).

FRESH TOMATO GRAVY

4 strips bacon, cut into ¼-inch slivers
2 tablespoons olive oil
3 cloves garlic, minced
2 tablespoons minced shallots, chopped
½ green bell pepper, cored, seeded, and finely chopped
2 cups peeled, seeded, and finely chopped fresh ripe tomatoes
½ cup heavy (or whipping) cream, Chicken Stock (see page 329), or canned broth
2 tablespoons chopped fresh basil (or 1 teaspoon dried)
Salt and freshly ground pepper, to taste

1. Fry the bacon in a nonreactive heavy skillet over medium heat until golden brown, about 2 minutes. Drain the bacon on paper towels; discard the bacon fat.

2. Add the olive oil, garlic, shallots, and bell pepper to the skillet and cook over medium heat until fragrant and soft but not brown, about 2 minutes. Stir in the tomatoes and cook over high heat for 1 minute. Stir in the cream and basil and simmer the sauce until thick and well-flavored, about 3 minutes. Correct the seasonings, adding salt or pepper.

Manchego Cheese Grits

This recipe is guaranteed to make believers out of skeptics who question the palatability of grits. I like to think of it as Floridian polenta. Manchego cheese is a sheep's-milk cheese from Spain. If unavailable, substitute Romano or mild Cheddar.

SERVES 8 TO 10

2 tablespoons olive oil

2 cloves garlic, minced

½ cup finely chopped onion

½ green bell pepper, cored, seeded, and finely chopped

½ red bell pepper, cored, seeded, and finely chopped

1 jalapeño chili, seeded and minced (optional)

2 cups milk

2 cups Chicken Stock (page 329), canned broth, milk, or water

Salt and freshly ground black pepper, to taste

1 cup quick-cooking grits

2 eggs, beaten

1 cup freshly grated Manchego cheese

½ teaspoon of your favorite hot sauce (optional)

1. Heat the oil in a large heavy saucepan over medium heat. Add the garlic, onion, bell peppers, and chili and cook until soft and fragrant, but not brown, 2 to 3 minutes.

2. Stir in the milk, chicken stock, and a little salt and pepper and bring to a boil. Add the grits in a thin stream, stirring constantly. Bring the mixture back to a boil. Reduce the heat and simmer the grits, uncovered, stirring occasionally, until cooked, 3 to 4 minutes. Remove the pan from the heat and let the grits cool slightly.

3. Stir the beaten eggs into the grits, followed by the cheese. Correct the seasonings, adding salt and pepper to taste. For a touch of heat, add the hot sauce. Spoon the mixture into a buttered 12 x 8-inch baking dish. (The recipe can be prepared several hours ahead to this stage.)

4. Preheat the oven to 400°F.

5. Bake the grits until thoroughly heated through and lightly browned, 15 to 20 minutes. Serve at once.

Guava Cheesecake

Hibiscus Granita

Happy Endings

Cuban Coffee Brûlée

Floridians are great dessert lovers and we come by our passion naturally. The Sunshine State leads the nation in sugar production, with more than 427,000 acres of cane fields. The sugar industry has made Clewiston, Florida, north of Lake Okeechobee, one of the wealthiest communities (in terms of per capita income, at least) in the state. Tall shocks of whole sugarcane can be found at most of our ethnic markets, while *guarapo* (fresh sugarcane juice) is sipped at *loncherias* (Cuban snack bars) throughout the state.

If sugar is the backbone of Floridian dessert making, fresh fruit provides its soul. There are few places in the United States where cooks have such a rich selection from which to choose. Florida ranks first in U.S. orange, lime, tangerine, grapefruit, and mango production. It's the only state in the Union that grows the key lime, a small, yellow, bracingly tart fruit popularized by our most famous dessert, key lime pie.

The Sunshine State is America's primary source for a host of exotic tropical fruits as well—from kumquats, carambolas, and canistels to lychees, longans, and passion fruits. One farm in Homestead, Florida, grows 51 different varieties of bananas. Another specializes in space-age fruits, such as monstera deliciosa, also known as ceriman, a green-scaled, phallic-shape fruit that tastes like a cross between lime, banana, and honey; and jackfruit, which looks like an armadillo, tastes vaguely like an apricot, and can weigh up to 100 pounds.

Florida's growing Latin American communities play an increasingly significant role in Floridian dessert-making. In many areas, flan and its numerous variations are better-known than key lime pie. Nicaragua's famous *tres leches*, "three-milk cake," has been adopted by Hispanic restaurants of all stripes and

HOW TO BUY AND USE LIMES

When buying limes, look for firm, shiny, unblemished fruits that feel heavy in your hand. As a general rule, the thinner the skin, the juicier the pulp. Store limes in a closed plastic bag in the refrigerator. Tightly wrap cut limes in plastic, as contact with oxygen destroys the vitamin C.

The lime offers the cook two dynamic flavors: the sour juice and the aromatic oils in the rind. These oils are concentrated in the "zest," the dark outer rind: remove it with a zester (a tool with a perforated flat blade) or a grater. When large quantities of grated lime zest are required, remove the zest in broad strips with a vegetable peeler, then grind it in a spice mill. Avoid the white pith, which is bitter.

To juice a lime, roll it firmly on a work surface to rupture the juice sacs inside. Limes are drier than lemons, so you'll need to press hard. Depending on the size, a Persian lime contains 1 to 3 tablespoons juice. To make 1 cup of key lime juice you'll need 10 to 18 key limes. Lime can be substituted for lemon in most recipes, but keep in mind that its juice is more acidic.

Lime juice has a natural affinity with melon, chicken, and seafood. Sprinkle a few drops on cut bananas or avocados to prevent them from discoloring.

even Anglo eating establishments. Visit a south Florida ice cream parlor and you're sure to find ice creams and sorbets made from a dozen different Caribbean fruits.

Here are some of the traditional and new Floridian desserts that are captivating the American palate.

Maida Heatter's Key Lime Cake

Maida Heatter, America's grande dame of desserts, lives right here in Miami Beach. Whenever she comes for dinner, she brings us a bag of the largest, juiciest key limes I've ever seen, picked from a tree that grows outside her kitchen. This cake is the perfect dessert for people who have overdosed on key lime pie.

SERVES 10

Fine, dry bread crumbs, for coating pan
3 cups sifted all-purpose flour
2 teaspoons baking powder
½ teaspoon salt
8 ounces (2 sticks) unsalted butter, at room temperature
2 cups sugar
4 extra-large or jumbo eggs
1 cup milk
Finely grated zest of 3 limes, preferably key limes

GLAZE:
½ cup fresh key lime juice, or ¼ cup each fresh regular lime juice
*   and fresh lemon juice*
¾ cup sugar

1. Adjust a rack one-third of the way up from the bottom of the oven. Preheat the oven to 350°F. Thoroughly butter a 10-inch tube pan. Sprinkle the pan with the bread crumbs.

2. Sift together the flour, baking powder, and salt and set aside.

3. In the large bowl of an electric mixer beat the butter until soft. Gradually add the sugar and beat until light and fluffy. Beat in the eggs, one at a time, scraping down the sides of the bowl after each addition.

4. On the lowest speed, alternately add the sifted dry ingredients in three additions with the milk in two additions, scraping the bowl as necessary, beating just to mix after each addition.

5. Stir in the grated lime zest by hand. Pour the batter into the prepared pan, pouring half the batter on one side of the tube pan and half on the other. Level the top by briskly rotating the pan back and forth.

6. Bake the cake until a cake tester inserted in the middle comes out clean, about 1¼ hours. Remove the pan from the oven and let the cake cool slightly in the pan on a wire rack, 10 to 15 minutes.

7. Meanwhile, prepare the glaze. Stir the lime juice and sugar in a bowl just to mix.

8. Place a cake rack over the tube pan and invert the cake onto it. Place the rack over a large sheet of foil.

9. Using a pastry brush, brush the glaze all over the warm cake, until completely absorbed. Brush on any glaze that drips onto the foil.

10. Let the cake cool completely. Use a flat-sided baking sheet or a very large spatula to transfer the cake to a round platter or cake plate. Let the cake stand loosely covered with plastic wrap for several hours, preferably overnight, so that the glaze has time to penetrate to the interior of the cake. When ready, the outside of the cake will be completely dry. Cut into slices for serving.

SPANISH LIMES

On my first trip to the weekly farmers' market in Coconut Grove, I discovered a singular delicacy: a bag of what looked like miniature limes clinging to twig-like stems. The Bahamian and Cuban children around me devoured them at eye-blurring speed. I later learned the name of this strange fruit: Spanish lime.

Known as *momoncillo* in Spanish and *gineep* in Caribbean English, Spanish lime is a small (seldom more than an inch in diameter), lime-green fruit with one large seed in the center. Despite its lime-like appearance and sour taste, it's actually a member of the grape family.

Spanish limes are in season in summer and fall. To partake, bite or tear the skin off (pinch it with your teeth) and chew the coral-colored flesh off the seed. It may seem like a lot of work at first. But once you get the hang of it, Spanish limes become as addictive as pistachio nuts.

FLORIDA LIMES

Is there any flavor more conducive to warm-weather feasting than lime? Bracingly tart and distinctively aromatic, it refreshes like no other fruit when the temperature and humidity rise. Lime juice is the primary ingredient in countless warm weather dishes, from Daiquiris to ceviche.

The association of lime with warm-weather cooking is no accident. Limes are believed to have originated in India or Malaysia. Columbus prized the fruit enough to bring it with him on his second voyage to the New World in 1493. The tree spread rapidly throughout the Caribbean to Florida and Central America, where it remains an essential ingredient. Prior to Hurricane Andrew, Florida grew 90 percent of the nation's limes. Although many groves were severely damaged by the storm, the industry is

making a comeback.

The fruit most of us think of as lime is the Persian or Tahitian lime, a shiny, dark green, seedless hybrid. Persian limes are quite large, averaging 4 to 8 to a pound. Peak season is summer, when the fruit is larger and juicier, but Persian limes are available year-round. The 10-pound box that wholesales for $6 in the summer, however, could cost as much as $40 in the winter.

Here in Florida, we are partial to the key lime, a small (10 to 16 to a pound), yellowish fruit with seeds and a bracingly acerbic juice. Also known as Mexican lime or West Indian lime, the key lime was culti-

vated extensively in the Florida Keys in the nineteenth and early twentieth centuries. Many Floridians still have key lime trees in their backyards. Key

lime is the preferred lime

throughout the Caribbean and Central and South America.

Key limes do have their drawbacks, however. The trees are full of thorns and the fruits are full of seeds. The juice has a mildly bitter aftertaste that can be off-putting. Key limes are acidic, of course, but because they're picked at a riper stage than Persian limes, they also have a touch of sweetness. Key limes are available irregularly throughout the year (peak season is summer) at specialty produce shops and progressive supermarkets. If unavailable, the flavor can be approximated by combining equal parts of Persian lime juice and lemon juice.

This brings us to the tangerine lime, which sometimes turns up at ethnic markets. A large, round, green fruit with orange-colored pulp and acidic orange-colored juice, it is actually a type of sour orange (see page 72).

Chocolate-Banana Sin Cake

Chocolate and bananas are one of those unexpected flavor combinations that sends you rushing back for seconds. This dessert features a sinfully rich flourless chocolate cake topped with caramelized manzanos, or apple bananas (if unavailable, use regular bananas), and rum-scented whipped cream. The cake tastes best at room temperature.

SERVES 8 TO 10

CAKE:

1 pound semisweet chocolate, chopped

8 tablespoons (1 stick) unsalted butter,
cut into tablespoons, at room
temperature

4 large eggs, separated

4 tablespoons granulated sugar

1 tablespoon cornstarch

2 teaspoons vanilla extract

¼ teaspoon cream of tartar

BANANA TOPPING:

1 pound manzanos (apple bananas) or
other ripe bananas

2 tablespoons fresh orange juice

3 tablespoons unsalted butter

3 tablespoons granulated sugar

1 cup heavy (or whipping) cream

3 tablespoons confectioners' sugar, or to taste

1 tablespoon light rum, or to taste

1 piece (1 ounce) semisweet chocolate,
for shaving

YES, WE HAVE NEW BANANAS

William Lessard's farm is a 45 minute drive south of Miami. But walking between his banana plants, their broad green leaves canopied 18 feet overhead, it feels like a jungle in Southeast Asia. The former fighter pilot became impassioned with growing bananas while stationed in a Philippine rain forest. Today, he grows 51 different exotic banana varieties on his 7½-acre farm in Homestead. Lessard is one of a small but growing number of progressive growers who are changing the way Americans think about bananas.

To most people, banana means the *Gran Enano* (literally "big dwarf"), the long, gracefully arched fruit popularized by Chiquita. But bananas come in a dazzling array of shapes, sizes, and flavors. There are tiny *finger bananas,* no bigger than your pinky, and giant *Hua Moas*, starchy cooking bananas that are as big around as your arm. There are red-skinned *Macaboo* bananas (also known as Jamaican Reds) and striped *Ae Aes,* that are variegated like candy canes. There are bananas that taste like apples, strawberries, pineapples, and even baked potatoes.

Odd as it may seem, bananas are the berries of a tropical plant grown in India, Asia, Africa, and Central and South America. The first bananas arrived in the U.S. in the early 1800s. The fruit is so popular today that Americans eat more than 25 pounds per person a year.

Red, finger, and apple bananas can be found at specialty green grocers and large supermarkets. Look for plantains at Hispanic and Caribbean markets and in the produce section of large urban supermarkets. You'll need to mail away for the more esoteric varieties.

The W.O. Lessard Nursery (19201 S.W. 248th Street., Homestead, Florida 33031) sells exotic banana sampler packs. Each pack includes 15 pounds of bananas (5 to 10 different varieties) and costs $40, including shipping by second-day air. For further reading, Lessard has written *The Complete Book of Bananas* ($35), profiling 50 banana varieties, with 41 full-color plates.

1. Preheat the oven to 350°F. Butter a 10-inch spring-form pan, and sprinkle with sugar.

2. Prepare the cake: Melt the chocolate in the top of a double boiler over simmering water. When the chocolate has completely melted, whisk in the butter a tablespoon at a time. Let the mixture cool slightly.

3. Meanwhile, beat the egg yolks with 2 tablespoons of the granulated sugar in a mixer at high speed until the mixture is ivory colored and as thick as marshmallow topping, about 5 minutes. Stir in the cornstarch and vanilla.

4. Beat the egg whites, adding the cream of tartar after 20 seconds, and adding the remaining 2 tablespoons sugar as the whites stiffen to soft peaks. Gently fold the egg yolk mixture into the chocolate mixture; Fold in the egg whites as gently as possible.

5. Spoon the batter into the prepared pan. Bake the cake until firm on top, but the center is still a little soft, about 30 minutes. Remove the pan from the oven, set on a wire rack, and let the cake cool to room temperature. Run a knife around the inside edge of the pan and remove the sides. The cake will sink a little in the center.

6. Meanwhile, prepare the topping: Peel the bananas and cut them into ¼-inch slices. Toss the bananas with the orange juice to prevent discoloring.

7. Combine the butter and granulated sugar in a large skillet over high heat and cook until the mixture begins to caramelize, 2 to 3 minutes. Stir in the bananas and cook, turning, until golden brown, 3 to 4 minutes. Let the banana mixture cool completely.

8. Beat the cream in a chilled bowl with a mixer. As the cream stiffens, beat in the confectioners' sugar and rum to taste. Continue beating until stiff.

9. Spoon the caramelized banana mixture on top of the cake. Using a pastry bag fitted with a star tip, pipe rosettes of the whipped cream all over the top of the cake. Use a vegetable peeler or paring knife to shave the chocolate over the cake. Cut into wedges for serving.

Banana Strudel

H ere's a tropical remake of an Austrian classic. My favorite banana for this one is the red banana, but any ripe banana will do. Sometimes, I substitute macadamia nuts for the pecans.

MAKES 2 STRUDELS,
ENOUGH TO SERVE 8 TO 10

6 ripe bananas
½ cup raisins
Juice and grated zest of 1 lemon
1 cinnamon stick (2 inches long)
2 tablespoons dark rum
3 tablespoons (packed) light brown sugar, or to taste
1 tablespoon cornstarch
2 tablespoons banana liqueur (optional)
8 sheets filo dough
⅓ cup melted unsalted butter
¼ cup granulated sugar
¼ cup finely chopped toasted pecans or macadamia nuts
(see page 311)
¼ cup confectioners' sugar (optional)

1. Peel the bananas and cut them into ½-inch dice. Combine the bananas, raisins, lemon juice, lemon zest, cinnamon stick, rum, and brown sugar in a nonreactive heavy saucepan. Simmer the mixture, uncovered, over medium heat until the bananas are just tender, 2 to 3 minutes. Remove from the heat and correct the flavorings, adding sugar or lemon juice to taste.
2. Make a paste with the cornstarch and banana liqueur, if using (if not, substitute water). Return the banana mixture to the heat. Whisk the paste into the mixture and boil over high heat until the mixture thickens, about 20 seconds.

A TASTING OF EXOTIC BANANAS

A n afternoon on Bill Lessard's banana farm will quickly dispel the notion that all bananas taste the same. Here are my notes from a recent tasting of exotic bananas grown in south Florida.

MANZANO: This short (4-inch-long), thick, pale yellow-skinned fruit is often called apple banana. Its fragrant flesh has a distinct apple flavor. Great for pies and out-of-hand eating.

MYSORE: A tiny (3-inch-long, ½ inch in diameter), finger-shaped banana originally from

Mysor in western India. Sweet and musky, with a vanilla-pineapple flavor. The flesh is pale yellow and slightly fibrous.

RAJAPURI: A small, stubby banana (4 inches long and 1 inch in diameter). Tangy and vibrantly flavored, with a fruity acidity reminiscent of cherries or orange. Pale yellow, smooth-textured, and creamy. This is one of my favorites.

PYSANG RAJA: A medium-size banana with a sharp nipple at the flower end. The skin clings tightly to the fruit. (Unlike most bananas, this one is most easily peeled from the flower end.) Sweet but rather bland.

HA'A: A medium-size, torpedo-shaped banana with a nipple at the stem end and a point at the flower end. The flesh has an orange tinge and is hard to peel. Sweet-flavored and nicely acidic, but its musty smell is off-putting.

ORINOCO: Named for the Orinoco River in Venezuela, this one sure doesn't look like a Chiquita! Eight inches long, angular, with three sharp ridges, the *orinoco* has a firm white-yellow flesh with a flavor that hints at strawberry.

Transfer the filling to a bowl and let it cool to room temperature; remove the cinnamon stick. Cover and chill the filling completely in the refrigerator, at least 1 hour.

3. Assemble the strudels: Lay 1 sheet of filo dough on a dish towel on a baking sheet, with a long edge toward you. Keep the remaining filo covered with a cloth. Lightly brush the sheet of filo with some of the melted butter. Sprinkle with some of the granulated sugar and pecans. Lay another sheet of filo on top, brush with butter, and sprinkle with sugar and pecans. Repeat with a third and fourth sheet of filo.

4. Mound half of the filling along the long edge closest to you and roll up the filo half way, lifting the dish towel to help with the rolling. Tuck in the ends and continue rolling the strudel; it should look like a giant eggroll. Carefully roll it onto the baking sheet. Assemble the second strudel in the same way.

5. Brush the tops of the strudels with the remaining butter and sprinkle with the remaining sugar and nuts. Cover with plastic wrap and chill until firm, about 30 minutes.

6. Preheat the oven to 375°F.

7. Using a sharp knife, lightly score the tops of the strudels without cutting all the way through to the filling. Bake the strudels until crisp and golden brown, 30 to 40 minutes. Transfer the strudels to a wire rack to cool for at least 5 minutes. Cut the strudels diagonally into slices. Sprinkle with confectioners' sugar, if desired and serve.

The Fontainebleau Cheesecake

The Fontainebleau Hotel (now the Fontainebleau-Hilton) is the most famous hotel in Miami Beach—indeed, one of the most famous in all of Florida. Built on the oceanfront estate of tire baron Harvey Firestone, the Fontainebleau boasts more than 1,200 rooms and a gracefully curved facade that shocked the architectual world when the hotel opened in 1954. In the early years, Dean Martin, Joey Bishop, Peter Lawford, Sammy Davis Jr. and Frank Sinatra — the so-called Rat Pack—made the hotel's La Ronde Room their stomping ground. Sinatra was such a regular here, that the hotel named an oceanfront suite for him. Less famous, but no less praiseworthy was the Fontainebleau's first pastry chef, Maurice Guillot, who created an exquisitely rich cheesecake that still has guests clamoring for seconds today. The double baking method helps keep the cake uncommonly creamy and moist. There are many possible toppings and sauces. I like the Mango Sauce on page 322.

SERVES 10

2 pounds cream cheese (preferably Philadelphia brand), at room temperature

1½ cups sugar

4 extra-large eggs, at room temperature

¾ cup half-and-half

1¼ teaspoons vanilla extract

Juice and grated zest of 1 large or 1½ small lemons

1. Preheat the oven to 425°F. Generously butter a 9-inch springform pan.

DECO DINING

Ten years ago, the Art Deco District on Miami Beach was a ghost town after sunset. These days, "SoBe" (short for South Beach), is jammed with cosmopolitan tourists and locals on the prowl for chic food and steamy nightlife. What has brought them here is a major restaurant revolution.

Since 1987, more than a hundred new restaurants have opened in the historic Art Deco District. If fact, the opening of a new South Beach restaurant has become almost a weekly occurrence.

South Beach is a triangular, one square mile area at the southern end of Miami Beach. Bordered by Lincoln Road to the north, the Atlantic Ocean to the east, and Biscayne Bay to the south and west, the Deco District is home to more than 800 historic Art Deco buildings. Most were constructed in the 1930's and 40's, when glass and concrete blocks were the preferred building materials, when corners were rounded, and color schemes ran to pastel pink, turquoise, and aquamarine.

In the fifties, the Deco District was eclipsed by high-rise resort hotels, like the Eden Roc and the Fontaine-bleau, a mile north of South Beach. By 1980, the Deco District had become a refuge for fixed income retirees.

The turn-around came in the mid 1980s, when developers began buying up and renovating hotels on Ocean Drive. The TV series Miami Vice brought national attention to the Deco District, as many of the episodes took place here. Modeling agencies moved in, using the pastel-colored buildings and broad white sand beach as a backdrop for fashion shoots. The Art Deco District became the premiere spot for people-watching while sitting at a sidewalk café.

Chefs and restaurants still come and go here, like songbirds with the seasons. But South Beach will remain a dynamic dining destination for many years to come.

2. Beat the cream cheese in a mixer at medium speed until light and fluffy, about 5 minutes. Add the sugar and beat until it is completely incorporated. Beat in the eggs, one by one, scraping the bowl after each addition, waiting until one egg is completely incorporated before adding the next. Beat in the half-and-half in a thin stream, followed by the vanilla, then the lemon juice, and lemon zest.

3. Pour the batter into the prepared springform pan. Wrap a single piece of aluminum foil around the outside, bottom, and side of the pan. Place the pan in a roasting pan. Add enough very hot water to come about halfway up the side of the springform pan. Place the roasting pan in the oven and reduce the heat to 350°F.

4. Bake the cheesecake until the top puffs like a soufflé, about 40 minutes. Remove the cake from the oven and let rest for 20 minutes. Leave the oven on.

5. Return the cheesecake to the oven and bake until set and slightly puffed, about 20 minutes more. Jiggling should be minimal. Remove the cheesecake from the oven and let cool to room temperature. Refrigerate the cheesecake until completely cold, at least 6 hours, but preferably overnight.

6. Dip a sharp slender knife in hot water and run it around the inside edge of the springform pan. Unmold the cheesecake. Cut it into wedges for serving, using a sharp slender knife or dental floss stretched between your hands. (If using the former, wipe it off and dip it in hot water between slices.)

Guava Cheesecake

One of the oldest desserts from Key West is guava duff, a boiled pudding of Bahamian ancestry, made with the fragrant pulp of the guava. Fresh guava is difficult to obtain in most parts of the country, but the recipe gave me the idea for a cheesecake flavored with guava paste. Guava paste is sold in flat tins at Hispanic markets and in the canned fruit section of many supermarkets. Unused guava paste keeps for months in the refrigerator.

SERVES 10

CRUST:

1¼ cups chocolate ice box cookie crumbs or
*   graham cracker crumbs*
⅓ cup melted butter
2 tablespoons sugar

FILLING:

1 cup guava paste
⅓ cup fresh lemon juice
2 pounds cream cheese, at room temperature
2 cups sugar, or to taste
4 extra-large eggs
2 teaspoons vanilla extract
1 tablespoon grated lemon zest

GLAZE:

¼ cup red currant jelly
About 1 tablespoon water

1. Preheat the oven to 350°F. Butter an 9-inch springform pan.

2. Prepare the crust. Mix together the cookie crumbs, melted butter, and sugar in a mixing bowl to form a crumbly dough. Press the dough over the bottom and up the side of the springform pan. Bake the crust until almost dry, about 10 minutes. Set aside to cool. Leave the oven on.

3. Meanwhile, prepare the filling: Melt the guava paste in the lemon juice in a nonreactive heavy saucepan, whisking steadily, over medium heat, 2 to 3 minutes. Let the mixture cool slightly.

4. Beat the cream cheese in a large bowl with a mixer. Add the sugar and beat until light and fluffy. Beat in the eggs, one at a time, beating until each is incorporated before adding the next, and scraping down the sides of the bowl frequently. Beat in the vanilla, lemon zest, and melted guava paste. Correct the flavorings, adding sugar to suit your taste. Pour the filling into the prepared pan.

5. Bring 1 quart of water to a boil.

6. Wrap a sheet of aluminum foil around the bottom and sides of the springform pan to prevent water from seeping in. Place the pan in a large roasting pan and pour in 1 inch of boiling water.

7. Bake the cheesecake until the top is firm and the filling no longer jiggles when the pan is shaken, about 1¼ to 1½ hours. If the top of the cheesecake starts to brown before the filling sets, tent the cake with aluminum foil (see page 223). When the cake is done, turn off the heat, open the oven door a few inches, and let the cheesecake cool for 20 minutes.

8. Transfer the cheesecake to a wire rack to cool completely. Cover and refrigerate for at least 6 hours, preferably overnight.

9. Prepare the glaze: Melt the red currant jelly in the water in a small saucepan, whisking steadily, over medium heat, until the mixture is the consistency of heavy cream. Thin with additional water, if necessary.

10. Gently brush the top of the cheesecake with the glaze. Cover and chill for at least 30 minutes.

11. To serve, run a slender knife around the sides of the springform pan. Remove the sides and serve.

A New Pineapple Upside-Down Cake

H ere's a modern version of a traditional pineapple upside-down cake. Fresh pineapple slices are caramelized in butter and sugar in a nonstick frying pan, and then baked under a light cake batter. The result makes a great coffee cake for breakfast or brunch. Pineapples are no longer grown commercially in Florida, but a century ago they were an important cash crop.

SERVES 6 TO 8

6 tablespoons (¾ stick) unsalted butter

6 tablespoons sugar

1 ripe pineapple, peeled, halved, and cored (see facing page)

CAKE:

8 tablespoons (1 stick) unsalted butter, at room temperature

½ cup (packed) light brown sugar

3 large eggs

1 tablespoon dark rum

1 teaspoon vanilla extract

1 teaspoon grated lemon zest

1 cup all-purpose flour

1 teaspoon baking powder

1. Preheat the oven to 350°F.

2. Melt the butter in a 10-inch nonstick frying pan with an ovenproof handle, tilting the pan to coat the bottom and sides. Remove the pan from the heat and sprinkle the bottom with the sugar.

3. Cut the pineapple halves crosswise into ½-inch slices, reserving any juices. Arrange as many slices as will fit over

HOW TO PEEL A PINEAPPLE

My local supermarket sells pineapples already skinned and cored. I always feel like I'm cheating when I buy one, but it certainly saves time. Before I buy a whole pineapple, I turn it upside down and smell the root end. It should smell fragrant and pineappley. I avoid any that feel really hard or for that matter have soft spots.

To peel a pineapple, grab the leaves in one hand and the fruit in the other and twist in opposite directions. This neatly removes the leaves from the fruit.

Slice off the top and bottom of the pineapple. Stand the fruit on end. If possible, work on a grooved cutting board, so you can collect any juices. Using a sharp knife, cut the rind off the fruit in long strips, like barrel staves.

To core a pineapple, cut it lengthwise in half. Using a long knife, make lengthwise V-shaped cuts to remove the core.

the bottom of the frying pan, curved portions facing the same way. Cut the remaining pineapple into circles and triangles to fill in the holes. Work symmetrically, so you have a decorative pattern when the cake is inverted.

4. Place the pan with the pineapples over high heat and cook until the bottoms of the pineapple and pan juices are a deep golden brown, about 5 minutes. To check for doneness, lift a pineapple slice with a fork and inspect the underside. Rotate the pan as necessary to insure evening browning.

5. Prepare the cake batter. Beat the butter in a large bowl with a mixer. Add the brown sugar and beat until light and fluffy. Beat in the eggs, one at a time, scraping down the sides of the bowl between additions. Beat in the rum, vanilla, lemon zest, and any reserved pineapple juice. Add the flour and baking powder and beat just until mixed.

6. Pour the batter over the pineapple. Place the pan in the oven and bake the cake until firm and a skewer inserted in the center comes out clean, about 25 minutes.

7. Remove the pan from the oven and let cool for 5 minutes. Place a round platter over the pan and invert the cake onto it. I like to let the cake cool to room temperature before serving, but you can also serve it warm. Cut into wedges for serving.

Tres Leches (Three-Milk Cake)

The most famous Nicaraguan dessert is *tres leches*. Three different kinds of milk are used in its preparation—fresh milk, evaporated milk, and sweetened condensed milk—which explains the name. Universally appealing, this Nicaraguan dessert has been adopted by many Cuban and other Hispanic restaurants in South Florida. This recipe comes from the Miami restaurant Los Ranchos.

....
SERVES 8 TO 10
....

CAKE:

1 cup sugar

5 large eggs, separated

⅓ cup milk

½ teaspoon vanilla extract

1 cup all-purpose flour

1½ teaspoons baking powder

½ teaspoon cream of tartar

MILK SYRUP:

1 can (12 ounces) evaporated milk

1 cup sweetened condensed milk

1 cup heavy (or whipping) cream

1 teaspooon vanilla extract

1 tablespoon light rum

MERINGUE:

1 cup sugar

½ teaspoon cream of tartar

3 egg whites

1. Preheat the oven to 350°F. Generously butter a 13 x 9-inch baking dish.

2. Prepare the cake: Beat ¾ cup of the sugar and the egg yolks until light and fluffy, about 5 minutes. Fold in the milk, vanilla, flour, and baking powder.

3. Beat the egg whites to soft peaks, adding the cream of tartar after 20 seconds. Gradually add the remaining ¼ cup sugar and continue beating until the whites are glossy and firm, but not dry. Gently fold the whites into the yolk mixture. Pour this batter into the buttered baking dish.

4. Bake the cake until it feels firm and an inserted

toothpick comes out clean, 40 to 50 minutes. Let the cake cool completely on a wire rack. Unmold the cake onto a large, deep platter. Pierce the cake all over with a fork.

5. Prepare the milk syrup: Combine the evaporated milk, sweetened condensed milk, cream, vanilla, and rum in a mixing bowl. Whisk until well mixed. Pour the syrup over the cake, spooning the overflow back on top until all is absorbed.

6. Prepare the meringue: Place ¾ cup plus 2 tablespoons of the sugar in a heavy saucepan with ¼ cup water. Cover and cook over high heat, for 2 minutes. Uncover the pan and cook the sugar to the soft ball stage, 239°F on a candy thermometer, 6 to 8 minutes.

7. Meanwhile, beat the egg whites to soft peaks with the cream of tartar. Add the remaining 2 tablespoons sugar and continue beating to stiff peaks. Pour the boiling sugar syrup in a thin stream into the whites and continue beating until the mixture is cool to the touch. The hot syrup "cooks" the whites.

8. Using a wet spatula, spread the top and sides of the cake with a thick layer of the meringue. Refrigerate the cake for at least 2 hours before serving.

Coconut Brownies
with Coconut Snowballs

These brownies owe their richness to the use of coconut cream instead of butter. For further decadence, I serve them à la mode, with ice cream balls rolled in toasted coconut.

SERVES 8

2 ounces semisweet chocolate

2 ounces unsweetened chocolate

¾ cup canned coconut cream, such as Coco Lopez

1½ cups sugar

3 large eggs, beaten

2 teaspoons vanilla extract

1 tablespoon dark rum

1 cup sifted all-purpose flour

½ teaspoon ground cinnamon

⅛ teaspoon ground cloves

1 teaspoon baking powder

Coconut Snowballs (recipe follows)

1. Preheat the oven to 350°F. Generously butter an 8-inch square cake pan.

2. Melt the chocolates in the coconut cream in the top of a double boiler over simmering water.

3. Combine the sugar, eggs, vanilla, and rum in a large mixing bowl and whisk until smooth. Whisk in the chocolate mixture. Sift the flour into the mixture, along with the spices and baking powder and whisk just to mix. Pour the batter into the prepared pan.

4. Bake the brownies until the top is crusty, but the center remains a little soft, about 35 minutes. Let cool completely in the pan on a wire rack. Cut the brownies into 8 rectangles. Serve the brownies topped with the Coconut Snowballs.

BUYING AND OPENING FRESH COCONUTS

When buying coconuts, avoid any with cracked shells, a sour or acrid aroma, or wet "eyes" (the three small circles at one end of the nut). The nut should feel heavy and you should be able to hear the coconut water slosh around when you shake it. A dry nut is past its prime.

Shelling a fresh coconut isn't difficult, but it helps to know a few tricks. First, punch in all 3 eyes, using a screwdriver and hammer. Drain out the liquid inside, and save it for drinking. (Mixed with a little sugar and rum, it makes a

COCONUT SNOWBALLS

ⓖⓖⓖ

I f you have the time, use freshly grated coconut, but acceptable results can be obtained with the packaged variety. This dish was inspired by a dessert from my wife's childhood: The "Snow Princess" served at the restaurant in Burdine's in Miami Beach. The Burdine's version came crowned with silver balls and a tiny doll.

2 cups shredded coconut
1 pint of your favorite ice cream

1. Preheat the oven to 350°F.

2. Spread the coconut over a baking sheet and bake until lightly toasted but not dark brown, 5 to 8 minutes. Transfer the coconut to a bowl and let cool.

3. Just before serving, place the coconut in a pie pan. Use an ice cream scoop to form 2-inch balls of ice cream. Shake the pan to coat the balls with the toasted coconut and use as a garnish for the brownies.

delicious cocktail—see the Saoco recipe on page 14.)

Next, break the nut into five or six pieces by whacking it with a hammer. (Wrap it in a dish towel to keep the pieces from flying.) Bake the pieces in a 400°F oven until the meat begins to pull away from the shell, 10 to 15 minutes. The same effect can be achieved by freezing the coconut for an hour or two.

Pry the meat away from the shell. Cut off the brown skin with a vegetable peeler or paring knife. The coconut meat is now ready for munching, grating, or shaving into thin strips with a vegetable peeler. One coconut yields 3 to 3½-cups grated flesh and ½ to 1 cup coconut water. Three cups grated flesh will make about 3 cups coconut milk.

Mango Napoleons

W hat could be better than a fresh, ripe, juicy mango? How about a fresh, ripe, juicy mango sandwiched between layers of crisp filo dough and citrus-flavored pastry cream? This recipe was invented by my friend, Rachel Gottfried, who has baking in her genes. Her parents owned the once famous Silvercup Bakery of New York.

SERVES 4

4 sheets filo dough
¼ cup Clarified Butter (page 327), melted

PASTRY CREAM:
½ cup heavy (or whipping) cream
½ cup sour cream
¼ teaspoon grated lemon zest
¼ teaspoon grated orange zest
3 to 4 tablespoons confectioners' sugar,
*   plus additional confectioners' sugar, for dusting*

1½ cups diced ripe mangos
Rachel's Hot Fudge Sauce (recipe follows)

1. Preheat the oven to 375°F.

2. Lay 1 sheet of filo dough on a large cutting board and lightly brush it with the clarified butter. Lay another sheet of dough on top and brush with melted butter. Repeat with the third and fourth sheets.

3. Using a 3-inch round cookie cutter, cut out 12 circles. Transfer the rounds to a baking sheet. Bake the filo circles until crisp and golden brown, about 10 minutes. Transfer the circles to a wire rack to cool. (The pastry can be prepared up to 6 hours ahead of serving. Let it cool completely, then store in an airtight cookie tin.)

4. Prepare the pastry cream: Combine the heavy cream, sour cream, citrus zests, and confectioners' sugar in a chilled mixing bowl. Beat the mixture to soft peaks with an electric mixer. Correct the flavorings, adding sugar to taste. Cover and refrigerate until assembling, no more than 3 hours later (see Note).

5. Just before serving, assemble the napoleons. Place a filo circle in the center of a dessert plate. Spread a spoonful of the pastry cream on top, working as gently as possibly. Arrange a spoonful of diced mango on top, and top with a little more pastry cream. Set a second filo dough circle on

BUYING MANGOS

When buying mangos, look for unblemished, smooth-skinned fruits that are free of soft spots. Mangos are usually picked green. Let them ripen at room temperature, in a sealed paper bag. (Mangos won't ripen below 55°F.) Contrary to popular belief, a red or orange skin isn't the only sign of ripeness. Some Thai varieties, like the Okrung or Tong Dam, remain green even when ripe. When a mango is ripe, it will be very fragrant and squeezably soft. A ripe mango can be stored in the refrigerator for up to 5 days. Diced or puréed mango can be frozen.

Mangos not only taste good; they're good for you, being rich in potassium and vitamins A and C. A 1-pound (medium) mango contains about 135 calories, and yields about 1½ cups diced fruit or 1 cup mango purée.

top. Top with more pastry cream, mango, pastry cream, and finally another filo circle. Lightly sprinkle the top of the napoleon with confectioners' sugar. Assemble the remaining napoleons the same way. Spoon a little of Rachel's Hot Fudge Sauce around the base of each and serve.

Note: Although the pastry and filling can be prepared ahead of time, the napoleons should be assembled at the last minute.

RACHEL'S HOT FUDGE SAUCE

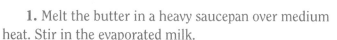

This recipe is simplicity itself, but it never fails to fetch raves. I like it on just about everything—from the Coconut Snowballs on page 293 to the tips of my fingers.

MAKES 1½ CUPS

6 tablespoons (¾ stick) unsalted butter
1 cup evaporated milk
⅔ cup unsweetened cocoa powder
2 cups confectioners' sugar
Pinch of salt
1 teaspoon vanilla extract

1. Melt the butter in a heavy saucepan over medium heat. Stir in the evaporated milk.

2. Remove the pan from the heat and sift in the cocoa powder, sugar, and salt, whisking steadily. Return the pan to medium heat and bring the sauce to a boil. Reduce the heat and simmer until thick and well-flavored, about 2 minutes.

3. Remove the pan from the heat and whisk in the vanilla. Cover and keep warm until you're ready to serve.

FLORIDA MANGOS

From June through September it's mango season in south Florida and our backyard trees will hang heavy with these dark, oval fruits. Fruit stands will spring up along roadsides, selling mammoth mangos for as little as 50 cents apiece. At the height of the season, I cut mangos over my breakfast cereal, dice them into salsas, whir them into milkshakes, and generally pig out on a fruit that's, for me, one of the few saving graces of Florida's steamy summer.

Novelist Tom Robbins once described a mango as "a ripe peach doused with kerosene." Although somewhat of an overstatement, certain Asian varieties have a kerosene or turpentine aftertaste—a quality that is much prized in India and Southeast Asia. A ripe mango does, indeed, have a peachy fragrance and sweetness, although the flavor is more luscious and concentrated. The fruit's sweetness is balanced by a musky acidity that some people liken to pineapple.

The first popular Florida mango was the large, oval, sweet, but fibrous *Haden*, named for one Captain John J. Haden, who planted imported Indian mango seeds at his home in Coconut Grove in 1902. The best-selling commercial variety is the *Tommy Atkins*, a large, oval, purplish-red fruit with a pleasant flavor but sometimes fibrous flesh.

Thanks to staggered ripening times, mango lovers can enjoy Florida mangos for four to five months a year. Early ripeners include the *Tommy Atkins* and the yellow-skinned *Florigon*—the latter remarkable for its intense flavor and creamy consistency. Mid-June to mid-July brings the red, medium-size, fine-flavored *Van Dyke*.

Mid-July ushers in my personal favorite, a large, oblong, red-skinned, dark-orange-fleshed, lusciously tart, and virtually fiber-free mango called *Kent*. Another midsummer treat is the *Palmer*, an elongated, S-shaped mango with a yellowish flesh and an aromatic flavor that hints at papaya. August brings a huge, oval, pink- or orange-tinged, sweet, delicate-tasting mango called *Keitt*, which will last through September. After that, extensive plantings in the Caribbean and Central and South America make mangos available virtually year round.

Mango Crisp

Crisps are a venerable American dessert. When I lived in New England, I made apple, pear, and cherry crisps. Now that I've moved to Miami, it seems only natural to make crisps from mangos.

SERVES 8 TO 10

4 pounds very ripe mangos (about 6 cups cubed fresh)
3 tablespoons fresh lime juice
¼ cup granulated sugar
2 tablespoons cornstarch
1 tablespoon minced candied ginger

TOPPING:
8 tablespoons (1 stick) cold unsalted butter, cut into 1-inch pieces
1 cup all-purpose flour
½ cup granulated sugar
½ cup (packed) light brown sugar
½ teaspoon ground ginger
½ cup coarsely chopped toasted pecans
    (optional; for toasting, see page 311)

1. Preheat the oven to 375°F. Generously butter a 11 x 7-inch baking dish.

2. Peel the mangos and cut the flesh into 1-inch dice. Place the mangos in a large bowl and toss with the lime juice.

3. Combine the sugar, cornstarch, and candied ginger in a mixing bowl and mix well. Stir this mixture into the mangos. Spoon the mango mixture into the prepared baking dish.

4. Using an electric mixer fitted with a paddle, a food processor, or 2 knives, combine the topping ingredients through the ginger and mix until the mixture resembles coarse crumbs with pea-size bits of butter in it. Mix in the pecans, if using, and spoon the topping over the mango mixture.

5. Bake the crisp until the crust is golden brown, 50 to 60 minutes. Remove the pan from the oven and let cool on a wire rack. The crisp can be eaten warm, but I prefer it at room temperature or chilled.

Nontraditional Key Lime Pie

Whipped cream or meringue? The question is hotly debated whenever the subject of key lime pie comes up. For example, I prefer meringue, while my wife, Barbara, favors whipped cream. So, this recipe offers both possibilities. Traditional key lime pie recipes call for the filling ingredients to be beaten but not cooked. Nowadays for safety's sake, we're better off cooking eggs rather than serving them raw.

....

SERVES 8 TO 10

....

CRUST:

1¼ cups cinnamon graham cracker crumbs

⅓ cup (5⅓ tablespoons) melted unsalted butter

FILLING:

3 egg yolks

1 can (14 ounces) sweetened condensed milk

½ cup plus 2 tablespoons fresh key lime juice,
*　　or 5 tablespoons each regular lime juice*
*　　and fresh lemon juice*

2 teaspoons grated lime zest, preferably from key limes

KEY LIME PIE

Key lime pie is Florida's most famous dessert. Its distinguishing ingredient is a small, yellow, seed-filled lime that grows throughout Florida, the Caribbean, and Latin America. The juice of the key lime is more acrid than that of the common Persian lime—it's ideal for offsetting the sweetness of the pie's other main ingredient, sweetened condensed milk.

Key lime pie is surprisingly simple and easy to make. The filling contains only three ingredients: key lime juice, sweetened condensed milk, and egg yolks. (I add lime zest to further intensify the lime experience.) Old-timers don't even bother to cook the filling. (These days I recommend cooking key lime pie to eliminate the small but worrisome risk associated with eating raw egg yolks.)

Most cooks serve this filling in a graham-cracker crust, but there all agreement ends. Floridians are sharply divided on the proper topping. Some argue for meringue, which has the advantage of using up the egg whites. Others insist on whipped cream to echo the creaminess of the filling.

Popular lore holds that key lime pie was invented at the end of the Civil War, the result of combining the indigenous citrus fruit with a newly invented convenience food—sweetened condensed milk. But no one has ever unearthed a nineteenth-century key lime pie recipe.

Food historian Meryle Evans believes that what was to become Florida's signature pie originated in the 1930s—the result of a campaign by the Borden Company to persuade Americans to use sweetened condensed milk for pie-making. "As fresh milk became more widely available in the United States," explains Evans, "the company sought new ways to market its canned products." According to Evans, a 1928 "Borden Condensed Milk Magic Recipes" booklet contained a recipe for lemon pie made with sweetened condensed milk. Lime pie recipes began to circulate in the 1930s. The earliest Florida key lime pie recipe Evans has found appeared in a Key West Women's Club cookbook in 1939.

Whatever its origins, key lime pie remains an unbeatable Floridian dish.

MERINGUE TOPPING:
3 egg whites
¼ teaspoon cream of tartar
½ cup granulated sugar

WHIPPED CREAM TOPPING:
1 cup heavy (or whipping) cream
3 tablespoons confectioners' sugar
½ teaspoon vanilla extract
½ teaspoon grated lime zest,
preferably from key limes

1. Preheat the oven to 350°F.

2. Prepare the crust: Combine the graham cracker crumbs and butter in a mixing bowl and mix to form a crumbly dough. Press the mixture into an 8-inch pie pan. Bake the crust for 5 minutes. Remove the crust from the oven, but leave the oven on.

3. Meanwhile, prepare the filling. Combine the egg yolks and sweetened condensed milk in a mixing bowl and beat with a mixer at high speed until light and fluffy, about 5 minutes. Gradually beat in the lime juice and zest.

4. Pour the mixture into the crust. Bake the pie for 6 to 8 minutes, or until the filling is set and an inserted skewer comes out clean and hot to the touch. Remove the pie from the oven. If choosing the meringue topping, increase the temperature to 400°F and proceed with Step 5. If choosing the whipped cream topping, turn off the oven, set the pie on a rack to cool to room temperature, and skip to Step 6.

5. Prepare the meringue: Beat the egg whites to soft peaks with a mixer, starting on low speed, gradually increasing the speed to high, and adding the cream of tartar after 20 seconds. Beat in the sugar in a thin stream and continue beating until the whites are glossy and firm, but not dry. Spread or pipe the meringue on top of the pie. Bake the pie until the meringue is nicely browned, 3 to 5 minutes. Let the pie cool to room temperature. Refrigerate, uncovered, for at least 4 hours before serving.

6. Prepare the whipped cream topping: Place the cream in a chilled bowl and beat until soft peaks form. Add the confectioners' sugar, vanilla, and lime zest and beat the cream until stiff. Spread or pipe the whipped cream on top of the pie. Refrigerate, uncovered, until serving. For the best results, serve within 1 hour of adding the whipped cream.

Coconut Cream Pie

This will probably be the richest, coconuttiest coconut cream pie you've ever tasted. The secret? The filling is made with coconut cream. For the very best results, use finely grated fresh coconut, but store-bought, sweetened and shredded coconut makes a perfectly tasty pie, too.

SERVES 8 TO 10

1 cup milk

1 cup canned coconut cream, such as Coco Lopez

2 large eggs

6 tablespoons granulated sugar

3 tablespoons all-purpose flour

2 cups shredded (finely grated) fresh coconut

1 teaspoon unsalted butter

1 Coconut Pie Crust (recipe follows)

1 cup heavy (or whipping) cream

3 tablespoons confectioners' sugar

1 tablespoon light rum

½ cup shredded (finely grated) coconut, toasted,
      for garnish (see sidebar, facing page)

1. Preheat the oven to 350°F.

2. Scald the milk and coconut cream in a heavy saucepan. Beat the eggs in a large mixing bowl. Whisk in the granulated sugar, followed by the flour. Add the 2 cups shredded coconut and whisk until smooth.

3. Whisk ¼ cup of the scalded milk mixture into the egg mixture to warm it. Whisk the egg mixture into the milk mixture remaining in the saucepan. Boil the filling, whisking steadily, until thick and bubbly, about 2 minutes. Transfer the filling to a bowl, dot the top with the butter, and let cool.

4. Spoon the filling into the coconut crust and let it cool completely. Cover and refrigerate until thoroughly chilled, 2 hours.

5. Whip the cream in a chilled bowl, adding the confectioners' sugar and rum as it thickens. Continue to beat until stiff peaks form. Spoon the cream into a pastry bag filled with a large star tip. Decorate the top of the pie with rosettes of whipped cream and sprinkle evenly with the toasted coconut. Refrigerate, uncovered, until ready to serve.

Note: Canned coconut cream tends to solidify when cold. If the coconut cream is too hard to pour, set the can in a bowl of hot water to warm it.

TOASTING COCONUT

To toast shredded coconut, spread the coconut on a baking sheet, place it in a preheated 350°F oven, and brown, stirring frequently for 5 to 8 minutes.

COCONUT PIE CRUST

This crust is a tropical version of a classic *pâte brisée*. It not only works well for coconut cream pie, but all sorts of fruit and dessert pies. Store-bought sweetened, shredded coconut can be substituted for fresh in this recipe.

MAKES ONE 9-INCH PIE CRUST

1½ cups all-purpose flour

¼ cup shredded (finely grated) coconut

¾ teaspoon salt

2 tablespoons sugar

3 tablespoons cold unsalted butter, cut into ½-inch pieces

2 egg yolks

4 to 5 tablespoons canned coconut cream, such as
    Coco Lopez

1. Place the flour, shredded coconut, salt, sugar, and butter in a food processor. Run the machine until the butter is completely cut in; the mixture should feel sandy, like cornmeal.

2. Add the egg yolks and coconut cream and pulse until the dough comes together into a smooth ball, 1 to 2 minutes. If the dough seems too dry (it should be soft and pliable), add a little more coconut cream.

3. Gather the dough into a ball and wrap in plastic. Refrigerate for 1 hour, or freeze for 15 minutes.

4. Preheat the oven to 400°F.

5. Roll out the dough on a lightly floured work surface to 11 inches in diameter. Use it to line a 9-inch pie pan. Prick the bottom of the crust with a fork and decoratively crimp and trim the edges. Line the crust with aluminum foil and fill with baking weights, beans, or rice.

6. Blind-bake the crust for 12 to 15 minutes (see Note). Remove the weights and foil. Continue baking until nicely browned, about 5 minutes. Transfer the pie shell to a wire rack to let cool.

Note: Blind-baking refers to cooking a pie crust without the filling. The uncooked crust is first lined with foil or parchment paper and baking weights, beans, or rice, which are added to weigh down the dough as it bakes and prevent bubbling. The foil and weights are removed for the last 5 minutes of baking to allow the crust to dry out.

NUTS ABOUT COCONUTS

Florida's official state tree is the sabal palm, but it could well be the coconut palm. This graceful tree symbolizes the best of the Sunshine State: our semi-tropical climate and our exotic commingling of Caribbean and North American food ways. When I return to Miami after a trip, there's nothing like the sight of a palm tree to make me feel like I'm home.

To many Americans, coconut means the processed, shredded, sweetened stuff found in candy bars and sprinkled on cupcakes. Moving to Florida introduced me to a host of new coconut products, from jelly coconuts to coconut milk.

What most Americans mean by coconut is actually the core of a mature nut, a hard sphere covered with shaggy brown "bark," with a half-inch layer of firm white meat inside. But visit an Hispanic produce market, like Miami's famous El Palacio de los Jugos and you'll encounter the nut in its natural state: a large, green oblong of mostly fiberous husk, weighing five to six pounds a piece. A machete-wielding vendor whacks the top off one of these behemoths, proffering a straw for sipping the clean, sweetish "water" in the center. To complete the coconut experience, use a shard of shell or a spoon to scoop out the soft, white, custardy "jelly"—the part that would one day become the squeaky-crisp meat of a hard-shelled nut.

Green coconuts are harvested after only six months on the tree. Ethnic markets throughout south Florida carry green coconuts as well as hard ones. Cuban vendors sell these thirst quenchers—the botanical equivalent of canteens—at open-air markets and street fairs. Green coconuts can be found in Hispanic and Caribbean markets in most major cities.

For much of the world, coconut meat is not an end in itself, but a source of fresh coconut "milk." The analogy to a dairy product is an apt one: The fat in coconut milk is closer in chemical composition to butterfat than it is to vegetable fat. As with cow's milk, coconut milk has a cream that rises to the top. Complete instructions for making coconut milk are found on page 331.

Although making fresh coconut milk isn't difficult, it does take time. When fresh coconut isn't available or time is short, substitute canned unsweetened coconut milk, which works well in most recipes. Look for it in Caribbean, Brazilian, and Asian markets. Indian markets and health food stores sell unsweetened dried coconut, which can be used to make coconut milk. The readily available sweetened varieties should be avoided for this purpose.

Coconut milk is often confused with sweetened coconut cream. The latter is a sugary product made in Puerto Rico and elsewhere in the Caribbean. It's an essential ingredient in a *piña colada* and other tropical drinks, but can't be substituted for unsweetened coconut milk. The best-known brand of coconut cream is Coco Lopez.

Exotic Banana Cream Pie

There once was a time when banana meant a supermarket Chiquita. My, how times have changed! Today's consumer often has the choice of a dozen types of exotic bananas, from tiny sweet finger bananas to manzano bananas that taste like apples. This pie can be made with any of the new bananas or with the more commonplace varieties. Folding beaten egg whites into the custard makes the filling exceptionally light.

SERVES 8

CRUST:

1¼ cups ice box chocolate cookie crumbs

2 tablespoons granulated sugar

5 tablespoons unsalted butter, melted

FILLING:

1 teaspoon unflavored gelatin

2 tablespoons water

1 cup milk

3 egg yolks

3 tablespoons (packed) light brown sugar

2 tablespoons all-purpose flour

1 tablespoon dark rum

¼ teaspoon ground cinnamon

2 egg whites

¼ teaspoon cream of tartar

2 tablespoons granulated sugar

1 pound bananas, preferably exotic varieties

¼ cup fresh orange juice

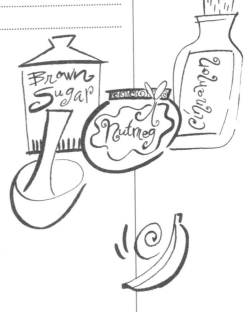

TOPPING:

1 cup heavy (or whipping) cream

3 tablespoons confectioners' sugar, or to taste

1 tablespoon banana liqueur, or to taste

Freshly grated nutmeg

1. Prepare the crust: Combine the cookie crumbs, sugar, and butter in a mixing bowl and mix to form a crumbly dough. Press the mixture into an 8-inch pie pan.

2. Prepare the filling: Sprinkle the gelatin over the 2 tablespoons water in a small saucepan. Let stand until soft and spongy, about 5 minutes. Warm the mixture over low heat, stirring, until the gelatin dissolves.

3. Meanwhile, scald the milk in a heavy saucepan. Combine the egg yolks, brown sugar, and flour in a mixing bowl and whisk until smooth. Whisk the scalded milk into the yolk mixture in a thin stream. Return the mixture to the pan and boil over medium heat for 1 minute, whisking constantly. Remove the pan from the heat and whisk in the rum, cinnamon, and dissolved gelatin.

4. Beat the egg whites to soft peaks, adding the cream of tartar after 20 seconds. Add the granulated sugar and continue to beat the whites until glossy and firm, but not dry. Fold the egg whites into the filling while it is still hot so that the whites are "cooked."

5. Peel and thinly slice the bananas. Toss the bananas with the orange juice in a bowl to prevent discoloring.

6. Drain the sliced bananas and arrange half of them on the bottom of the crust. Spoon in half of the filling mixture. Add the remaining bananas and top with the remaining filling. Smooth the top with a spatula. Let the filling cool to room temperature. Cover and refrigerate until thoroughly chilled, 2 hours.

7. Beat the cream to stiff peaks in a chilled bowl with a mixer. As the cream stiffens, beat in the confectioners' sugar and banana liqueur to taste. Continue beating until stiff.

8. Using a pastry bag fitted with a star tip, pipe rosettes of whipped cream all over the top of the pie. Grate a little fresh nutmeg on top. Cut into wedges and serve.

HOW TO RIPEN A BANANA

As bananas and plantains ripen, a chemical process called hydrolysis converts their starches into sugars. Hydrolysis works fastest at room temperature and can be slowed down by refrigeration. It is accelerated by the presence of ethylene gas, which is found naturally in the skins of apples and bananas.

For speedy ripening, store the bananas at room temperature in a sealed paper bag with apple peels or banana peels. At peak ripeness, the skin will be completely yellow and covered with tiny brown spots, called sugar spots. The skin of a fully ripe red banana will be as colorful as a tropical sunset.

FLORIDA'S EXOTIC FRUIT REVOLUTION

This one looks like an armadillo, its elongated body armored with tiny scales. That one has knobby protuberances, like some prehistoric hedgehog. This one boasts five fins, like a sea creature on steroids. No, you're not at the zoo; the creatures in this edible menagerie are a jackfruit, atemoya, and carambola (star fruit). Grown in a South Florida agricultural district called the Redlands, they're the American fruits of the future.

ATEMOYA: Looks like a knobby, dusky green artichoke. The wet white flesh tastes like a cross between vanilla pudding, grapes, and honeydew melon. Studded with shiny black seeds, atemoya is a hybrid of the cherimoya and sugar apple. In season August through October.

BLACK SAPOTE (also known as chocolate pudding fruit): A round green fruit, 2 to 6 inches in diameter. When fully ripe, the skin will be black and shriveled. The pulp of a ripe fruit looks like chocolate pudding and tastes like dates or persimmons. In season December through March.

CANISTEL (also known as egg fruit): A thin-skinned, heart-shaped, orange-fleshed fruit that tastes like baked sweet potato. When ripe, the fruit will be squeezably soft. There's one hard, shiny, brown seed in the center. In season December through March and sporadically during the summer.

CARAMBOLA: See page 240.

JABOTICABA: A small, round berry-like fruit native to Brazil. The dark purple skin encases a pulpy-white, Concord-grape-flavored flesh with seeds like grape pips. In season January through May.

JACKFRUIT: A huge armadillo-shaped fruit with a tough, scaly skin. The musky yellow flesh is wetly crunchy and slightly fibrous. Jackfruit tastes like a cross between melon, honey, and apricot.

LONGAN: A small brown-skinned fruit similar to a lychee, but firmer and with a cucumber-melon flavor. In season July and August.

LOQUAT: A small, orange teardrop-shaped fruit in season in spring. Loquat tastes like a cross between apricots, plums, and honey and is more luscious than all three. Each fruit contains one to four hard, shiny, brown seeds.

LYCHEE: Native to China, the lychee is a small red ball with leathery skin. The translucent white flesh is sweet and perfumed. There's a single shiny hard brown seed. In season mid-May through July.

MAMEY SAPOTE: Much prized by Cuban-Americans, the mamey looks like an elongated coconut. A rough brown skin encases a bright orange flesh. Mamey is ripe when squeezably soft; the flavor lies somewhere between that of melon and sweet potato, with a hint of marzipan. In season January through September.

MONSTERA DELICIOSA: The weirdest of Florida's weird fruits, monstera looks like a giant green banana covered with pentagonal scales. It ripens from the bottom up and is ready to eat when the scales pop off. The cream-colored flesh is softly fibrous and tastes like a cross between a banana, lychee, melon, and honey.

MUNTINGIA (also known as strawberry fruit): A small pinkish-red berry with the flavor of

Black Sapote Pie

cotton candy. In season May
through October.

PASSION FRUIT: A lemon-size fruit with a leathery yellow, brown, purple, or green casing. The perfumed, tart, orange flesh is riddled with tiny crunchy black seeds, which are edible. The pulp is usually strained and enjoyed in juice form. In season July through March.

SAPODILLA (also known as sapote): A round or egg-shaped, brown-skinned fruit that tastes like a pear that's been injected with maple syrup. In season March through July.

SUGAR APPLE: Related to the atemoya, this oval fruit is covered with light green, knobby protuberances and is filled with a moist, sweet, custardy pulp. In season August through October.

WHITE SAPOTE: A member of the citrus family, this luscious fruit is round and slightly flattened, with a thin orange or light green skin and soft, creamy pulp that tastes like orange sherbet. It has several large seeds. In season May through July.

*T*he black sapote (pronounced sa-PO-te) has everything one could ask of an exotic fruit—a handsome, cocoa-colored flesh; a creamy, pudding-like consistency, and a mild, mellow flavor suggestive of custard, persimmons, and dates. Although it is widely enjoyed in Latin America, it has yet to catch on in this country. One of the reasons is looks: It isn't ready to eat until it is black, spotted, and squishily soft. In other words, you shouldn't eat it until it looks like you should throw it out. In its unripe state, the black sapote looks like a leathery green tomato. Let it ripen at room temperature until extremely soft. Black sapotes are in season in early spring. This pie can be made with a wide variety of custardy tropical fruits, including white sapote, canistel (egg fruit), and atemoya.

SERVES 8

2 cups seeded, mashed ripe black sapote pulp (2 to 3 black sapotes)
½ teaspoon vanilla extract
¼ teaspoon grated lemon zest
About 1 tablespoon honey
1 Graham Cracker Crust (see Note)
1 cup heavy (or whipping) cream
3 tablespoons confectioners' sugar
1 tablespoon light rum
1 piece (1 ounce) semisweet chocolate, for shaving

1. Mash or purée the black sapote pulp with the vanilla, lemon zest, and honey to taste. Spoon this mixture into the prepared pie crust.

2. Whip the cream, adding the confectioners' sugar and rum as it thickens, until stiff peaks form. Spoon into a pastry bag fitted with a large star tip. Pipe rosettes of whipped cream over the top of the pie. Using a vegetable peeler or paring knife, cut thin shavings of chocolate and scatter on top. Refrigerate, uncovered, until ready to serve.

Note: The graham cracker crust used for this pie is the same as the crust used in the Nontraditional Key Lime Pie on page 298. Because the black sapote pie is not baked once the filling is added to the crust, increase the crust-baking time in Step 2 of the Key lime recipe to 8 to 10 minutes.

Coconut Soufflé

My wife, Barbara, has an insatiable appetite for soufflés. Fortunately, this one can be made in about 20 minutes, and it tastes as great as it looks. Have the can of coconut cream at room temperature and shake well before using.

SERVES 4

1½ tablespoons unsalted butter, melted

1 cup toasted coconut (see page 301)

4 egg yolks

4 tablespoons sugar

2 tablespoons all-purpose flour

1 cup canned coconut cream, such as Coco Lopez

6 egg whites

½ teaspoon cream of tartar

Tangerine Chocolate Sauce (recipe follows)

1. Preheat the oven to 400°F.

2. Brush the inside of a 5-cup soufflé dish with half of the melted butter, taking special care to coat the inside rim. Place the dish in the freezer for 5 minutes.

3. Brush the soufflé dish with the remaining melted butter. (This double buttering prevents the soufflé from sticking as it rises.) Sprinkle the inside of the dish with ⅓ cup of the toasted coconut.

4. Place the egg yolks in a medium-size bowl and whisk in 2 tablespoons of the sugar and the flour. Scald the coconut cream in a medium-size heavy saucepan over high heat.

5. Whisk the scalded coconut cream into the yolk mixture in a thin stream. Return the yolk mixture to the pan, set over medium heat, and bring the mixture to a boil, whisking steadily. Cook the mixture until bubbly and thickened, about 2 minutes. Remove the pan from the heat and keep hot.

6. Starting the mixer on low, beat the egg whites, adding the cream of tartar after 20 seconds. Gradually increase the speed to medium, then to high. Sprinkle in the remaining 2 tablespoons sugar as the whites start to stiffen. Continue beating until the whites are firm and glossy, but not dry.

7. Whisk one-quarter of the whites into the hot yolk mixture to lighten it. Gently fold this mixture back into the remaining whites with a rubber spatula.

8. Gently spoon one-third of the soufflé mixture into the prepared soufflé dish. Sprinkle ⅓ cup of the toasted coconut on top. Spoon half of the remaining soufflé mixture into the dish and sprinkle with the remaining coconut. Spoon in the remaining soufflé mixture. (Any extra can be baked in buttered ramekins.) Smooth the top of the soufflé with a wet spatula. Wipe off the outside of the soufflé dish with a wet cloth. Run the tip of a paring knife around the inside edge of the dish to clear a path for the rising soufflé.

9. Bake the soufflé until puffed and golden brown, 15 to 20 minutes. Don't open the oven door during the first 10 minutes. When you open the door, do so just a crack and close it as quickly and gently as possible. To test for doneness, gently poke the dish with a wooden spoon. The soufflé should jiggle just slightly. Serve the soufflé immediately, with the Tangerine Chocolate Sauce on the side.

TANGERINE CHOCOLATE SAUCE

This recipe is dedicated to my Belgian friend, Robert Van Wittenberghe, who's a great fan of the Belgian tangerine liqueur, Mandarine Napoléon. You can also use fresh tangerine juice. Besides the Coconut Soufflé, try this sauce over ice cream or as a fondue-style dip for fruit.

MAKES ¾ CUP

⅓ cup heavy (or whipping) cream
4 ounces semisweet chocolate, finely chopped
1 to 2 tablespoons tangerine liqueur

1. Scald the cream in a small heavy saucepan over medium heat. Whisk in the chocolate and cook over low heat until completely melted, about 3 minutes.

2. Whisk in the tangerine liqueur, to taste. Serve warm. Any leftover sauce can be stored, covered, in the refrigerator. Reheat in the top of a double boiler over simmering water.

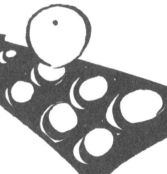

Icky Sticky Coconut Pudding with Rum-Toffee Sauce

One of the hallmarks of the new Floridian cuisine is its playfulness. Consider this pudding, a signature dessert at the restaurant Mark's Place, in North Miami. The pudding can be baked in individual small molds or a large cake pan.

SERVES 6

5 tablespoons unsalted butter, at room
temperature
¾ cup sugar, plus 3 tablespoons for sugaring
the molds
4 ounces pitted dates (½ cup), very finely
chopped
1 cup shredded (finely grated) fresh coconut
1 cup water
1 teaspoon baking soda
2 large eggs
1⅓ cups flour
2 teaspoons baking powder
½ teaspoon salt
1 teaspoon vanilla extract
Warm Rum-Toffee Sauce (recipe follows)
¼ cup coarsely chopped macadamia nuts,
lightly toasted (see sidebar)

1. Preheat the oven to 400°F. Grease six 6-ounce timbale molds or ramekins or one 9-inch round or square cake pan using 1 tablespoon of the butter. Lightly sugar the molds with the 3 tablespoons sugar.

2. Combine the dates, coconut, and water in a saucepan over high heat. Bring the mixture to a boil. Remove the pan from the heat, stir in the baking soda, and set aside.

3. Cream the remaining 4 tablespoons butter in a mixing bowl. Beat in the remaining ¾ cup sugar, little by little, and continue beating until light and fluffy. Beat in the eggs one at a time. Sift the flour with the baking powder and salt onto the mixture, then fold it in gently. Gently stir in the coconut mixture and vanilla.

4. Spoon the pudding mixture into the molds or mold and cover with buttered aluminum foil. Bake the puddings on a baking sheet until set and an inserted skewer comes out dry, 20 to 25 minutes. Uncover the molds and prick the

HOW TO TOAST NUTS

Like many foods, nuts taste richer when lightly toasted. There are two easy ways to toast nuts: One way is to brown them in a heavy, dry frying pan over low heat. Shake the pan as the nuts roast to cook them evenly on all sides. This method works best for small seeds and nuts, such as sesame seeds, pine nuts, and chopped macadamia nuts or pecans.

The second method is to roast the nuts in a 350°F oven or toaster oven. Spread out the nuts in a single layer in a roasting pan. Shake the pan from time to time so the nuts brown evenly. Depending on the size of the nuts, browning will take 5 to 10 minutes.

puddings with a knife tip or skewer. Pour 1 tablespoon of the Warm Rum-Toffee Sauce over each pudding. Return the pudding to the oven, uncovered, for 1 minute.

5. Let the puddings cool for 5 minutes. Then unmold them onto individual plates or a platter. Spoon the remaining sauce over the puddings and sprinkle with the toasted macadamia nuts.

WARM RUM-TOFFEE SAUCE

Mark serves this toffee sauce over Icky-Sticky Coconut Pudding, but it's also delicious over bananas or ice cream.

MAKES 1½ CUPS

¾ cup plus 2 tablespoons packed light brown sugar

6 tablespoons heavy (or whipping) cream

8 tablespoons (1 stick) unsalted butter

½ teaspoon vanilla extract

3 tablespoons dark rum

Combine all of the ingredients in a heavy saucepan over medium heat. Boil until thick and well blended, about 3 minutes. Serve warm. Any leftover sauce can be stored, covered, in the refrigerator. It will keep for up to 1 week. Reheat in a small heavy saucepan over low heat.

Raphil's Rice Pudding

R aphil's was a landmark deli in the glory days of Miami Beach. Sandwiches from Raphil's fed the workers who built the Fontainebleau and Eden Roc hotels. Deli platters from Raphil's sustained the great entertainers—from Frank Sinatra to Milton Berle—who performed in Miami each winter. Crime boss Meyer Lansky was a regular. During the season, the line to get in would stretch down the block. I never had the privilege of meeting Raphil's colorful co-founder, Phil Seldin. But his partner, Ray Malschick, and his family, have regaled me with stories about the man who would have been my father-in-law. This is a soft, exceptionally creamy pudding—almost like custard. I can't think of a better comfort food.

SERVES 8

1 cup Valencia-style or arborio (short-grain) rice

1 cinnamon stick (2 inches long)

3 strips lemon zest

1 vanilla bean, split

1 can (12 ounces) evaporated milk

1 can (14 ounces) sweetened condensed milk

1 whole star anise pod (optional)

½ cup raisins, soaked in warm water to cover (optional)

½ cup pine nuts, lightly toasted (optional; see page 311)

1 to 2 tablespoons sugar, or to taste

Ground cinnamon or freshly grated nutmeg, for sprinkling

1. To wash the rice, place it in a large heavy saucepan with cold water to cover by 2 inches. Swirl it around with a spoon; the water will become cloudy. Pour it off and add more water. Continue rinsing the rice until the water runs clear. Drain off the water, leaving the rice in the pan.

2. Add 2½ cups of fresh water, the cinnamon stick, lemon zest, and vanilla bean and bring to a boil over high heat. Reduce the heat, cover, and gently simmer the rice until most of the water is absorbed, about 20 minutes.

3. Stir in the evaporated milk. Gently simmer, uncovered, until most of the liquid is absorbed, about 8 minutes. Stir the rice occasionally.

4. Stir in the sweetened condensed milk, and if using, the star anise, raisins, and pine nuts. Gently simmer, uncovered, until most of the liquid is absorbed and the rice is very tender, about 6 minutes. The pudding should remain very moist. Stir occasionally.

5. Remove the cinnamon stick, lemon zest, vanilla bean, and star anise pod. Stir in the sugar, to taste. Transfer to a bowl and let the rice pudding cool to room temperature. You can serve it at room temperature or chilled.

6. To serve, transfer the rice pudding to a serving bowl or individual bowls. Sprinkle with the ground cinnamon and serve at once.

Brandy Flans

K ey lime pie is Florida's most famous dessert, but flan is the most popular in our Hispanic communities. This one is flavored with Spanish brandy, which is beloved by Florida's Hispano-Americans. The molten caramel called for in this recipe can give you a bad burn, so I suggest wearing heavy gloves to protect your hands when lining the ramekins.

1½ cups sugar
3 large whole eggs
1 egg yolk
2 cups milk
1½ tablespoons brandy, preferably Spanish
1 teaspoon vanilla extract
½ teaspoon ground cinnamon,
 or to taste

1. Preheat the oven to 350°F. Have ready six 8-ounce ramekins.

2. Make the caramel: Place 1 cup of the sugar in a heavy saucepan with 3 tablespoons water. Cover and cook the sugar over high heat for 1 minute. Uncover the pan and continue cooking until the mixture turns dark golden brown, about 4 minutes.

3. Pour a little of this mixture into each ramekin. Tilt and rotate the ramekins to coat the bottom and sides. Set aside.

4. Meanwhile, bring 1 quart of water to a boil.

5. Whisk together the remaining ½ cup sugar, the whole eggs, and egg yolk in a mixing bowl. Whisk in the milk, brandy, vanilla, and cinnamon. Correct the flavors, adding sugar or cinnamon to taste. Pour this mixture into the ramekins.

6. Place the ramekins in a small roasting pan and pour in boiling water to a depth of ½ inch. Loosely cover the pan with aluminum foil. Bake until the flans puff slightly and an inserted skewer comes out clean, about 20 minutes.

7. Remove the flans from the roasting pan, and let cool to room temperature. Cover and refrigerate until cold, at least 6 hours. The flans set up even better if you allow them to chill overnight. Just before serving, run a sharp knife around the inside of each ramekin. Place a plate on top and invert. Gently shake the dish; the flan should slip out easily. Spoon the caramel sauce around the flan and serve.

Ginger-Molasses Flan

Part cheesecake and part flan, this gingery dessert is 100 percent delicious. I got the idea to add the molasses while visiting the ruins of a nineteenth-century sugar mill, founded by Florida's first senator, David Yulee, in Homosassa Springs on the west coast of Florida. (Molasses is an important by-product of sugar-making.) As I mentioned in the Brandy Flans recipe, you may wish to wear heavy gloves when lining the cake pan with caramel.

SERVES 6 TO 8

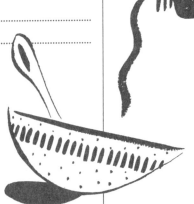

¾ cup sugar

8 ounces cream cheese, at room temperature

1 tablespoon grated fresh ginger

1 tablespoon finely chopped candied ginger

1 cup light, unsulphured molasses

3 large eggs

1 cup half-and-half

3 to 4 tablespoons sugar, or to taste

1. Preheat the oven to 350°F. Have ready an 8-inch round cake pan.

2. Combine the sugar and 3 tablespoons water in a heavy saucepan. Cover and cook the sugar over high heat for 1 minute. Uncover the pan and continue cooking until the mixture turns dark golden brown, about 4 minutes.

3. Pour the caramel into the cake pan. Tilt and rotate the pan to coat the bottom and sides; set aside.

4. Meanwhile, bring 1 quart of water to a boil.

5. Beat the cream cheese, fresh ginger, and candied ginger in a mixing bowl until light and fluffy. Beat in the molasses. Beat in the eggs, one at a time, scraping the sides of the bowl after each. Beat in the half-and-half. Add the sugar to suit your taste. Pour the custard mixture into the caramel-lined cake pan.

6. Place the flan in a roasting pan and pour in boiling water to a depth of ½ inch. Bake until the mixture is set and an inserted skewer comes out clean, about 30 minutes. Remove the flan from the oven and roasting pan, and let cool to room temperature. Cover and chill in the refrigerator for at least 6 hours, preferably overnight.

7. Just before serving, run the tip of a paring knife around the inside rim of the cake pan. Place a platter over the cake pan and invert. Give the pan a shake; the flan should slide out easily. Spoon the caramel sauce around the flan. Cut into wedges and serve.

Cuban Coffee Brûlée

Every few years a dessert comes along that captivates the American palate. A while back, it was the flourless chocolate cake, then wine-poached pears, then tiramisù. To judge from my dining out in Miami and elsewhere, a current dessert darling is crème brûlée. This version was inspired by the luscious crème brûlée served at the Grand Café in the Grand Bay Hotel in Coconut Grove. A complete discussion on making Cuban coffee can be found on page 16), but any strong espresso-type coffee will do.

1½ cups heavy (or whipping) cream
1 vanilla bean, split, or 2 teaspoons vanilla extract
1 cup brewed strong Cuban coffee or espresso
6 egg yolks
½ cup granulated sugar
1 cup (packed) light brown sugar

1. Preheat the oven to 325°F. Have ready six 6-ounce ramekins.

2. Place the heavy cream and vanilla bean (if using) in a heavy saucepan over medium heat. Slowly scald the cream. Turn off the heat and let it stand for 10 minutes. Remove the vanilla bean and rinse it off. Blot dry and store; it can be reused once or twice. (If using vanilla extract, add it to the egg yolk mixture below.) Stir in the coffee and heat the mixture, but do not let it boil.

3. Meanwhile, bring 1 quart of water to a boil.

4. Combine the egg yolks, vanilla extract (if using), and granulated sugar in a large bowl and whisk just to mix. Whisk in the coffee mixture in a thin stream. Strain this mixture into the ramekins. Wipe off any drips around the edges with a damp cloth. Place the ramekins in a small roasting pan and pour in boiling water to a depth of ½ inch. Loosely cover the pan with aluminum foil.

5. Bake the crème brûlées until almost set, but still jiggly in the center, 30 to 40 minutes. Transfer the ramekins to a wire rack and let cool to room temperature. Cover and refrigerate for at least 6 hours, preferably overnight.

6. Just before serving, preheat the broiler.

7. Push the brown sugar through a strainer to coat each crème brûlée with a thick sprinkling of sugar. Fill a roasting pan with crushed ice and nestle the ramekins in it. Run the crème brûlées under the broiler, as close to the heating element as possible, until the sugar melts, about 2 minutes. Let the crème brûlées cool slightly and serve.

Mango Ice Cream

Here's a good way to use up bruised or blemished mangos. Peach ice cream can be made the same way, substituting 2 cups diced peeled peaches for the mangos.

SERVES 4 TO 6

2 cups peeled, seeded, diced ripe mangos
About 1½ cups sugar
2 tablespoons fresh lime juice
2 cups milk
5 egg yolks
1 cup heavy (or whipping) cream

1. Combine the mangos, ½ cup of the sugar, and the lime juice in a nonreactive mixing bowl. Cover and refrigerate for 1 hour.

2. Prepare the custard: Scald the milk in a heavy saucepan. Whisk together the egg yolks and ¾ cup sugar in a mixing bowl. Whisk in the scalded milk in a thin stream.

3. Return the yolk mixture to the pan, and cook, uncovered, over medium heat, until thick enough to coat the back of a wooden spoon, about 3 minutes. Do not let the mixture boil or it will curdle. Strain the custard into a bowl, and let cool to room temperature.

4. Stir the mango mixture into the custard mixture. Stir in the cream. Taste the mixture for sweetness, adding sugar if necessary. Freeze the mixture in an ice cream maker, following the manufacturer's instructions.

Island Spice Ice Cream

The Opa-Locka Flea Market, held weekends in a
northwest Miami neighborhood, is the closest thing
to a Caribbean street market I've encountered in the
U.S. The stalls go on for acres, many manned by Haitians,
others by Cubans or Central Americans. This recipe was
inspired by the bags of star anise, cinnamon, and cloves,
sold ready-mixed by Haitian vendors. The flavorings are as
refreshing on a hot day as the ice cream itself.

SERVES 6 TO 8

2 cups milk

2 cinnamon sticks (2 inches long)

1 whole star anise pods

6 whole cloves

3 strips orange zest

5 egg yolks

¾ cup sugar

1 cup heavy (or whipping) cream

1. Combine the milk, cinnamon, star anise, cloves, and
orange zest in a heavy saucepan. Cook over low heat until
the spice flavors are well infused in the milk, about 20 minutes. Bring the milk just to a boil, and remove the pan from
the heat.

2. Meanwhile, whisk the egg yolks with the sugar in a
mixing bowl. Whisk in the scalded milk in a thin stream.
Return the mixture to the saucepan.

3. Cook the custard over medium heat until it thickens
to the consistency of heavy cream, about 3 minutes. (It will
thickly coat the back of a wooden spoon.) Do not let it boil,
or it will curdle. Strain the mixture into a clean bowl and let
cool to room temperature. Cover and chill the custard in the
refrigerator until cold.

FLORIDA'S WORLD OF EXOTIC FRUITS

C ashews are native to the West Indies, cinnamon to Ceylon; jaboticaba is a grape-like berry from Brazil. But to experience first hand the exotic trees from which these are derived, you need go no farther than the Preston B. Bird and Mary Heinlein Fruit & Spice Park in Homestead, Florida.

Founded in 1944, the Fruit & Spice Park is a twenty acre orchard and research center planted with more than 500 varieties of exotic fruits, nuts, and spices imported from all over the world. Citrus trees here range from commonplace orange to the bizarrely shaped Buddha's hand citron. Still too common? How about wampi (a small aromatic berry) or ice cream beans (whose slender pods contain a sweet white flesh reminiscent of ice cream).

The Fruit & Spice Park also hosts agricultural and arts festivals and ongoing workshops whose topics range from coconut breeding to tropical fruit wine making. It is located at 24801 S.W. 187th Avenue, Homestead, Florida: (305) 247-5727, and is open daily from 10 a.m. to 5 p.m.

4. Stir the heavy cream into the custard. Freeze the mixture in an ice cream maker according to the manufacturer's instructions.

Sour Cream Ice Cream with Mango Sauce

F ood mavens who came of age in the seventies will remember a simple but stunning dessert consisting of fresh strawberries dipped in sour cream, then in brown sugar. The combination gave me the idea for this dizzyingly rich ice cream, which is accompanied by a fresh mango coulis.

SERVES 8

2 cups heavy (or whipping) cream
1 pint sour cream
2 tablespoons minced candied ginger
1 tablespoon grated lemon zest
¾ cup (packed) light brown sugar
Mango Sauce (recipe follows)

1. Combine the heavy cream, sour cream, ginger, lemon zest, and brown sugar in a chilled mixing bowl and whisk just to mix.

2. Freeze the mixture in an ice cream maker according to the manufacturer's instructions.

3. To serve, scoop out balls with an ice cream scoop and place in chilled bowls or dessert plates. Pour the mango sauce over the ice cream and serve.

MANGO SAUCE

ⓖⓖⓖ

Here's a Floridian's answer to the classic raspberry sauce served in restaurants up North. Besides ice cream, mango sauce is delicious spooned over a slice of pound cake topped with fresh berries.

MAKES ABOUT 1½ CUPS

2 cups diced ripe mango
2 to 3 tablespoons confectioners'
sugar, or to taste
1 tablespoon fresh lemon juice,
or to taste
½ to 1 cup fresh orange juice
or water

1. Purée the mango with the confectioners' sugar and lemon juice in a food processor. Add enough of the orange juice to obtain a pourable sauce. Correct the flavorings, adding sugar or lemon juice to taste.

2. Force the sauce through a strainer, pressing with the back of a wooden spoon to extract the juice from the pulp. Cover and refrigerate until serving.

Banana Gelato

Fruit sorbets and ice creams are among my favorite desserts. Yet, until now I'd never been able to make a banana ice cream that didn't taste chalky or grainy. One day I mentioned the problem to

Washington, D.C.-based chef Roberto Donna, who told me about this banana gelato. The sugar syrup keeps the mixture from becoming grainy. The Tangerine Chocolate Sauce on page 310 makes a great accompaniment.

SERVES 6 TO 8

1 cup water
¼ cup sugar, or to taste
2 tablespoons chopped candied ginger
1½ tablespoons grated lemon zest
5 ripe bananas
4 to 5 tablespoons fresh lemon juice, or to taste

1. Combine the water, sugar, candied ginger and lemon zest in a heavy saucepan. Boil the mixture until thick and syrupy, about 5 minutes. Let cool to room temperature.

2. Peel and dice the bananas into the syrup. Stir in the lemon juice. Purée the mixture in a food processor. Correct the flavorings, adding sugar or lemon juice as necessary.

3. Freeze the banana mixture in an ice cream maker following the manufacturer's instructions.

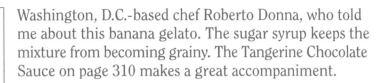

Tangerine-Mint Sorbet

This sorbet isn't too sweet, so it can be served as a mid-meal refresher or a light dessert. The zest is the oil-rich outer rind of the tangerine; remove it in strips with a vegetable peeler.

SERVES 4 TO 6

¾ cup sugar, or to taste

1 cup water

2 tablespoons light corn syrup

½ cup chopped fresh mint, plus 2 tablespoons for garnish

5 strips tangerine zest

3 cups fresh tangerine juice

3 to 4 tablespoons fresh lime juice, or to taste

1. Combine the sugar, water, and corn syrup in a saucepan and boil over high heat until clear, 2 to 3 minutes. Add the ½ cup mint leaves and the tangerine zest, cover the pan, and infuse over very low heat for 15 minutes. Strain the mixture into a large mixing bowl and let cool.

2. Stir in the tangerine juice and lime juice. Correct the flavorings, adding lime juice or sugar to taste.

3. Freeze the mixture in an ice cream maker according to the manufacturer's instructions. For a fanciful presentation, serve the sorbet in hollowed-out tangerine shells.

Carambola Sorbet

The carambola, also known as star fruit, is Florida's answer to California's kiwi fruit. Recognizable by its slender fins, it yields perfect five-point stars when sliced.

PORTRAIT OF A TROPICAL FRUIT GROWER

The driveway leading to Marc and Kiki Ellenby's house is lined with trees you've probably never heard of—such as caimito (star apple), chocolate sapote, and jackfruit—not to mention more commonplace fruits, like carambola (star fruit) and ten varieties of avocado. Welcome to LNB Groves, one of the most progressive tropical fruit farms in Florida.

Marc Ellenby became impassioned with tropical fruits as a graduate student in horticulture at the University of Florida. In 1980, the family bought their first farm, 8½ acres of prime orchard land in Homestead, Florida. The Ellenbys began planting atemoyas and sugar apples, custardy fruits much prized by Miami's Hispanics. In 1983, they added lychees and longans, followed by the first sweet star fruit varieties in 1985. "We tried to choose fruits with an established ethnic base and expand the market from there," explains Mark.

Today, Marc, his wife Kiki, and children, Adena, Aliya, Jody, and Levi, farm more than 150 acres.

Experimentation and innovation are the hallmarks of their operation. As a founding member of the Tropical Fruit Growers of South Florida, Marc helped write the Tropical Fruit Policy Act. Passed by the State Legislature in 1990, the act protects and promotes Florida's burgeoning exotic fruit industry.

In the wake of hurricane Andrew, Mark planted three types of fast growing exotic bananas. He's now experimenting with passion fruit, jackfruit, and sapodilla. But you never know what you're going to find at LNB Grove.

SERVES 6 TO 8

1 teaspoon unflavored gelatin
¼ to ½ cup cold water
¼ to ½ cup sugar, or to taste
3 tablespoons light corn syrup
3 pounds carambolas, diced and seeded, plus 1 carambola,
    thinly sliced, for garnish
2 to 3 tablespoons fresh lime juice, or to taste

1. Sprinkle the gelatin over the water in a small saucepan. Let stand until spongy, about 10 minutes.

2. Melt the gelatin mixture over low heat until smooth and liquid, 2 to 3 minutes. Stir in ¼ cup sugar sugar and corn syrup, and cook over low heat until the mixture becomes clear. Let cool completely.

3. Purée the carambolas in a food processor or blender. For a smoother sorbet, strain the mixture.

4. Combine the gelatin mixture with the purée and 2 tablespoons lime juice. Correct the seasoning, adding sugar or lime juice to taste. Freeze the mixture in an ice cream maker according to the manufacturer's instructions.

5. Scoop the sorbet into martini glasses. Garnish each with a carambola slice.

Note: A similar sorbet can be made with atemoya, sugar apple, monstera deliciosa, or any other tropical fruit. Adjust the sugar and lime juice to suit the sweetness of the fruit.

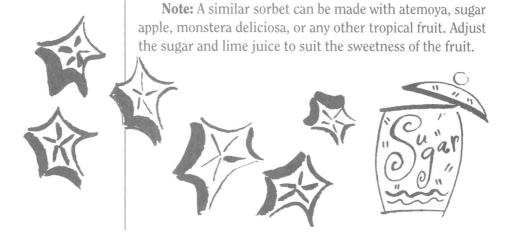

Hibiscus Granita

Granitas are the simplest of all frozen desserts, made by scraping a frozen liquid into icy crystals that melt on your tongue like snowflakes. Hibiscus flowers bloom wild all over Florida. We have several plants in our yard. Hibiscus flowers are the principal flavoring in Red Zinger tea, which inspired the following recipe.

SERVES 4

2½ cups water
3 Red Zinger tea bags (see Note)
2 to 3 tablespoons fresh lemon juice
2 to 3 tablespoons honey

1. Bring the water to a boil and remove the pan from the heat. Add the Red Zinger and let steep for 5 minutes. Remove the tea bags and stir in the lemon juice and honey, to taste.

2. Place the bowl in the freezer and freeze the granita, breaking it up 2 or 3 times with a fork as it freezes. The freezing process will take 1 to 2 hours. Just before serving, scrape it again into icy crystals with a fork. Serve in chilled wine glasses.

Note: Red Zinger tea is made by Celestial Seasonings and is readily available in supermarkets nationwide.

Basic Recipes

Orange Syrup

Coconut Milk

Bouquet Garni

Fish Stock

Clarified Butter

Butter is clarified to remove the water and milk solids. This raises the butter's smoking point, which is useful for sautéing. Here are two methods for clarifying butter.

MAKES A LITTLE LESS THAN 1 CUP

½ pound (2 sticks) unsalted butter

Method 1: Melt the butter in a saucepan over low heat. Skim off any white foam that rises to the surface. Carefully pour off the clear yellow liquid—the clarified butter—leaving the milky residue in the bottom of the pot.

Method 2: Melt the butter in a tall narrow saucepan over low heat. Skim off any foam that rises to the surface. Cook the butter over high heat until it stops bubbling, then immediately pour it into another container. With this method, the butter acquires a pleasantly nutty flavor when it's ready. If it starts to brown, immediately remove the pan from the heat.

Basic Chicken Stock

This is an all-purpose stock suited to a wide variety of soups, stews, casseroles, and sauces. To make dark stock, roast the bones and vegetables in a hot (400°F) oven until dark brown. To make broth, use a whole chicken instead of bones.

MAKES 2 QUARTS

4 pounds chicken backs, necks,
*   or wings, well rinsed*
1 large onion, quartered
2 carrots, cut into 1-inch pieces
2 ribs celery, cut into 1-inch pieces
3 cloves garlic, cut in half
1 tomato, quartered
Bouquet Garni (see page 334)

1. Combine all of the ingredients for the stock in a large pot and add water to cover (8 to 10 cups). Bring the mixture to a boil. Skim off the foam that rises to the surface.

2. Reduce the heat and gently simmer the stock, uncovered, for 2 to 3 hours. Add cold water as necessary to keep the bones covered and skim the stock often to remove any fat or scum that collects on the surface. Do not let the stock boil, or it will become cloudy.

3. Strain the stock through a strainer lined with several layers of cheesecloth into a large bowl, and let cool to room temperature. Cover and refrigerate. Remove any fat that congeals on the surface. I like to freeze stock in 1-cup containers, so I'll always have the right amount on hand.

Fish Stock

F ish stock should be made with delicately flavored fish, like snapper, pompano, or grouper. Bottled clam broth (also called clam juice) makes an acceptable substitute in most recipes.

MAKES 1 QUART

2 pounds fish trimmings, frames
     (skeletons), or heads
1 tablespoon olive oil
1 onion, finely chopped
2 ribs celery, finely chopped
2 cloves garlic, finely chopped
½ cup dry white wine
Bouquet garni (see page 334)

1. Cut the fish trimmings into 1-inch pieces, and the fish frames into 2-inch pieces. If using fish heads, have your fishmonger cut them in half and discard the gills. Rinse all in cold water until all traces of blood are gone.

2. Heat the oil in a nonreactive large saucepan. Add the onion, celery, and garlic and cook over medium heat until soft but not brown, about 3 minutes. Increase the heat to high and add the fish. Cook, stirring, for 1 to 2 minutes to sear the fish.

3. Add the wine and boil for 1 minute. Add the bouquet garni and enough water to cover (4 to 5 cups). Bring the stock to a boil, and skim off any foam that rises to the surface.

4. Reduce the heat and gently simmer the stock until well flavored, about 20 minutes. Do not cook fish stock too long, or it will become bitter.

5. Strain the stock through a strainer lined with several layers of cheesecloth into a large bowl, and let cool to room temperature. Cover and refrigerate until cold. Skim off any fat that congeals on the surface. I like to freeze fish stock in 1-cup containers, so I always have the right amount on hand.

Shrimp or lobster stock: Prepare as described above, substituting shrimp shells or lobster heads for fish bones. Add 1 tablespoon Cognac for flavor and 1 tablespoon tomato paste for color.

Coconut Milk

Coconut milk isn't the clear liquid in the center of a coconut, as is commonly but erroneously stated. That liquid is coconut water. The milk is a creamy extract made by mixing freshly grated coconut with boiling water. Coconut milk is used throughout the tropics as an alternative to milk and cream.

MAKES 3 CUPS

Freshly grated flesh of 1 coconut
3 cups boiling water

1. Combine the grated coconut and boiling water in a blender or food processor and purée for 2 minutes. Let this mixture stand for 15 minutes.

2. Strain the mixture through a strainer lined with several layers of dampened cheesecloth. Twist the cheesecloth tightly to extract as much milk as possible. (The process can be repeated using another 3 cups of boiling water to make a second, thinnner batch of coconut milk.) Store the coconut milk in the refrigerator, where it will keep for 3 to 4 days. It can also be frozen.

To Peel and Seed a Tomato

To Peel a Fresh Tomato: Cut out the stem end and cut a small *X* in the bottom. Plunge the tomato in a pot of rapidly boiling water for 20 to 60 seconds (depending on the ripeness of the tomato), or until the skin feels loose. Rinse the tomato under cold running water and pull the skin off with your fingers.

To Seed a Tomato: Cut it crosswise in half. Working over a bowl in which a strainer is resting, squeeze each half, cut side down, in the palm of your hand to wring out the liquid and seeds. Reserve the tomato liquid for sauces, soups, and stocks. The tomato is ready for chopping or dicing.

Two pounds fresh tomatoes (4 to 5 tomatoes) yield about 3 cups peeled, seeded, and chopped tomatoes.

Orange Syrup

Orange juice can lend a Floridian touch to a wide variety of sauces, salad dressings, and desserts. In order to achieve an intense orange flavor without diluting the sauce, I boil freshly squeezed orange juice until it reduces to a thick syrup. The result is similar to commercial orange juice concentrate, but without the latter's bitterness. Orange Syrup will keep for several weeks in the refrigerator and can be frozen. Freeze it in ice cube trays to have premeasured portions.

Annatto can be found at most Hispanic and Caribbean food markets and in the ethnic food section of many supermarkets. It's sometimes sold by its Spanish name, *achiote*, or, when ground, as *bijol*. As with most spices, it is best bought at a store that has a good turnover. Avoid dust-covered bottles and try to use the annatto within 6 months of purchase.

To make annatto paste for marinades, gently simmer 3 tablespoons seeds in ¼ cup sour orange juice or vinegar until soft, 10 to 15 minutes. Add 1 teaspoon salt and purée in a spice mill or mortar. To increase the flavor, lightly roast the seeds in a dry skillet over medium heat for 2 to 3 minutes before grinding.

MAKES ½ CUP

4 to 5 Florida oranges (enough to make 2 cups juice)

Squeeze the oranges; you should have 2 cups. Strain the juice into a nonreactive heavy saucepan. Briskly simmer the juice until thick and syrupy and reduced to about ½ cup, 5 to 8 minutes. Cover and store the orange syrup in the refrigerator.

Grapefruit syrup: Prepare as above, using 2 cups freshly squeezed grapefruit juice.

Tangerine syrup: Prepare as above, using 2 cups freshly squeezed tangerine juice.

Annatto Oil

Use annatto oil for frying onions, browning pork or chicken, or for perking up salad dressings. Stored in a jar, annatto oil will keep for months—even at room temperature. Warning: Take care not to spill annatto oil. The orange stains are murder to remove from clothing and carpet.

MAKES 1 CUP

1 cup vegetable oil or light olive oil
½ cup annatto seeds

1. Heat the oil in a heavy saucepan over medium heat. Add the annatto seeds and cook until the oil is reddish gold and the seeds begin to crackle, about 3 minutes.
2. Strain the oil into a clean container with a lid.

Bouquet Garni

Bouquet garni is an herb bundle used to flavor soups, stews, and stock. A traditional French bouquet garni contains bay leaf, thyme, and parsley. My version is spiced up with peppercorns, whole allspice berries, and cloves. Traditionally, the flavorings are tied in cheesecloth, but a high-tech bouquet garni can be made by wrapping the ingredients in aluminum foil and perforating it with the tines of a fork.

1 to 2 bay leaves

2 sprigs fresh thyme or 1 teaspoon
    dried

4 sprigs fresh parsley

10 black peppercorns

3 whole allspice berries

2 whole cloves

Tie together all of the ingredients in a square of cheesecloth or wrap them in a small sheet of aluminum foil. If using the foil, perforate the bundle with the tines of a fork to release the flavors.

A GLOSSARY OF FLORIDIAN MENU TERMS

Look at a menu at many Florida restaurants and you might feel like you're in a foreign country. Here are some of the more popular ethnic specialties.

ACHIOTE: Annatto seed, a rust-colored spice with an earthy flavor that's used in Spanish-Caribbean cooking.

ADOBO: A Cuban marinade made with sour orange juice, garlic, cumin, and oregano.

AJIACO: A soulful stew of Cuban root vegetables, pumpkin, corn, salt pork, and salt beef.

ALBONDIGAS: Hispanic meatballs.

ANNATTO: See *achiote*.

AREPAS: A Colombian cornmeal dish that's a cross between polenta and a pancake.

ARROZ CON LECHE: Literally "rice with milk"; rice pudding.

ARROZ CON POLLO: Chicken and rice, plus peas, pimentos, and other ingredients (a sort of chicken paella).

BACALAO: Salt cod.

BACALAITOS: Salt cod fritters.

BAJO: Nicaraguan boiled dinner made with brisket and cornmeal.

BATIDO: A Hispanic milkshake made with fruit, ice, and sweetened condensed milk.

BATIDO DE TRIGO: A milkshake made with puffed wheat.

BOLICHE: Cuban pot roast (usually stuffed with chorizo sausage).

BOLLITOS: Cuban black-eyed pea fritters.

BUNUELOS: Cuban "doughnuts." Figure 8-shaped fritters made of yuca and malanga dough, served in star anise-scented syrup.

CARAJILLO: Cuban coffee with brandy.

CASCOS DE GUAYABA: Poached guava shells (usually served with cream cheese or salty farmer's cheese).

CAZUELITA DE FRIJOLES: A small earthenware pot of red beans baked with sour cream (Nicaraguan).

CEBOLLITO: Nicaraguan pickled onion sauce. Traditionally served with *churrasco*.

CERDO FRITO: Nicaraguan-style pork marinated in vinegar and annatto seed, then fried.

CEVICHE: Uncooked lime-marinated seafood.

CHICHARRONES: Pork cracklings. Can also be made with chicken.

CHILE CRIOLLA: A piquant Nicaraguan salsa made with vinegared onions and chilies.

CHIMICHURRI: A pesto-like sauce made from parsley, garlic, and olive oil. Traditionally served with *churrasco*.

CHORIZO: Spicy Spanish sausage.

CHURRASCO: Marinated grilled beef tenderloin.

COLADA: Sweet strong Cuban coffee served with thimble-size cups for sharing among friends.

CONGRI: Cuban red beans and rice. Nicaraguans call this dish *gallo pinto*.

CREMA CATALANA: Spanish crème brûlée.

CROQUETAS: Cuban croquettes. Often flavored with shredded ham and nibbled throughout the day as a snack.

DJON-DJON: Tiny black dried mushrooms used by Haitians. Often cooked with rice.

ELENA RUZ: A Cuban sandwich of turkey, cream cheese, and strawberry jam on a sweet roll. Named for a Havana socialite, it tastes a lot better than it sounds.

EMPANADA: A fried or baked turnover popular throughout Latin America. Often filled with *picadillo*.

ENCHILADO: Seafood in Cuban-style creole sauce flavored with tomato, onion, garlic, oregano, and cumin.

ESCABECHE: Cuban pickled fish.

FRIJOLES NEGROS: Black beans. Often served as a Cuban soup. Sometimes served as a soupy topping for rice.

FUFU: Cuban mashed boiled green plantain served with garlic and pork cracklings. In the Dominican Republic this dish is known as *mangú*.

GALLETAS: Cuban crackers.

GRIOTS: Haitian fried spiced pork.

GUARAPO: Sugarcane juice.

INDIO VIEJO: "Old Indian," a creamy Nicaraguan stew of brisket, onions, butter, cream, and eggs.

JAMON SERRANO (or sometimes just *serrano*): Country-style (salt-cured) ham. Smithfield ham is often used by Hispanic-Americans in this country.

LANGOSTA: Spiny lobster (also called *Florida lobster*).

LAMBI: Conch (in French and Creole).

LECHON ASADO: Roast pork (literally, roast suckling pig).

MADUROS: Fried sweet (ripe) plantains.

MARINARA: A sweet and sour sauce made with tomatoes, peppers, and onions. Traditionally served with *churrasco*.

MARIQUITAS: Fried green plantain chips that taste like potato chips. Nicaraguans call them *tajadas*.

MASITAS DE PUERCO: Cuban fried spiced pork.

MEDIA NOCHE: Literally, "midnight," a Cuban sandwich lavished with ham, cheese, pickles, and roast pork.

MOJITO: A famous Cuban cocktail made with rum, lime, *yerbabuena*, and soda water.

MOJO: A vinaigrette-like Cuban sauce made with garlic and sour orange juice.

MOROS: Literally, "Moors" (short for Moors and Christians)—Cuban black beans and white rice.

MUCHACHO RELLENO: Colombian-style stuffed eye of round.

NACATAMAL: Nicaraguan *tamal* flavored with prunes, raisins, olives, rice, and pork, wrapped and steamed in a banana leaf.

NATILLA: Cuban custard.

PAELLA: Similar to the Spanish dish, but the Cuban version owes its golden color to annatto seed.

PALOMILLA: Cuban shell steak marinated in sour orange juice and garlic.

PASTEL: Puerto Rican plantain pastry cooked in a banana leaf.

PASTELITOS: Nicaraguan meat pies flavored with olives, capers, raisins, and sugar.

PICADILLO: Ground beef stewed with olives, capers, and raisins.

PINOLILLO: A Nicaraguan drink made with cocoa, cinnamon, cloves, and toasted cornmeal.

PIO QUINTO: Literally, "Pope Pius V" cake. A Nicaraguan trifle: sponge cake made with toasted cornmeal, soaked with rum, and topped with custard and prunes.

PUDIN: Egg custard.

QUESO FRITO: Nicaraguan fried cheese (often served with tortillas).

RABO ESTOFADO: Cuban braised oxtail.

ROPA VIEJA: Literally "old clothes"—Cuban shredded skirt steak stewed with peppers, onions, and tomato sauce.

SANCOCHO: A Colombian stew of meat, corn, and root vegetables. (Similar to Cuban *ajiaco*.)

SOPA DE MONDONGO: Colombian tripe soup.

TAMAL: Cornmeal pastry cooked in a corn husk.

TASAJO: Salt beef (Cuban corned beef—usually served shredded in tomato sauce).

TOCINO DE CIELO: Cuban egg yolk-enriched custard.

TORREJAS:Cuban fried bread in star anise-scented syrup.

TORTILLA: In Nicaraguan parlance this refers to a thick cornmeal flatbread (like a Mexican tortilla, only thicker). In Cuban parlance, it's a sort of frittata made with potatoes and onions.

TOSTONES: Mashed, fried plantains.

TRES LECHES: "Three milks" cake, Nicaragua's most famous dessert. Made with fresh milk, evaporated milk, and sweetened condensed milk, *tres leches* consists of sponge cake imbibed with a creamy syrup and topped with clouds of meringue.

VACA FRITA: Literally "fried cow"—crispy shredded fried skirt steak.

VIGORON: A Nicaraguan appetizer consisting of boiled yuca, pork cracklings, and pickled cabbage.

YUCA CON MOJO: Boiled cassava root with garlic-lime sauce.

Index